Cultivating Foundation Support For Education

Mary Kay Murphy, Editor

Council for Advancement and Support of Education

ISBN 0-89964-263-2

Printed in the United States of America.

In 1974, the American Alumni Council (founded in 1913) and the American College Public Relations Association (founded in 1917) merged to become the Council for Advancement and Support of Education (CASE).

Today, approximately 2,850 colleges, universities, and independent elementary and secondary schools in the U.S. and 23 countries belong to CASE. This makes ours the largest nonprofit 501(c)(3) education association in terms of institutional membership. Representing the member institutions in CASE are more than 13,000 individual professionals in institutional advancement.

Nonprofit education-related organizations such as hospitals, museums, libraries, cultural or performing arts groups, public radio and television stations, or foundations established for public elementary and secondary schools may affiliate with CASE as Educational Associates. Commercial firms that serve the education field may affiliate as Subscribers.

CASE's mission is to advance understanding and support of education for the benefit of society. Central to its mission are its member colleges, universities, and independent schools. CASE fulfills this mission by providing services to beginning, mid-level, and senior advancement professionals; direct services to member institutions; and public affairs programs that bond higher education to the public interest.

CASE offers books, videotapes, and focus issues of the award-winning monthly magazine, CURRENTS, to professionals in institutional advancement. The books cover topics in alumni administration, communications and marketing, fund raising, management, and student recruitment. For a copy of the catalog, RESOURCES, write to the CASE Publications Order Department, 80 South Early Street, Alexandria, VA 22304. For more information about CASE programs and services, call (202) 328-5900.

Cover illustration by Michael David Brown

Council for Advancement and Support of Education
Suite 400, 11 Dupont Circle, Washington, DC 20036

Contents

Foreword

While foundations are an important part of the fund-raising programs at most educational institutions, this source of funds is not inexhaustible, and the competition for grants is keen. Over 25,000 foundations exist, but some 5,000 of the largest hold approximately 97 percent of the assets and make approximately 92 percent of the grants. How can *your* institution persuade a foundation to help you build a new arts center, sponsor important research, or fund an innovative program?

Cultivating Foundation Support for Education, an important addition to the fund-raising literature, supplies the answers. In this book, Editor Mary Kay Murphy brings together an impressive corps of specialists who represent many perspectives—grant makers, grant seekers, consultants, marketing and public relations professionals as well as research specialists. All are leaders in their areas with an important message related to successful foundation fund raising. And Professor James Donahue of Georgetown University introduces the book with a reminder of the ethical considerations of a foundation fund-raising program.

This book will help you find the areas where your institution's needs and interests intersect with those of foundations. It will show you how to cultivate foundation contacts, prepare your proposal, and follow through with good stewardship after you receive the grant.

As you learn more about this important area of fund raising, bear in mind this historical perspective. In Chapter 1, Elizabeth Boris of the Council on Foundations says:

> Foundations are relative newcomers [in the philanthropic world].... The concept of a freestanding, endowed institution that uses the income from the donor's gift...to benefit humankind through systematic, scientific philanthropy was the product of an era of optimistic belief in the ability of capitalism and science to make the world right.... Their goal was to find the causes of and cures for society's ills, not to treat the symptoms.

Boris cites some impressive foundation-supported accomplishments—the eradication of hookworm, for example, and the development of the polio vaccine.

Foundations exist to give money away, but that doesn't necessary mean they're going to give it to your institution, or that they *should* give it to your institution. Perhaps the most important thing to remember as you cultivate your foundation prospects is that foundations have their own priorities, which may not be the same

i

as yours. Deborah Callard of the Fund for Johns Hopkins Medicine discusses foundation interests today:

> Some of the largest foundations...are developing programs that reflect deep concern about such important social issues as the underclass, the homeless, teenage pregnancy, and the environment.... Increasing numbers of foundation programs have also addressed health... and educational issues.... Unfortunately, these concerns do not always coincide with an institution's most pressing needs.

Despite these shifting emphases, foundations continue to invest significant resources ($353 million in 1986) in higher education—and for good reason. If our society is to solve the problems that confront it, it must have the educated citizens, medical and scientific research, scholarship, and public service programs that our colleges and universities provide.

Gary H. Quehl
President, CASE
January 1989

Preface

When I began my job as director for foundation relations at Georgia Tech, I read every reference book I could find on how to raise foundation support for education. That was eight years ago. Now I am working as director for development, but the lessons I learned in that job have served me very well in other areas of fund raising.

I never found a book with the kind of information in it about raising money from foundations that we have been able to provide to you, our reader. To learn the secrets contained in this book, I attended conferences all over the country, met colleagues in the field, and worked with program officers and volunteers for several years.

Like favorite recipes from the world's best cooks, these secrets have been shared by some of the country's most effective and highly regarded program officers and grant seekers. Why would such people give away their secrets and tell all about the business of successful foundation fund raising? I believe they told because they want those of us who raise money for educational institutions to be successful. They believe in the benefits of higher education and want to help us in our quest for foundation dollars.

Those who worked on this book think it is unique in the publications world. No book in current print has exactly the focus that is this book's: identifying techniques and strategies to raise foundation money for the support of education. We are hopeful and confident that our friends in the not-for-profit world will benefit from the information in this book, even if theirs is not an educational organization.

Our audience includes directors of foundation relations and development, vice presidents for development, foundation program officers, trustees, faculty, prospect researchers, and college and university presidents—all who are a part of the process and play a role in seeking foundation support for education.

We selected topics to enlighten those just entering the field as well as to stimulate and challenge those who are working in well-established foundation fund-raising programs. We invited those on the grant-seeking and the grant-making sides to share their sharpest insights. They are the best of the best in their areas of specialty, and it is a special privilege to include their work in this volume.

I would like to thank my supervisors at the Georgia Institute of Technology for supporting my work on this book. Certainly I thank Virginia Carter Smith and her diligent staff at CASE for their many contributions to the project. Finally, I thank the remarkable array of authors whose work we are privileged to include in this volume. We think their contributions rank in the range of "blockbuster." We hope you will agree and that both you and your organization will benefit from the publication of this book.

Happy cultivation to you. May all of your responses be in the form of foundation grants for your institution.

Mary Kay Murphy
Atlanta, Georgia
January 1989

Ethics and Foundation Fund Raising: The Search For Moral Standards

James A. Donahue
Assistant Professor of Ethics
Department of Theology
Georgetown University

A recent headline in the "Philanthropy News" section of the *Chronicle of Higher Education* announced some rather somber news for development officers in American colleges and universities. It read: "Companies' Once-Strong Support for Charitable Giving Seen Eroded by Changes in Society and Economy." The headline simply states what development professionals already know: that corporate philanthropic money is getting scarcer; that the competition for what resources do exist is getting fiercer; and since corporate philanthropy in America is being pinched by tightened economic constraints, a greater share of philanthropic funding to higher education will have to come from foundations.

This increased competition for limited foundation dollars is viewed as a mixed blessing by many in the fund-raising profession. Some contend that competition brings out the best in people, that it challenges both individuals and institutions alike to perform to the best of their ability. The best and the strongest will survive, and the resources will go where they can be utilized best.

Others believe that while this optimistic view of competition may be good in theory, the reality is often quite different. In the real world, the competition that results when increased numbers contend for limited available resources almost inevitably leads to greater pressure on the fund raiser to secure funding. The result of the heightened tensions and anxieties about achieving the necessary financial security is oftentimes the temptation to compromise moral standards.

1

Foundation fund raising is currently undergoing a time of strain, and the moral standards that guide the profession are being severely tested. My purposes in this essay are two: to explore the nature of the ethical challenges that exist in foundation fund raising, and to develop some "ethical rules of thumb" that can guide institutional development officers and foundation officials alike as they engage in the competitive business of seeking and granting foundation support. When these ethical guidelines are spelled out, there is a better chance that the granting of foundation support will be more equitable and fair for all involved.

Many professional organizations like the Council for Advancement and Support of Education (CASE) and the National Society of Fund-Raising Executives (NSFRE) are already in the process of defining ethical standards for their own constituencies. These efforts are to be applauded. My remarks here are meant to supplement these ongoing efforts.

Essential values in foundation fund raising

A good way to begin the search for moral standards in foundation fund raising is to analyze exactly what foundations do and to explore the nature of the relationships formed between foundations and those who are seeking funding. When we look at this, we can see that *certain values are essential for and are built into the very structure of foundation fund raising,* and that without these values the "system" of foundation fund raising breaks down and becomes chaotic and arbitrary. The values at the heart of fund raising include: competition, trust, fairness and equality, and honesty and integrity.

A look at how these values function will clarify the moral standards that fund raisers and foundation officers alike can utilize in their work.

Competition. There are some who think that competition is the root of all unethical behaviors in financial matters and that if competition in some way can be eliminated, there will be no pressure to cut moral corners. Consequently, ethical behaviors will follow. While any system that is highly competitive will be vulnerable to abuse, and, indeed, the pressures to succeed are great, it is unfair to blame all ethical wrongdoing in the financial marketplace on competition.

Competition is one of the cornerstones of the system of foundation fund raising. Foundations announce their intention to provide funding for a range of projects and invite those who are in need and fall within the stated range of this funding to apply for support. Those institutions that apply must compete with fellow applicants.

Much has been written about the virtues and vices of competition, particularly as it relates to the free market economic system. The "pure" free market economists (Milton Friedman, among others) argue that competition gives everyone in the system the same fair advantage and that when competition operates in an unfettered way, it brings out the best in people. That is, in a system of open competition, people will work to their best capacities and the products they produce, since they must win out over those of their competitors, will necessarily be of high quality. Competition, so the logic goes, challenges us to work to the best of our potential.

Critics contend that pure competition never has and never will exist, and that there is little protection in a system of pure competition for those who do not have a fair advantage. They argue that, because of the misfortunes of history and social structures, some people or groups are disenfranchised in a purely competitive situation. Moreover, abuses of power always occur in a competitive marketplace, and these need to be prevented. To do this, we need some type of intervention in and regulation of the practices within the system.

Making an analogy between the competition in the "system" of foundation fund raising and the competition in the economic market system can provide insights for fund-raising practitioners. In the development world, institutions compete with one another to make the best possible case for their project or institution and to argue that they deserve funding over their competitors. From the foundation's perspective, competition among institutions works to the benefit of all. Institutions are challenged to present a product that is worthy of funding and one that is "better than" that of another institution. By defining funding project areas, guidelines, and limitations according to clearly articulated criteria, the foundation is enabled to confer benefits on those most deserving.

Are there flaws in this logic of foundation giving? In theory, pure competition is a powerful and important element in fund raising that can bring out the best in both institutions and individuals. In theory, it leads to the creation of the best program possible and the best foundation grant possible. In the real world, however, we must remember that there can and will be imbalances in the system. The prestigious "name" institutions oftentimes are the frequent recipients of grants, and when success builds upon success, the strong get stronger and the weak get weaker. Abuses can arise; unfair practices can emerge.

These deficiencies are not inevitable, but they are natural flaws that can emerge in any human enterprise. Controls are needed to modify the propensity to abuses and inequality in the competition for foundation funds.

Be careful to note an important distinction between healthy and harmful competition. Excesses of any kind are harmful, and so it is with competition. When competition becomes severe, it can prevent the fund raiser from working to the best of his or her ability. It creates undue pressure and anxiety and requires institutions to grasp for performance that is perhaps unattainable and not realistically within their reach. This kind of reach for the unattainable can create a mentality that skews the fund raiser's perspective and leads to behavior that is morally compromising. That is, if we are convinced that we must attain a goal that is, in fact, not truly within our reach, our desire for success can sometimes take over, leading us to do things that we would not ordinarily do.

Trust. Trust must be the foundation of competition in foundation fund raising. For competition brings out the best in people only when everyone has a fundamental trust in each other and in the system—that is, each applicant believes that his or her institution has a fair chance at being funded and will be treated fairly in comparison with other institutions. When this trust is missing, suspicion is generated, and suspicion breeds an adversarial attitude.

Institutional grant seekers must be able to trust the foundations' assurances that the announced criteria upon which projects will be funded are accurate and precise and that they will be used to distinguish the priority of one project or institution over another. Unless foundations are clear about what these standards are and provide assurance to potential applicants that these criteria will be applied fairly and consistently, applicants will not have any trust in the process. Nothing could be more damaging to the foundation world than to create a situation in which "special privilege" or "inside connections" are seen as the criteria for approving projects. This leads to cynicism on the part of applicants and eventually to attempts to develop ethically questionable strategies, such as influence seeking and peddling, that threaten the entire fund-raising system.

Foundations and institutions can take some basic measures to create an environment of trust. These include: being clear and precise about the criteria for evaluation of grant applications; avoiding the divulging of information to some institutions or individuals that would be unavailable to others; being consistent in the way foundation staff treat applicants; making sure that whatever is said is true and what is promised can actually be delivered.

Developing trust takes time. Both foundations and institutions, as well as the individuals associated with them, will be judged trustworthy only after they have shown themselves to be trustworthy over time. When trust is there, competition brings out the best in people; when it is not, the entire system is marred.

Trust is a two-way street between foundation and institution. Each has to operate with the confidence that the other party is being candid and forthright. When this trust exists, those who participate in the competition for grants know that they can count on the other participants to observe the moral rules of the game.

Fairness and equality. When those who participate in foundation fund raising have trust in the system, they believe that they will be treated fairly and justly, that all will be treated with the same respect and dignity regardless of their particular set of circumstances and their relative strength or weakness within the system. This means that foundations have a moral responsibility to give equal consideration to all applicants that apply for funding, and that all applicant institutions are required to abide by the same rules of the game.

The issue of fairness arises frequently in foundation fund raising. It arises when foundations judge the merits of institutional proposals; it is reflected in the selection of the judges who approve foundation grants; it is reflected in the strategies that institutions use when they compete with one another for grants; it is manifested in the standards that fund-raising officers require of their development staffs.

The contemporary literature on ethics contains a great deal about fairness and equality. While there is no consensus as to what makes for fairness, some basic agreement seems to exist on the following:

• Fairness means treating everyone with fundamental respect. For foundations this would mean giving each applicant a thorough and substantive consideration.

• Fairness means that each applicant should be judged regardless of prestige, power, previous status, relative position in the world of education, or other reasons extraneous to the announced criteria for grant awards. These concerns are not totally irrelevant to making judgments about foundation proposals, but each applicant ought to be given a fair chance at getting foundation funds as long as the institution observes the criteria determined by the foundation. This is to ensure that the strong and powerful institutions with proven successful track records in securing grants will not have an unfair advantage.

• Fairness requires that everyone compete according to the same rules of the game. Competing institutions must agree to "play fair." This includes not resorting to techniques that are deemed inappropriate in that they are not available to other competitors, such as using personal relationships with inside people or relying on "insider information" that is secured illegally.

Each of these manifestations of fairness might seem initially to be so restricting that following them will almost certainly lead to failure. Everyone knows, for example, that the name of the foundation game is to try to find ways that will put your application at a competitive advantage. As I have indicated, this is proper and essential. But the point is that this advantage has to be secured in ways that are available to all and are not based on techniques that are harmful to the competitive system as a whole. Issues such as "influence peddling," "insider information," "falsifying claims and promises," and "dirty tricks" contaminate the system and lead to the creation of more compromising behaviors.

Honesty and integrity. When all is said and done, the ethical standards of the individuals in foundation fund raising set the ethical norms for the industry. When both development officers and foundation officials operate according to standards that are fair and just, all involved in the system are forced to abide by those standards. When individuals engage in unethical practices, the moral climate of the industry is diminished.

It is vitally important, therefore, that the development/foundation profession create ways to ensure that individuals develop sound ethical standards. There are several methods to achieve this.

Good ethics begin with good people. Each institution should strive to attract people to development positions who have sound moral standards; in fact, the institution should *demand* those standards as necessary features of job performance and evaluation. There is no substitute for having people with integrity and honesty working in the fund-raising field.

But there is more to good ethics than just good people. Ethics is something that both the institutions and the profession of fund raising as a whole can address by articulating formal ethical standards and developing ways of ensuring that these standards are followed. Both the institution and foundation officers and their staffs should make sure that ethical issues are addressed and that everyone is well-informed as to what is expected ethically from the representations of the institution or the foundation.

Fund-raising professionals are already beginning to develop codes of conduct; their regional and national meetings are addressing common ethical issues in the profession. These initiatives are important; they help the institution and the profession provide a structure in which honesty and integrity can be demonstrated. If honesty and integrity are demanded by the profession, then there is a greater likelihood that they will become part of the fabric of institutional decision making.

The three crucial moments of the foundation/institution relationship

It is one thing to name the values and standards that apply in the foundation/institution relationship; it is quite another to know how they actually function in the practice of foundation fund-raising.

These values come into play at three distinct moments in the foundation/institution relationship which are, in fact, decision points where adhering to clear ethical standards is important: the point when the foundation identifies areas for grants; the application process; and the time after a grant award.

Identifying areas for funding. Foundations are enormously powerful institutions in our society. When they make decisions about what areas of need they will respond to by providing grant money, they make choices that significantly affect the future directions of our society. When they decide that one area of research in medicine, or in economics, or in the humanities, is in need of investigation, they create great opportunities for progress in that particular area. When foundations make decisions that certain building programs for colleges and universities are to be funded, they play an important role in defining the direction of a significant sector of higher education.

The decisions that foundations make about funding priorities are basically moral decisions, based on an understanding of the responsibility that goes with the role that foundations play in the larger scheme of society. Like a corporation or a public agency or a religious institution, foundations have a duty to advance the development of the moral integrity of society in some distinctive way.

Foundations exercise this responsibility when they make decisions about granting categories. It becomes attendant on them, therefore, to assess their choices in light of their effects on the long- and short-term future of society. This can be done by defining granting areas in accord with societal need at times, as well as in accord with societal want and preference. In other words, the well-being of the human community is an important criterion that foundations must keep in mind when they decide what to grant as well as to whom to grant. At times, it may be the lesser-known institutions or the least popular causes that cry out for attention and support. Foundations need to find ways to assure that those who make granting decisions will be aware of these types of considerations. The larger social welfare and health are at stake in these decisions.

The application process. Applying for a grant is a little like writing a resume for a job. The individual wants to sell himself or herself to a potential employer. In doing so, the job seeker may compromise his or her ethical standards in obvious ways, such as fabricating academic credentials, or in less obvious ways such as exaggerating previous job responsibilities. So, too, an institutional applicant may be tempted to cheat in one of these ways.

6

Most institutions would hesitate to include false statements in a grant application; this is clearly wrong, and foundations have ways of verifying the accuracy of information provided in a proposal, so an institution would have little to gain and much to lose by going this route. But exaggeration is not such a simple issue. Since institutions, like many individuals, often have an inflated view of themselves, they tend to state their case in glowing terms, perhaps exaggerating the success of an earlier project. When the result is to describe an institution as something it is not, the applicant may be creating a relationship based on skewed perceptions that can lead to situations where expectations and actions clash. In this light, then, it is difficult to condone exaggeration in foundation fund raising. A relationship that is based on honesty and reality will be stronger and more successful over the long term.

How, then, can an institution that has chosen complete honesty compete successfully if other applicants are exaggerating their claims? This is where trust is essential. When the grant seeker believes that the foundation is capable of piercing through the exaggerations of competing institutions to judge a case on the merits, the application process works well. When the grant seeker does not believe this, chaos reigns. It is up to foundation staff to assure potential applicants—through actions as well as through words—that they will not be misled by exaggerations. Doing this goes a long way towards creating a strong and effective funding process.

Candor, then, is the responsibility of both parties: The applying institutions must be honest, and foundation staff must be able to discount those that are not honest.

After the grant has been received. The possibilities for ethical wrongdoing do not end with the award of the grant. On the contrary, numerous opportunities arise in the use of the grant money and the reporting of this use. To use a grant for a different purpose than that stipulated in the award is clearly wrong. Such a misuse compromises the whole system of foundation fund raising.

But a more troubling issue is the way foundation grants are reported and categorized in the financial records of the receiving institution. In efforts to reach stated goals or to project to the public a successful track record, institutions may take liberties with the way gifts are reported and classified. For example, the fiscal years to which grants are applied are sometimes blurred, the status of the award altered to qualify for matching funds or to meet an announced campaign goal.

In the short run, this kind of "creative reporting" might be useful to meet pressing goals or to provide a much-needed image uplift; in the long run, however, it is difficult to see how an institution can fortify its ethical character by such practices. Deceptive practices run the obvious risk of being discovered by the auditors or the public. An equally serious problem, however, is the effect this kind of behavior has on the institution's long-range character, both in the eyes of its internal constituency and in the eyes of the public. It inevitably weakens the institution's stature over the long term.

It would be nice to believe that reporting errors are unintentional and rare. But we live in an imperfect world, and reporting deceptions do occur, if not frequently at least often enough to be a cause of concern. We need to develop ways in which the profession, the foundations, and the institutions themselves can monitor behavior and enforce sanctions when infractions have been committed.

Summary and conclusion

Ethics in foundation fund raising is complex. A comprehensive ethical analysis needs to focus on three levels: the individual fund raisers and foundation staffers, the institutions that seek the grants and the foundations that make them, and the society of which these individuals and institutions are a part.

Once we understand the web of these interactions and relationships, the primary ethical question becomes: "What actions best serve the well-being of this entire system?" This question can help us face thorny ethical dilemmas and find solutions that will serve the interests of all who seek to make the world a better place through the work of foundation fund raising.

Section 1

Targeting the Foundation Market

Chapter 1

Foundations as Part of an Overall Fund-raising Program

Elizabeth Boris
Vice President, Research
Council on Foundations

T o deal successfully with foundations, you must understand the philanthropic context. In the philanthropic world, foundations are relative newcomers, arising in the early years of this century with the creation of the
Rockefeller, Sage, and Carnegie endowments. The concept of a freestanding, endowed institution that uses the income from the donor's gift (and often some of
the principal) to benefit humankind through systematic, scientific philanthropy
was the product of an era of optimistic belief in the ability of capitalism and science
to make the world right.

The early foundations consciously sought to go beyond the widespread tradition of charity that was practiced at all levels in American culture. Their goal was
to find the causes of and cures for society's ills, not to treat the symptoms. Their
method was to support research and model programs, not to provide alms.

Today there are over 25,000 foundations of four major types:
- private independent foundations like Ford and Rockefeller;
- corporate foundations like Aetna and Dayton Hudson;
- operating foundations like the Getty Museum and the Kettering Foundation;
and
- community foundations like the Cleveland Foundation and the New York
Community Trust.

Under the law, all are considered to be private foundations except the last. (Community foundations are classified as public charities.) Private foundations are usually
formed by an individual, a family, or a company; they may have a mission as broad
as benefiting mankind throughout the world or as narrow as finding a cure for
schistosomiasis. Independent foundations (foundations formed by an individual

or a family) are the most numerous of the four types. There are only about 1,100 corporate foundations (vehicles used to carry out a company's philanthropy) and 907 operating foundations (institutions that run a charitable program such as a museum, a home for the aged, or a research program).[1]

Community foundations, as public charities, come under a different set of regulations. They are formed by a group of donors who wish to benefit a particular community or region. While community foundations are the fastest growing segment of the foundation field, they are still a small part, with only 300 institutions.[2]

As you might expect from institutions that sprang from the fortunes of some of this country's most successful entrepreneurs, foundations are exceptionally varied. They range from the Ford Foundation with more than $4 billion dollars in assets to small funds with several hundred dollars.

There is a world of difference between the small family foundations and the large professionally staffed foundations, but they all follow the nonprofit model of governance. They are governed by a board, which may be called the board of directors or the board of trustees or, in community foundations, the distribution committee. In a family foundation, the board may represent the family and friends of the donor; in other operating and nonoperating foundations, the board may include experts from various fields, national and local notables; in a corporate foundation, the company executives; in a community foundation, the community itself. In all cases, the board is responsible for the foundation's policies and operations.

Foundations have supported an impressive history of accomplishments during this century—the abolishment of hookworm, the development of public television, the discovery of the polio vaccine, and many others. As a share of the national economy, however, foundation assets have declined from $1.16 of every 100 dollars in household and nonprofit assets in 1962 to $.86 in 1981.[3] Today, foundations are providing a smaller share of the private funding for nonprofit activities, approximately 6 percent in 1986 compared to 10 percent in 1970.[4]

Foundations currently have assets of more than $103 billion and make grants of over $6 billion. Most foundations, however, are small and do not employ professional staff. There are only slightly over 5,000 foundations that have assets of more than $1 million or grants that equal $100,000 or over. We estimate that about 2,000 foundations currently employ about 8,000 staff members. Clearly, most of the foundation programs are being run by the donors, their families, and the lawyers and bank trust officers who are often given the responsibility for managing foundations.

Since the 5,148 largest foundations hold approximately 97 percent of the assets and make approximately 92 percent of the grants, most college and university fundraising programs focus on these.[5] The exceptions include small local foundations that concentrate their giving in the immediate community, small foundations that focus on the particular topic or program that requires funding, and small foundations that serve as pass-through vehicles for very large gifts of wealthy donors.

Compared to the rest of the nonprofit sector, foundations are indeed a very small part. There are approximately 821,000 organizations with revenues of $253 billion that make up the nonprofit sector. About 26.9 percent of their revenue comes from private contributions (including gifts from individuals, foundations, and corporations); the same amount of revenue comes from government. Dues, fees, and charges make up about 37.8 percent, and other receipts, including endowment and investment income, comprise about 8.4 percent of revenues.[6]

Charitable giving is an important part of nonprofit revenues and has grown from $21 billion in 1970 to $87 billion in 1986. Foundations account for almost 6 percent of those revenues, but individuals account for the bulk of private giving. The major recipients of private philanthropy, according to *Giving USA,* are religious organizations, education, and health, in that order.[7]

Foundation funding patterns reveal that higher education has long been a major beneficiary of foundation giving, although giving to higher education has been declining in recent years. According to the introduction to the 11th edition of the *Foundation Directory,* foundation grants in 1986 went to the following recipients: 26.4 percent to welfare; 21.9 percent to education; 20.5 percent to health; 14.7 percent to culture; 8.8 percent to social science; and 1.3 percent to religion.[8]

Why set up a foundation program?

An obvious answer is that a major proportion of foundation grants is made to colleges and universities, and it is not always easy for an institution to decide on the appropriate funding source to approach. An institution that expects to develop funding relationships with foundations should develop a systematic approach that includes:
- learning about foundations generally;
- doing the research necessary to identify likely foundation prospects; and
- developing and maintaining in-depth knowledge about the programs and priorities of that targeted group of likely funders.

The particular situation of each institution—its resources and how much money it needs to raise—should determine the extent of its foundation program, which might be a separate, well-staffed program or just one or more people who have been trained and are responsible for research in this area of fund raising.

An institution may benefit from putting a special emphasis on foundation fund raising, not only because there are more than 25,000 very diverse foundations, but because each college or university has a wide variety of programs and other types of needs that could be addressed to different funding sources. For this reason, each institution needs a coordinated approach that reflects a clear sense of institutional priorities.

Another important factor to consider is that while some foundations (especially family foundations with ties to a specific institution or community) are willing to support the same program or institution, year in and year out, most prefer to maintain flexibility in funding possibilities. For this reason, a well-developed foundation program must be an ongoing activity, not a one-time thing.

On the other hand, not every institution needs a foundation fund-raising program. Although foundations give a high proportion of their grants to colleges and universities (35.7 percent or $791 million in 1986), this is a small amount compared to that available from governments, contracts, and other sources.[9] Also, because of government cutbacks in funding for social programs run by nonprofits, increasing numbers of those organizations have turned to foundations for funding. As a result, competition for foundation grants is keener than ever.

If your institution has not sought foundation funds in the past, you should carefully analyze your needs and determine which ones are likely candidates for support from alumni, government, or special campaigns. Needs that do not easily lend themselves to funding from these other sources or that might benefit from a challenge to encourage funding from other sources are probably the best candidates for foundation grants.

If you hope to get a foundation grant, you must understand that foundations tend to fund projects and programs that help them to achieve their goals and objectives. When your institution receives a grant, it becomes a partner with the foundation in meeting its program goals. It is this convergence of interests—the institution's and the foundation's—that results in a successful application. Identifying and articulating those mutual interests is the challenge of the development officer.

You will find a wide variety of interests, missions, and operating styles in the foundation world. This is a world that glories in individualism, and, to make it even more difficult, most foundations are small family-run organizations that do not have professional staff to guide you through the application process.

Understanding foundations

Because foundations have so little to spend in relation to the larger economy, many foundations—particularly the larger staffed ones—have the philosophy that this is very special money and that it must be carefully targeted if it is to make a difference. You can think of foundation funding as the risk capital for improving society. At its best, foundation funding can be the force that encourages creativity and innovation, especially in areas overlooked by other sectors of the economy or too controversial for institutions that must rely on the verdict of the bottom line or the ballot box.

In order to develop a systematic approach to foundation fund raising, you must consider these basic factors:

- the types of foundations (corporate, community, independent, and operating) and the different constraints that apply to each;
- the differences between staffed and unstaffed foundations and the resulting impact on the grant-making process;
- the variations in foundation size that affect not only the amounts of the awards, but the philosophy and operating style of the foundation;
- geographic limitations that cause some foundations to give locally, regionally, nationally, or internationally;
- programmatic emphases—some foundations focus on education, others on health, and so forth;
- differences in operating philosophy and style that may affect the types of grants

made and the types of recipients;

• the regulatory framework that mandates the amount that must be paid out each year, limits grants for certain activities such as lobbying, requires certain procedures for grants to individuals and for scholarship and fellowship funds, and so on.

You also need to be aware of institutional change points that may affect these basic factors, such as death of the donor, infusion of additional money, addition or change of staff, change in board chair or board members, and evaluation or refocusing of the foundation's programs.

How to learn about foundations

Some of the chapters that follow cover this topic in greater depth, but however you wish to handle your research, the place to start is the Foundation Center and the materials it produces. In addition to the indispensable resource directories—the *Foundation Directory,* the *National Data Book,* and the *Grants Index* (all available online through the DIALOG computer network)—Foundation Center collections also include copies of foundation annual reports and the required tax form, the 990-PF, containing information on finances and grants. The Foundation Center has over 100 cooperating collections around the country and four regional offices in New York, Washington, D.C., Cleveland, and San Francisco (see pp. 87-90).

Specialized publications useful for the person new to foundation grant seeking include three of particular interest: *Foundation Fundamentals* by Patricia Read is the basic text for researching foundations; *Working in Foundations* by Teresa Odendahl, Arlene Kaplan Daniels, and myself describes the internal workings of foundations of different types; and *America's Wealthy and the Future of Foundations,* edited by Teresa Odendahl, contains a series of studies including a major survey of foundations, interviews with donors and their advisers that explore their motives for forming foundations, and other chapters on the legislative history of foundations and trends in their creation and growth over the past 25 years.

To round out your knowledge of how foundations work, read some of the classic works by F. Emerson Andrews, Merrimon Cuninggim, John Nason, David Freeman, John Russell, and the more gossipy works by Waldemar Nielsen. You can supplement the basic background provided by these books with *Foundation News* and foundation annual reports. (For further reading, see "Reference Sources" at the end of this chapter and the bibliography at the end of this book.)

Understanding institutional needs

To have a successful fund-raising program, you and your staff must thoroughly understand your institution's needs and priorities. Such an understanding is imperative when you are identifying potential funders and exploring other ways, in addition to grants, that foundations can help the institution. The foundation and the institution could undertake a cooperative venture, for example, or the foundation could provide the institution with services, such as loans, technical assistance, use of facilities, speakers, and so on.

You also need clear direction from the top about the priority attached to each proposal. This helps you match proposals to funders. You should usually avoid submitting more than one proposal at a time to the same funder, but if, for some reason, more than one is appropriate, you and your staff should carefully monitor the process in case a donor can fund only one project. You must know which has the higher priority. In some cases, foundations require that the president of the institution approve all requests for funding so that the foundation doesn't have to attempt to sort out the university's priorities among proposals submitted by various individuals and departments.

When you are seeking foundation funding, you should be clear on the following points:
- the various types of needs (capital, endowment, research, special programs, operating support, professional or curriculum development);
- amounts required in each category;
- institutional priorities;
- timing, date when the funds are needed;
- other types of (non-grant) needs that a foundation might be able to address.

Future issues and trends

Formation of foundations. Research reported in *America's Wealthy* verifies the declining rate of formation of new large foundations since the 1960s. Declining tax rates, the development of other charitable options that have greater tax deductibility, and increasing regulation are among the factors that played a role in the falloff. Paradoxically, the further reduction of the tax rate in 1986 caused the creation of some new foundations as donors sought to speed up planned contributions before the lower tax rates took effect. It will take several years before we can assess the long-term implications of the Revenue Act of 1986.

Several concerns emerged from this study. First, the growth in numbers of foundations, although substantial, was not great enough to maintain their position in the larger economy in the period from 1962 to 1981. Also, large foundations, those most likely to be staffed, have a smaller proportion of foundation assets than they did in 1962. There are more smaller foundations than in the past.

Second, the proportion of foundations formed during the donor's lifetime declined. As a result, there is less likelihood that foundations will receive large future gifts, a major source of foundation income in the 1970s. And during this period, lawyers and other advisers to wealthy donors usually considered a private foundation as the least desirable option for their clients' charitable giving.

These findings highlight the need to pay greater attention to the preservation and enhancement of existing foundation assets. They also indicate the need to educate donors and their advisers about the benefits and advantages of conducting philanthropy through a foundation. The Council on Foundations has developed programs to address both concerns. It will soon publish a major study of foundation investment policies and procedures and will intensify its efforts to provide educational programs dealing with this important topic. In addition, the Council has undertaken a three-year project to educate legal and other advisers about foundations and to encourage wealthy individuals to form or contribute to foundations.

Staffing trends. Since the early 1970s there has been a major change in the staffing patterns of foundations. Not only is there a greater number of foundations that have hired staff, but there is greater diversity among the staff. Biennial surveys conducted by the Council reveal that there are increasing numbers of women and minorities working in foundations. Our surveys show that the proportion of foundations headed by a woman has risen from 26 percent to 41 percent over the past seven years. And the proportion of women in foundation program positions has risen to 62 percent. Minorities account for about 2 percent of foundation chief executives and about 15 percent of program staff. Those who have advocated greater diversity of foundation staff expect that this change in composition will improve foundation sensitivity to issues that affect the well-being of women and minorities.

The big picture. The future of foundations is intimately tied up with the future of the nonprofit charitable sector as a whole. Many elected officials and other policy makers have little understanding of this sector and little appreciation of its current role, long history, and great accomplishments. Too little research has been conducted and too little attention has been given to the role that nonprofit institutions play in our society. The result of this neglect—graphically demonstrated in recently proposed legislation on lobbying, unrelated business income, and taxes—is that proposed regulations often have seriously detrimental, if unintended, consequences for nonprofits.

Colleges and universities are beginning to realize that they have a stake in the well-being of the whole sector. The creation of Centers for the Study of Philanthropy and programs that train nonprofit managers within colleges and universities is a welcome development that should benefit the entire sector in the long run.

Notes

[1] *National Data Book,* 11th ed. (New York: The Foundation Center, 1987), p. xi. Note: The number of corporate foundations is an unpublished estimate from the Foundation Center.

[2] Ibid.

[3] Ralph Nelson, "An Economic History of Large Foundations," in *America's Wealthy and the Future of Foundations,* ed. Teresa J. Odendahl (New York: The Foundation Center, 1987), pp. 127-177.

[4] Virginia Ann Hodgkinson and Murray Weitzman, *Dimensions of the Independent Sector* (Washington, DC: Independent Sector, 1986), p. 53. See also *Giving USA* (New York: American Association of Fund-Raising Counsel Trust for Philanthropy, 1987), p. 31.

[5] *The Foundation Directory,* 11th ed. (New York: The Foundation Center, 1987), p. i. Note: Figures for assets and grants come from information to be included in the 12th edition of the *Foundation Directory.*

[6] Hodgkinson and Weitzman, *Dimensions of the Independent Sector,* p. 32.

[7] *Giving USA,* p. 11.

[8] *Foundation Grants Index,* 16th ed. (New York: Foundation Center, 1987), p. xvi.

[9] Ibid.

Reference Sources

Andrews, F. Emerson. *Philanthropic Foundations.* New York: Russell Sage Foundation, 1956.

Corporate Philanthropy: Philosophy, Management, Trends, Future, Background. Washington, DC: Council on Foundations, 1982.

Council on Foundations, Inc. "Recommended Principles and Practices for Effective Grantmaking." *Foundation News 21,* September/October 1980, pp. 8-10.

Cuninggim, Merrimon. *Private Money and Public Service: The Role of Foundations in American Society.* New York: McGraw-Hill, 1972.

Edie, John A. *First Steps in Starting a Foundation.* Washington, DC: Council on Foundations, 1987.

The Foundation Directory, 11th ed. New York: The Foundation Center, 1987.

Foundation Grants Index, 16th ed. New York: The Foundation Center, 1987.

Foundation News—The Magazine of Philanthropy. Arlie Schardt, ed. Washington, DC: Council on Foundations, bimonthly.

Freeman, David F. *The Handbook on Private Foundations.* Washington, DC: Council on Foundations, 1981.

Giving USA. New York: American Association of Fund-Raising Counsel Trust for Philanthropy, 1987.

Heimann, Fritz F., ed. *The Future of Foundations.* Englewood Cliffs, NJ: Prentice-Hall, 1973.

Hodgkinson, Virginia Ann, and Weitzman, Murray. *Dimensions of the Independent Sector.* Washington, DC: Independent Sector, 1986.

Koch, Frank. *The New Corporate Philanthropy: How Society and Business Can Profit.* New York: Plenum Press, 1979.

Nason, John W. *Trustees and the Future of Foundations.* New York: Council on Foundations, 1977.

National Data Book, 11th ed. New York: The Foundation Center, 1987.

Nielsen, Waldemar A. *The Big Foundations*. New York: Columbia University Press, 1972.

Nielsen, Waldemar A. *The Golden Donors*. New York: Truman Talley Books, E. P. Dutton, 1985.

Odendahl, Teresa J., ed. *America's Wealthy and the Future of Foundations*. New York: The Foundation Center, 1987.

Odendahl, Teresa, and Boris, Elizabeth. "A Delicate Balance: Board-Staff Relations." *Foundation News*, September/October 1983, pp. 34-35.

Odendahl, Teresa, and Boris, Elizabeth. "The Grantmaking Process." *Foundation News*, September/October 1983, pp. 22-31.

Odendahl, Teresa Jean, et al. *Working in Foundations: Career Patterns of Women and Men*. New York: The Foundation Center, 1985.

Pekkanen, John. "The Great Givers, Part I and Part II." *Town and Country*, December 1979, pp. 141-148, and January 1980, pp. 37-44.

Roisman, Lois. "The Community Foundation Connection." *Foundation News*, March/April 1982, pp. 2-8.

Russell, John M. *Giving and Taking: Across the Foundation Desk*. New York: Teachers College Press, 1977.

Weaver, Warren. *U.S. Philanthropic Foundations: Their History, Structure, Management and Record*. New York: Harper and Row, 1967.

Whitaker, Ben. *The Philanthropoids: Foundations and Society*. New York: William Morrow, 1974.

Chapter 2

"It's a Jungle in Here!"

M. Joseph Roberson
Director for Corporate and Foundation Relations
University of Michigan

E ach profession has its own form of jungle in which individuals must operate. In our competitive economic and political system, those jungles require survival techniques.

Although we in development work are not fighting for our own personal survival, we may be fighting for the survival of our institutions—or at least for the goals and aspirations that make our institutions what they are. Operating with your eye on this kind of survival is an excellent personal motivator.

We've all heard the story of the two men on safari who are spotted by a hungry lion. As one prepares to run, the other says, "You can't outrun that lion!" "I don't have to outrun the lion," says the first man, "I only have to outrun *you*!" Sometimes it seems that the world of foundation relations fosters that sort of attitude—and a little jungle lore can help you keep away from the lions!

The most basic requirement for jungle survival is to know your environment— the easy paths through the undergrowth, who and where the predators are, who competes with you for nourishment, whom you can count on for help and support, how to find the water and avoid the quicksand, and what the pecking order is. If you want to survive—and maybe even prosper—you must begin by understanding your environment.

The internal environment

Every foundation officer works in a unique environment. While many institutions have significant similarities, none of them are exactly alike. Different programs, people, organizational structure, and traditions are only some of the things that make each institution different from all others.

When you analyze the internal environment of your institution, you will need to identify both the formal and the informal characteristics that make it distinctive.

Formal characteristics. Although these features are not as clearcut as they might once have been, most people will agree in general on these institutional characteristics. The difficulty is understanding how they should help shape the foundation relations plan.

• *Public/private.* There was a time when this distinction was an obvious one, but no longer. Today we have institutions that are "mostly private" or "publicly assisted," and so forth. We are hard pressed to find an institution that receives its support—aside from tuition—either solely from tax dollars or solely from private sources. Most "private" universities draw heavily on tax dollars, often federal but frequently state. And "public" universities and colleges seek funding from the traditionally private sources of foundations and corporations.

Moreover, most governmental bodies have accepted the principle of supporting, either directly or indirectly, private higher education, and most foundations and corporations have accepted the idea of support to public higher education. If we use tax dollar support as a criterion, then we have very few, if any, purely private or purely public universities. Institutions of higher education are more accurately characterized as predominately one or the other.

As you develop your foundation program, you need to have a clear picture of the private/public blend at your institution. Many foundations will support projects that are not considered to be the obligation of the public sector. In order to plan your program, you need to know which parts of your institution fit this criterion. For example, a public university might obtain support from a foundation for a program or facility the state will not fund, such as a conference center, student activities facility, or some other non-core facility. Private colleges and universities have a broader menu in the world of foundations. Core programs or basic educational facilities often get private support at these institutions.

• *Research/teaching.* Here, again, we find the characteristics blending. All institutions of higher education teach, and all do some form of research. Nevertheless, most institutions are organized primarily around one or the other. Faculty reward structures are different, and funding sources differ as well, depending on how teaching and research are blended at an institution.

Research universities receive funding from government and corporations in support of their research activities. Some foundations are research-oriented as well. Institutions of higher education that have a teaching orientation are more likely to achieve foundation support for curricular or programmatic purposes.

Careful analysis of your institution's blend should lead you *to* some foundations and *away* from others.

• *Other formal characteristics.* In addition, the size of your institution, its geography, the quality and diversity of the student body, and other such features are all part of the obvious institutional environment. Understanding these characteristics will help you focus your projects and market them to foundations.

Informal characteristics. The formal characteristics are important. Understanding them and their implications will strengthen your foundation program. However, these characteristics are the trail blazes in the jungle: You can't miss them. The real dangers are less obvious. If you don't see and comprehend the informal characteristics of your institution, you may find yourself in the land of no return—and there's no worse place for a development officer. Be aware of these boggy places in your jungle:

• *Centralized/decentralized.* In a centralized institution, the role of the president or CEO is a strong one—power passes downward through this person and his or her office. In a decentralized system, decision making and power are distributed among the different components (schools and colleges) of the institution. This does not mean that the president is necessarily a strong leader in the centralized system and not in the other. On the contrary, many believe that the CEO of a decentralized system must be a very strong leader because he or she does not receive authority from the position but from other factors (expertise, personality, etc.).

Neither one system nor the other is "better"; either can succeed or fail, depending on the nature and the needs of the institution. But it *is* important that you understand which system your institution uses and how it works.

When you know where the power resides, you can shape your foundation relations program accordingly. For example, if program and project decisions are made at the most basic level, you need to spend a lot of time with deans, department chairs, and faculty. If your institution has tighter control and decisions are made at the top, you need to establish clear paths of communication to the upper levels of the organization. This does not mean, of course, that you speak only to deans and faculty chairs or only to those on the upper level. You need to be in touch with all facets of your organization, but your time is limited, and you should spend it in the most productive way possible. Your program will benefit if you use your understanding of the institutional environment to establish your priorities.

• *Formal and informal power structures.* Whether your institution is centralized or decentralized or a blend of both, your college or university has both a formal and an informal power structure.

To understand the formal power structure, all you need is an organizational chart. The chart shows you who reports to whom and who is equal to whom. But it doesn't always show you where the real power is located. For this you need to understand the informal power structure.

All of our institutions have people who wield far more power than the organizational chart indicates. Such people were not assigned the power but got it by a variety of other means. One is seniority—a person who has been around a long time represents continuity and a sense of tradition. Sometimes power is in the hands of a "gatekeeper," a person who controls the flow of information to the decision makers. Who can forget the power Haldeman and Ehrlichman had because they were the only source of information President Nixon had?

In the academic arena, power is often cornered by the articulate, well-informed person. This person flourishes in open discussion. He or she always seems to have the most information and the best. The position of this person—a senior faculty member, a well-placed secretary, or a well-informed staff member—is often not relevant to the amount of power he or she possesses, which can be enormous.

You need to identify the people who have this power and gain their support. A person in the informal power structure can destroy your program just as surely as a person high on the organizational chart. Be sure to get such a person "on your side" early—at least at the time your proposal is going through the formal structure and perhaps even before.

Role of the foundation officer

The role a foundation officer plays in the overall institutional scheme is determined in part by the formal power structure and in part by the informal structure. Depending on the amount of power vested in the position at a particular institution, the foundation officer's role lies at some point on the directing/coordinating/advisory continuum.

Thus, at some institutions, the foundation relations office has a fair amount of decision-making power. It has significant input on decisions about what units apply for how much money, for what, and when. On other campuses, the office provides a coordinating function. It keeps track of various units' interests in Foundation X, what the programs are, and what amounts are being requested. Such a role may include implementing executive decisions, made by others, about who is next in line.

If the foundation relations office plays an advisory role, it stands clear of decision making but merely gives advice and observes who—if anyone—follows it.

Although few of us have such a narrow role that we *only* advise or *always* direct, you can probably define your job as being primarily at one point or another on the continuum. Regardless of where your situation places you, it is sometimes wise to function as though your only power and authority are executed through persuasion.

Whether you are on a large, decentralized research university campus or at a small, centralized teaching college, you will be better able to survive and thrive if your campus colleagues know you as *the* expert on foundations. If your power is based on extensive knowledge of the campus and foundations, you are on your way. For knowledge *is* power. Our higher education system prizes knowledge and expertise above all else. We value and reward faculty members who have a highly developed expertise in a discipline or profession. Thus, even if you have no formal decision-making authority, if you are *the* person on campus to turn to when the subject is foundation support, you will find that you do, in fact, have a great deal of power.

While your primary role, then, is that of institutional expert on foundations, you have another role as communicator. The word "communication" is overworked and misused second only to planning (and more on that later). It does not take a college education to understand that the key to most human endeavor is communication. Every course, seminar, training session, or other educational program in management tells us this. And yet few of us are very good at communicating.

Too many of us think that if we write a lot of memos and hold a lot of meetings, we are communicating. While some memos are necessary, too many result in overkill and inhibit communication. Memos become junk mail and many are ignored, particularly those for general distribution. Even the word processor, which can "personalize" every memo, can't help here as people quickly learn to recognize the efforts of the machine. If you make judicious use of memos, you are more likely to communicate than if you flood the institution with paper.

It is also safe to say that all of us attend too many useless meetings and too many long ones. In most of those meetings, very little communication takes place. People don't pay attention in slow-paced unfocused and too-frequent meetings. Often the only people who get anything done are those who bring something to do during interminable and pointless discussions. And if you get the reputation of holding too many meetings that last too long, people will come to your meeting with such low expectations that very little communication is likely to take place—even if you have determined that *this* meeting will be different.

Memos and meetings can enhance communication but only when they are used sparingly and skillfully.

The most effective communication is done face-to-face. The job of communicating is too important to be left to the pencil and the telephone. One way to fulfill your communication role is to be out of your office a lot. You should make regular visits to the important offices (as defined by your knowledge of your campus environment). Going to other people's offices is not only a courtesy to them but a show of confidence on your part. *You* are the institutional expert and as such you are comfortable in anyone else's territory.

I can't overemphasize the importance of on-campus communication. When you approach a foundation you are, in fact, attempting to market your institution's "products," and you must know those products as well as you can. You must establish good communications with your program people and keep them informed as to who is interested in their product and how you plan to find support for their projects.

Planning is another important role for the foundation officer. As with communication, we often mistake some activities for planning. Living in an academic jungle (where publication is a fact of life) encourages us to believe that making graphs, charts, matrices, lists, reports, and so on, is planning. The data contained in these documents—at least some of the data—are necessary but not sufficient for planning. Research is a planning tool but not the end result. When you mistake research for planning, you will be well-informed but not very effective.

Once the research is done, the planning begins. Now you understand institutional priorities, strengths, and weaknesses, and you have identified the key people in reaching your goal. You need to think about the steps you must take to obtain the grant: What are the cultivation activities? What is the proper timing? Whom should you involve and at what stage? Who will write the proposal? Who will make the presentation? What follow-up commitments will the foundation expect and the institution accept? If your proposal is turned down, what are your alternatives?

You cannot plan until you can answer these questions, and you cannot answer these questions unless you have analyzed and understood your institutional environment.

The external environment

Good institutional information provides you with a base from which you can begin to develop an understanding of the external environment—and that means the foundation. Like institutions of higher education, the foundation environment has both a formal and an informal structure.

The formal structure. You must understand the formal structure of any foundation with which you expect to have success. You must know its program areas, the size of its average grant, limitations, geographic preferences, application procedures, deadlines, and so on.

When you talk to anyone at the foundation, it should be obvious that you have carefully read its annual report and brochures. The president's letter in the annual report is particularly important as an indication of the foundation's major focus or potential future directions. Examining these materials will usually give you a good grasp of the formal structure of the foundation.

The informal structure. To be a successful foundation officer, you need to have all the formal information and much more. You need to understand the informal structure for each of your priority foundations.

• *Program officer influence.* In some foundations, once you have the program officer's approval, you have the gift. In others, the president's endorsement carries the weight. In still others, the board evaluates each proposal and makes a decision.

While it is never good strategy to alienate *any* program officer, some program officers are more equal than others. Having the program officer with the most clout support your proposal is to your advantage. Inside information on a program officer's pet project or his or her pet peeve can help the foundation relations officer immensely.

• *Foundation temperature.* Foundation people cannot see everyone who wants to see them. Otherwise, they would be so busy with meetings, they wouldn't be able to read proposals or recommend grants. But different foundations—and different people—deal with this problem in different ways. No annual report can tell you whether a given foundation is "warm" or "cold."

Some foundations encourage visits and discussions and practice constituency outreach; a half-hour with the president is not unheard of. Others are practically inaccessible, and it's considered a great accomplishment to get an appointment at all. If you can't reach a "cold" foundation personally, you must find other ways to get information on its informal structure—perhaps from a more fortunate colleague or from friends of the foundation or from a closer analysis of grant patterns.

As an institutional foundation officer, you can't consider a cold foundation "bad" or a warm foundation "good." But you do need to know toward which end of the temperature range a foundation tends, and then operate within that knowledge. Remember, foundations set the rules (both formal and informal), and it's your job to operate within those rules. That means if you are dealing with 30 foundations, you may be playing under 30 different sets of rules. But to be successful, that is what you have to do.

• *Future direction.* Every foundation officer has probably dreamed of being the only one who knows about a foundation's new area of interest; his or her well-prepared proposal is the first one submitted to tap this particular gold mine; the university gets the multimillion dollar grant; the foundation officer is invited to the White House, gets 10 percent of the grant, and is asked to share his or her expertise by writing an article for CASE.

Unfortunately, it doesn't happen like that—at least not often—but some people seem to know about new directions before the rest of us. All too often, by the time a new direction is formally announced, it is no longer new. It's not really a sixth sense—it's just that some of our colleagues are masters at using the informal foundation structure. They have friends on the program staff; they go over the president's message with a fine-tooth comb; they analyze grants for variations and patterns; and they find out which consultants are being hired by the foundation. Then they prepare the institution to take advantage of the new direction.

The institution itself can—and often does—help shape a foundation's future direction. The creative proposal, perhaps turned down initially, can start new trains of thought within the foundation. The world of higher education is supposed to be setting new directions, opening new horizons, and producing leadership. Many of these ideas can lead to new interests for foundations as they interact with the creative people on our campuses.

• *Giving cycles.* In many respects foundations are businesses. They have good years and bad years, depending on how they manage their investments. Foundation giving may increase or decrease dramatically, depending on the stock market. Some foundations have a very large percentage of their investments in market equities and are therefore very market-sensitive. Others invest a larger amount in bonds and are not affected as heavily by market fluctuation.

Your program

You have now completed the hardest part of your job. You understand your jungle—both the internal environment of your institution and the external environment of the foundation. Make the appropriate connection between these two information systems—that is, take your institutional strengths and priorities to the foundation with the most interest.

You are a survivor, soon to be a leader. But don't become complacent. Remember, no environment is static, especially not the jungle in here. Personnel changes and goal changes—both at your institution and at the foundation—make it essential that you stay alert. You can never tell when a new danger may show up or you may find a new path that will take you straight to the richest undiscovered part of the jungle.

Chapter 3

Managing for Results: Tools to Target and Refine a Foundation Relations Program

Arthur Caccese
Vice President for Development and College Relations
The College of Saint Rose

M anagement is a form of work. As the manager, you are the person who performs this work. In doing your work, you perform certain activities that we can call the "functions of management." Two elements are essential if you are to be an effective manager:

• a set of goals and the strategy, or strategies, to achieve them; and

• an understanding of those people whose motivation and direction will ultimately determine the success or failure of your plans.

In order to be an effective manager of the foundation relations program at your institution, you need to understand the principles and practices of management—and you must implement them as well. The demands of accountability and the imperatives of a competitive environment require you to do so.

What is management?

One of the earliest written descriptions of a manager at work comes from the Book of Exodus. In the passage below, Moses' father-in-law Jethro (possibly our first recorded management consultant) tells him how to deal with the increasing demands on his time:

The next day Moses sat as usual to hear the people's complaints against each other, from morning to evening.

When Moses' father-in-law saw how much time this was taking, he said, "Why are you trying to do all this alone, with people standing here all day long to get your help? You're going to wear yourself out—and if you do, what will happen to the people? Moses, the job is too heavy a burden for you to handle all by yourself.

"Now listen, and let me give you a word of advice....

"Find some capable, godly, honest men who hate bribes and appoint them as judges, one judge for each 1,000 people; he in turn will have 10 judges under him, each in charge of 100; and under each of them will be two judges, each responsible for the affairs of 50 people; and each of these will have five judges beneath him, each counseling 10 persons. Let these men be responsible to serve the people with justice at all times. Anything that is too important or too complicated can be brought to you. But the smaller matters, they can take care of themselves. That way it will be easier for you because you will share the burden with them." (Exodus 18: 13-22)

This passage illustrates the importance of teamwork, of delegation, and of planning. And as history has shown, Moses followed Jethro's suggestion and turned out to be quite an effective leader.

Management has been defined in many ways. Even today, with the popularity of the discipline of management at an all-time high, there is no commonly accepted definition. The definition of management I prefer is that suggested by Leslie W. Rue and Lloyd L. Byars: "Management is a process or form of work that involves the guidance or direction of a group of people toward organizational goals or objectives."[1]

These same authors identify five primary functions of management:

1. *planning*—deciding what objectives to pursue during a future time period and what to do in order to achieve those objectives;

2. *organizing*—grouping activities, assigning activities, and providing the authority to carry out activities;

3. *staffing*—determining human resource needs; recruiting, selecting, training, and developing human resources;

4. *motivating*—directing or channeling human behavior toward goals; and

5. *controlling*—measuring performance goals, determining causes of deviation, and taking corrective action where necessary.[2]

The successful manager

The effective manager possesses at least three primary abilities: the ability to manage time; the ability to work with and through others (interpersonal skill); and the ability to communicate.

The ability to manage time. Knowing how to manage time doesn't mean burning the midnight oil seven days a week or even filling every working moment with "productivity." What it does mean is working efficiently: setting priorities, thinking ahead, and achieving results through the efforts of others.

Joel S. Nadel has identified five common errors that can chronically undermine your ability to use your time effectively:

1. *Doing work beneath your capabilities.* On average, executives spend 53 percent of their time performing secretarial or clerical tasks. If these can be done by someone else, they should be.

2. *Tolerating too many interruptions.* Schedule your availability and your unavailability. Set aside a "quiet" period each day when you absolutely prohibit all visitors and phone calls, and another period when your door is open.

3. *Handling trivial assignments while keeping the big job "on hold."* Attack the most important project first thing in the morning and work on it as long as you can. The payoff: By 11 a.m., you'll feel as though you've accomplished a whole day's work.

4. *Working without a plan.* Take a few minutes at the start of each day to outline your objectives and priorities. By helping you organize your working day, those minutes will save you many hours.

5. *Saying "yes" too much.* Make "no" the automatic response to demands on your time. "Yes" should be the exception.[3]

In my own career, I've used two methods to organize my time more effectively: "elephant hunting" and "the 31 folders."

Elephant hunting is essential to effective time management. This means that you go after the big, high-payoff goals and minimize the time you spend stomping on ants—the "administrivia" that takes up so much of your time. The chart below may help you tell the ants from the elephants. When you're operating in cell 2, you're in elephant country.

		IMPORTANT	
		YES	NO
URGENT	YES	1. Important/Urgent	3. Not Important/Urgent
	NO	2. Important/Not Urgent	4. Not Important/Not Urgent

For example, here's how I would categorize the following activities:

1. *Important/urgent:* Getting a proposal out on time; resolving a conflict with your boss.

2. *Important/not urgent:* Long-range planning; developing subordinates.

3. *Not important/urgent:* Dealing with constant interruptions; answering telephone calls.

4. *Not important/not urgent:* Straightening papers again; socializing.

In the 31 folders method, you assemble folders numbered from 1 to 31 to represent the days of the month. This system enables you to handle each piece of paper only once. As you look at each piece of paper, decide to toss it, refer it, act on it, or file it—and do so immediately. For those papers that require follow-up action, decide when the next step should occur and put the piece of paper in the appropriate folder.

Each day you work with only those items in the folder for that particular day. The beauty of this procedure is that now you no longer have an in-basket. The folders are a sorted, organized, and prioritized in-basket. You can use the same system—and the same folders—to organize your personal life as well. The 31 folders system takes a little getting used to, but once you're comfortable with it you'll wonder how you ever managed without it.

Another great timesaver is to learn how to deal with meetings. Meetings are a major time-waster but, on the campus setting, they are how things get done—or don't get done. For committees to accomplish anything at all, they have to meet. Harold Taylor offers 10 tips for conducting a productive meeting:

1. Issue the agenda well in advance, and be sure to state the objective of the meeting. Include starting time, anticipated stopping time, and time allocated to each item to be discussed.

2. When making up the agenda, put important items first so that you won't have to rush through them at the end of the meeting.

3. Invite as few people as possible.

4. Start on time and don't summarize for late arrivals.

5. Don't let people air their views unless it will help reach the meeting's objective.

6. At the end of the meeting, summarize the decisions reached and the responsibilities assigned.

7. End the meeting when the objective is reached.

8. Keep minutes brief. Highlight the decisions reached and the actions to be taken. Include deadlines.

9. Issue minutes promptly after each meeting while it's still fresh in everyone's mind.

10. Always evaluate the success of a meeting. Ask yourself what could be improved the next time.[4]

Interpersonal skill. If you have interpersonal skill, you are effective at working with and through others—your boss, your peers, and your subordinates. The literature clearly shows that interpersonal skill is vitally important to promotion and career advancement. In fact, more senior managers are fired because of personality conflicts or differences in style with their bosses than for any other cause. The seven qualities below play a large role in interpersonal skill:

- honesty and directness;
- fairness;
- high expectations for yourself and others;
- a sense of humor;
- the ability to delegate;
- leader behavior; and
- knowing how to manage your boss.

Most of these are self-explanatory, but I'd like to elaborate briefly on "the ability to delegate." Delegating is a proven time and management technique. The principle here is a straightforward one. If a task can be done by someone else, it should be. All too often, however, we allow staff members to give their problems to us. This phenomenon is what my former boss at Rensselaer Polytechnic Institute referred to as "Who's got the monkey?"

Delegating is also an effective way to develop your subordinates. With the proper instruction—with clear directions and a deadline—delegating recognizes a subordinate's past performance as well as his or her potential. It is a tangible way to show your trust and your belief that he or she can handle the responsibility.

The ability to communicate. This managerial skill includes written, spoken, and listening proficiency. You simply cannot do your job successfully if you have trouble writing and speaking correctly and persuasively. Foundation relations officers have to be articulate representatives of their department and their institution, and they must be so on a variety of subjects—more so, I believe, than any other development officer.

To be effective, you must be able to communicate. And to communicate, you begin by listening. The art of listening is not as easy as you may think. All too many people are *not* listening, and this may be caused by any of the following factors, according to Margaret Tacarden of the social work department at Skidmore College:

- message overload;
- preoccupation;
- physical noise;
- faulty assumptions; and
- talking has more apparent advantages.

In his book, *Human Relations at Work*, Keith Davis offers the following 10 steps to effective listening:

1. Stop talking!
2. Put the speaker at ease.
3. Show the speaker that you want to listen.
4. Remove distractions.
5. Empathize with the speaker.
6. Be patient.
7. Hold your temper.
8. Go easy on argument and criticism.
9. Ask questions.

10. Stop talking! (This is first and last because all other steps depend on it.)[5]

Harvey K. Jacobson believes that while successful managers possess the three skills described above, a second set of qualities is necessary for the times in which we live and do our work:

- conceptual pluralism: flexible thinking that nurtures flexible action;
- a flare for cutting through the fog: reducing complex situations to their essentials;
- respect for the long term: weighing potential long-term consequences against immediate gains;
- judgment: the ability to interpret facts, assign proper weight, and come to sound conclusions;
- imagination: a willingness to dream and to take risks;
- an optimistic attitude: casting new ideas in terms of potential and opportunity;
- sensitivity to academe: an appreciation for the uniqueness of an academic institution;
- character: integrity and personal conduct;
- compatibility with the chief executive officer: being on the same psychological and ideological wavelength; and
- a sense of legacy: passing on the tradition of stewardship to others.[6]

In a 1986 paper, John W. Gardner outlines six ways in which leaders distinguish themselves from managers:

1. Leaders think longer term—beyond today's crises, beyond the quarterly report, beyond the horizon.

2. Leaders look beyond the unit they are heading and grasp its relationship to larger realities—the larger organization of which they are a part, conditions external to the organization, global trends.

3. Leaders reach and include constituents beyond their jurisdictions, beyond boundaries.

4. Leaders put heavy emphasis on the intangibles of vision, values, and motivation; and they understand intuitively the nonrational and unconscious elements in the leader-constituent interaction.

5. Leaders have the political skill to cope with the conflicting requirements of multiple constituencies.

6. Leaders think in terms of renewal. The manager tends to accept the structure and processes as they exist. The leader seeks the revision of process and structure required by ever-changing reality.[7]

We should all strive to be leaders and not merely managers.

The people factor: Staffing and motivating

Here are three rules that can help you deal effectively with your staff.

Rule 1: Recruit the best people. Don't look for bargains. The most successful managers—and the most successful institutions—spend a considerable amount of time identifying, recruiting, and training the people who work in the foundation program.

Rule 2: Keep your staff informed and involved. Don't keep secrets from them. The more your people know—and this means support staff too—the better able they are to do their jobs.

While I'd be the last to recommend more meetings, it is important to meet with your staff on a regular basis, both individually and departmentally. These meetings give you the opportunity to let the staff know how what they're doing fits into the larger picture and what projects are (or should be) on the front burner. You can find out how staff members are spending their time and what successes and frustrations they are experiencing. Remember that it's *your* job to provide the resources so that the staff can do *their* jobs. Information and shared vision are essential in this process.

Rule 3: Be concerned about the professional development of your staff. This means taking them seriously. If you are willing to rewrite job descriptions and to modify responsibilities so that people can move into other areas that interest them, you will find that your staff will be more committed to you, more productive, and that the entire operation will run more smoothly. The bottom line is that your program will be much more effective.

In an excellent chapter on maximizing staff performance, Michael Berger suggests that effective coaches know that getting the right person on the team, clarifying the roles, and training the team members are necessary but not sufficient to produce peak performance. "The player must be motivated to do what is expected. All the talent in the world will be useless unless it is channeled in the right direction."[8]

As managers we are often in a difficult position where motivation is concerned because, as Berger reminds us, "The manager's ability to provide financial rewards and promotions is often limited, and although it is nice to think that members of the staff will be internally motivated, this is often not the case."[9] How then can a manager develop creative ways to motivate employees?

One very effective activity that Rensselaer's development office undertook last year was to develop a list of "motivators." This year each manager has begun to implement them, and staff morale has risen dramatically. The point is to find out what your *staff* believes is important in the work environment and to establish these factors as motivators.

A good deal of research has been done on the motivation of employees. While academic institutions and the corporate community have very different cultures, it is possible to identify principles common to both. In the May 1983 CASE CURRENTS, Calvin Stoney identifies four rules for developing a motivation strategy:

1. integrate employee needs and organizational goals;
2. create conditions that facilitate performance;
3. develop a fair management style; and
4. recognize both good and bad performance.[10]

Your staff should *always* know how they are doing and where they stand. Good managers provide constant feedback—and they do so both formally and informally.

Coaching is an important skill that can help you develop your staff. Coaching departs from traditional appraisal and training because it assumes that *you* are responsible for the development of your subordinates.

Berger offers four principles for effective coaching:

1. Initiate contact with the employee to discuss his or her development.

2. Do mentoring on a regular, ongoing basis (with good and poor performers alike).

3. Offer advice on what to do and how to do it more effectively.

4. If the employee is having problems in bringing his or her performance up to standard, help determine the causes of those problems and plan strategies to overcome them.[11]

Developing the plan

Effective planning is really strategic planning. At a conference on executive management sponsored by the Council for Advancement and Support of Education (CASE), George Keller (author of *Academic Strategy: The Management Revolution in Higher Education*) defined strategic planning as a "coordinated effort to maintain a sustained competitive advantage in a time of rapid change." According to Keller, the four components of an effective strategic plan are:

- goals and objectives;
- a timetable for accomplishing goals and objectives;
- an evaluation process; and
- a feedback mechanism.[12]

Individual objectives are the basis for an effective plan. While management by objectives (MBO) is complicated, George S. Odiorne says that it is "deceptively simple in its underlying theory, which is: The first step in managing anything is to define your objective before you release any resources or spend any time trying to achieve it."[13]

Anthony T. Raia provides helpful guidelines for establishing objectives:

1. Adapt your objectives directly to organizational goals and strategic plans. Do not just assume that they support higher-level management objectives.

2. Quantify and target the results whenever possible. Do not formulate objectives the attainment of which cannot be measured or at least verified.

3. Test your objectives for challenge and achievability. Do not build any cushions to hedge against accountability for results.

4. Adjust the objectives to the availability of resources and the reality of organizational life. Do not keep your head either in the clouds or in the sand.

5. Establish reliable performance reports and milestones that measure progress toward each objective. Do not rely on instinct or crude benchmarks to appraise performance.

6. Put your objectives in writing and express them in clear, concise, and unambiguous statements. Do not allow them to remain in loose or vague terms.

7. Limit the number of statements of objectives to the most relevant key result areas of your job. Do not obscure priorities by stating too many objectives.

8. Communicate your objectives to your subordinates so they can formulate their own job objectives. Do not demand that they do your goal setting for you.

9. Review your statements with others to assure consistency and mutual support. Do not fall into the trap of setting your objectives in a vacuum.

10. Modify your statements to meet changes in conditions and priorities.[14]

Once you have developed a plan for your foundation relations program, however, you will quickly discover that your goals must be accomplished within the context of a budget. Be sure to spend budget dollars on the priority objectives for the year. All too often, the foundation relations officer suddenly finds that there is a budget overrun and the major objectives for the year have not been accomplished. Keep your eye on the essential goals of your program and devote your dollars to your priorities.

A related issue—and a particularly troublesome one—is the relationship between institutional priorities and time constraints. You find yourself spending your time meeting with faculty members who need help in securing small grants for their research projects, sabbatical leaves, or equipment. You're working with administrative units who need funds to develop new programs, to publish conference proceedings, or to sponsor workshops. But you can't afford to spend your time writing proposals for faculty, editing letters, doing research, and meeting with individuals on campus at the expense of the larger issues and projects for which you are responsible—*and* on which you will be evaluated.

It is important to keep in mind that your goal is to increase foundation support to the institution in the most efficient and effective way possible—not to serve as a consultant to the various people on campus who have projects to fund.

Implementing the plan

One of the first things that you, as program manager, need to do, is to develop—or identify—internal mechanisms to assist in the delivery of the foundation relations program. For example, what is the process on your campus for identifying priorities, dealing with competing interests, and developing strategies and approaches to prospective foundation donors?

One of the first things I did as director of foundation and corporate relations at Skidmore College was to initiate a grants committee. This group included the provost, the vice president for business affairs, the dean of faculty, the associate dean of faculty, the vice president for development and alumni affairs, the dean of special programs, the foundation and corporate researcher, and myself. We met monthly to establish priorities, to identify sources of support for the most important projects, and to suggest appropriate approaches to the identified foundations.

This committee has been quite successful because it includes individuals who can make decisions, who have a larger sense of the institution and its needs, and who are committed to increasing foundation support to the college. While there are other factors that need to be taken into account, I believe that the grants committee is a major reason for the impressive increases in foundation support to Skidmore College.

Such a committee has other benefits as well. It gives you visibility that would otherwise be difficult to achieve, and it provides an opportunity to educate individuals at the vice presidential level so that they will understand and be committed to your program and support you—and it—elsewhere on campus.

A successful foundations program requires support from the campus community and from constituent groups on campus—faculty, department chairs, deans, vice presidents, admissions staff, and students. These people are crucial to the successful delivery of your program. Thus, it is vital that you actively seek opportunities to be involved in the life of your institution apart from your formal responsibilities in development. In this way, people will get to know you as a competent individual in a context other than your role as a foundation officer. It is important that the people with whom you must work trust you and your judgment. To the extent that you can help these groups meet their goals, you will gain valuable support on campus.

An effective foundation relations program requires both short- and long-term objectives. One of the criticisms of MBO is that it leads to short-term thinking. While annual objectives for your program are essential, you also need to think about where you'd like the program to be three to five years from now. Setting long-term goals and periodically assessing your progress enables you to measure the growth and development of your program over time.

For the long-term effectiveness of your program, you must resist the tendency to move too quickly from identification to cultivation to solicitation; you must argue forcefully for careful cultivation of foundation prospects. Cultivation at its best is a process that involves the prospect in the life of the institution in a way that solidifies the relationship and leads to a commitment to your institution. Without an ongoing and thoughtful cultivation program (which encompasses, as well, careful stewardship after the grant has been awarded), your solicitations will be far less effective.

After you have completed the planning process, it's time to assemble your team. As foundation relations officer you should spearhead this effort. While individual situations should dictate exactly who makes each cultivation call, if the primary purpose of the call is information gathering, updating on institutional progress, or discussing possible areas of support, you represent the development office and with you should be either the president or the chief academic officer or dean. Perhaps you may want to ask one of your institution's key volunteers to be part of the team. Many institutions find this approach to be highly effective.

The same team that went on the cultivation call should be reassembled when you make the formal ask.

As you enter the action phase of your planning, you should make every effort to get out into the field—that is, visit the foundation prospects you have identified. Your relationship with a foundation's program staff is crucial when it is time to prepare the proposal.

When your president visits, he or she may not ask the specific questions to which you need answers: for example, questions about proposal content, the budget, and whether or not to include overhead. But when you have established a relationship with the foundation program officer, you can pick up the phone and ask for advice on how to prepare the proposal, what to include, and what not to include. Neither you nor your foundation program will be effective unless you maintain a very visible presence with the various foundations with which you have ongoing relationships—and from which your institution wishes to secure support at some point in the future.

The foundation program in relation to the plan

If you want to increase support to the institution from the private sector, your plan and your program need to work together. Your plan should include those ideas that define your philosophy, your priorities, and your objectives for the year. Your program should include the specific activities and people you employ to accomplish what you have spelled out as objectives in the plan. Unfortunately, at a number of institutions the plan and the program bear little resemblance to one another.

As a manager it is your job—possibly your most important one—to ensure that there is a synergistic relationship between the plan you develop and the program that will be used to carry it out.

At this point let me caution you against two common pitfalls to planning. Either those involved find every reason to avoid planning—and this happens, I fear, at all too many institutions—or they plan and plan and plan (and the key word here is *process*) until the planning becomes an end in itself.

Planning must be done, but your planning should be part of a process that leads to the accomplishment of your objectives.

Planning may be the most important task we face. Planning, after all, is the process of deciding what objectives to pursue during a future time period and what to do in order to achieve those objectives. The planning process is composed of two major segments: (1) setting objectives, and (2) determining the course of action to be used in achieving those objectives.

Rue and Byars describe planning as the management function that produces and integrates objectives, strategies, and policies. According to Rue and Byars, planning answers three basic questions: Where are we now? Where do we want to be? How can we get there from here?[15]

To answer the first question, you need to assess the present situation. To answer the second, you must determine the objectives of your institution or department. Answering the final question requires that you outline actions to achieve the objectives and, also, analyze the financial impact of those actions. Remember that planning is concerned with future implications of the decisions you make now; it does not—and cannot—address the decisions you will make in the future.[16]

Planning enables a manager or an organization to *affect* rather than merely *accept* the future. By setting the objectives and charting a course of action, the organization commits itself to "making it happen."

Conclusion

I'd like to conclude by suggesting two ideas for your consideration: Our institutions need to develop and preserve their own "cultures," and they need development professionals who are leaders.

An institutional culture. The idea of an institutional culture comes from the corporate sector. Marvin Bower, for years managing director of McKinsey and Company and author of *The Will to Manage,* offers an informal definition of "culture" in this context: "the way we do things around here."[17] In 1982 Thomas J. Peters and Robert H. Waterman, Jr., were the first to emphasize the importance of shared values as a performance factor in the business world.[18] Later in that same year, Terrence Deal and Allan Kennedy suggested that the most successful organizations—public and private—have strong and cohesive cultures that bind members together:

> Every business—in fact every organization—has a culture...culture has a powerful influence throughout an organization; it affects practically everything—from who gets promoted and what decisions are made to how employees dress and what sports they play. Because of this impact, we think that culture also has a major effect on the success of the business.[19]

As managers and leaders, we should be actively promoting our institution's culture. This helps build a team and provides both individual and institutional focus for plans and programs. If schools, colleges, and universities can learn anything from America's corporations, it is that a strong culture makes for consistently outstanding performance.

Development professionals as leaders. Successful managers realize that managing people is not so much about setting goals as it is about setting a course and sharing a vision.

In a fascinating interview in *INC. Magazine,* John Humphrey, cofounder and chairman of The Forum Corp. of North America, makes several controversial and thought-provoking statements. He claims that today's world requires a different kind of manager:

> In the old days, a good manager was someone who could translate plans into goals and then keep people focused on these goals.... Today, a good manager is someone who paints the field for his or her people. Good managers get their people excited, create a sense of urgency, a sense of empowerment. They provide lots of coaching—and continuous feedback. They offer people a vision they can believe in. They connect up with their people in a much more personal way, help them deal with the speed of change, empathize with them more—and break the rules when they have to be broken.... They don't set goals so much as they are clear about roles.[20]

Because change is the dominant factor in our lives today, we must adopt a different style of management. During periods of change, people anchor themselves to people—not to institutions. And as Humphrey reminds us, "The faster the speed of change, the more important the leader becomes to his people."[21] This new style of management, then, is more personalized, more continuous, less formal, less institutional, less procedural, less hierarchical.

As you endeavor to increase private support to your institution, you should direct your energies to recruiting and retaining foundation officers with superior organizational, interpersonal, and communication skills. In today's world, this job has become one of providing a vision for the program and persuasively articulating this vision to the foundations that will help make your dreams a reality.

Notes

[1] Leslie W. Rue and Lloyd L. Byars, *Management: Theory and Application,* rev. ed. (Homewood, IL: Richard D. Irwin, 1980), p. 88.

[2] Ibid, p. 7.

[3] Joel S. Nadel, *Executive Productivity* (Boca Raton, FL: Joel S. Nadel, 1982), pp. 1-2.

[4] Harold Taylor, *The Time Management Report* (Ridgewood, NJ: Forkner, 1981), p. 4.

[5] Keith Davis, *Human Relations at Work,* 5th ed. (New York: McGraw-Hill, 1978).

[6] Harvey Jacobson, "Skills and Criteria for Managerial Effectiveness" in *Handbook of Institutional Advancement,* 2d ed., ed. A. Westley Rowland (San Francisco: Jossey-Bass, 1986), pp. 24-26.

[7] John W. Gardner, *The Nature of Leadership: Introductory Considerations* (Washington, DC: Independent Sector, 1986), p. 8.

[8] Michael A. Berger, "Maximizing Staff Performance" in *Handbook of Institutional Advancement,* ed. Rowland, p. 60.

[9] Ibid.

[10] Calvin H. Stoney, "40 Carrots: To Motivate Employees, Try Listening to Their Needs," CASE CURRENTS, May 1983, p. 23.

[11] Berger, "Maximizing Staff Performance," p. 62.

[12] George Keller, CASE Seminar in Executive Management, Nashville, TN, July 1987.

[13] George S. Odiorne, *MBO II: A System of Managerial Leadership for the 80's* (Belmont, CA: Fearon Pitman, 1979), pp. 2-3.

[14] Anthony P. Raia, *Managing by Objectives* (Glenview, IL: Scott, Foresman, 1974), p. 30.

[15] Rue and Byars, *Management,* p. 116.

[16] David C.D. Rogers, *Corporate Strategy and Long Range Planning* (Ann Arbor, MI: Landis, 1973).

[17] Terrence E. Deal and Allan A. Kennedy, *Corporate Cultures: The Rites and Rituals of Corporate Life* (Reading, MA: Addison-Wesley, 1982), p. 4.

[18] Thomas J. Peters and Robert H. Waterman, Jr., *In Search of Excellence: Lessons from America's Best-Run Companies* (New York: Warner Books, 1982).

[19] Deal and Kennedy, *Corporate Cultures,* p. 4.

[20] *INC. Magazine,* "Interview with John Humphrey," September 1987, p. 54.

[21] Ibid.

Chapter 4

Does Your Institution Need A Foundation Program?

G. William Joyner, Jr.
Vice President for University Relations
Wake Forest University

D oes your institution need a foundation program? Maybe not! This is the answer more often than you might think. Unless certain conditions exist within your institution, your foundation program will *not* be successful and will therefore create problems and costs.

Prerequisites to a foundation program

A foundation program that doesn't work (or that doesn't work smoothly) will be a liability to your institution's fund-raising efforts. Therefore, if you are considering implementing such a program at your institution, you should study the prerequisites outlined below before you make your decision. Each ingredient is important.

1. Establish the proper perspective for your foundation program. I have often been asked by college presidents and vice presidents of development who are seeking a senior advancement officer: "Can this person deliver foundation money to us?"

The question itself signals a problem in their perception: A successful foundation program is one that fits within and complements a larger, structured development effort, and it must not be perceived as the most important part of that effort. Foundation relations is not a function of one individual.

Your cultivation and solicitation of individual donors must remain the focus of the fund-raising program at your college or university. The largest number of dollars comes from individuals, and the flow of dollars from this source is steady. The Council for Aid to Education reports that during 1985-86, individuals contributed

48.6 percent of all voluntary support for higher education, including both private and public institutions, while foundations contributed only 18.6 percent.

Your efforts to solicit individuals, successfully and repeatedly, should take precedence over all other facets of your development program, including considerations of staff, budget, and time. Individuals must be the key to satisfying your core academic mission; foundations become the complement to academic areas of mutual agreement.

Thus, a foundation program should be viewed as important to your development goals, but it should not be viewed as a reliable source of funds. Competition for foundation grants is fierce, and the truism "the rich get richer" is often applicable. So if you do decide to implement a foundation program at your institution, do not overestimate its potential, and do not look to your foundation officer to "deliver" grants with any degree of predictability or regularity. Foundations give grants; development officers don't get them! Keep your foundation program in the proper perspective.

2. Have a successful individual gifts program solidly in place. One of the primary reasons that your foundation program should be secondary to your individual gifts program is the fact that foundations will consider your success—or lack of it—in soliciting funds from individuals, especially from your alumni, as a critical factor during their review of your proposal.

When the F. W. Olin Foundation awarded one of its two 1987 grants to Wake Forest University, "strong annual fund support from trustees, alumni and others" was a key element in the decision. Your institution's financial base must be sound and growing, and the best indication of such a condition is a long and solid history of support from people close to your institution. The percentage of alumni and trustees who contribute must be high and their donations must be generous; your individual friends must have confidence in your institution's future and a willingness to invest in that future. Foundations may be willing to share in your success, but few foundations will be interested in breaking that ground themselves.

As the Olin Foundation expressed it: "The Foundation's grants, few in number but large in amount, do not lend themselves to substantial risk-taking. The Foundation's trustees prefer to make grants *to make strong institutions stronger* [emphasis added]." Foundation officials must be assured that there will be sources of funding other than their own grant, and a healthy history of individual giving is always an effective and convincing argument that such additional funding is secure.

3. Have an effective academic planning program in place. A good foundation program *responds* to needs; it neither creates nor discovers them. Your foundation program must be driven by a structured, sophisticated planning process that identifies and prioritizes the needs of your academic programs. This is true in the areas of curriculum enhancement, physical plant, faculty salaries, and student aid.

To win the competition for a foundation grant, you must make a sound argument supported by facts and figures that honestly and convincingly illustrate your need. It is impossible to make such an argument unless the need has been recognized and examined through a process of self-analysis. A proposal receiving serious consideration from a foundation may eventually involve a site visit by officials of the foundation. During such a visit, your senior administrators will be asked to substantiate the proposal. Without the base of a planning process, your administrators will be unprepared and unable to respond adequately.

The academic planning process provides another positive side effect: The recognition of established academic priorities by department chairs and departmental program planning committees will alleviate the pressure that you or your foundation officer will face from individual faculty members anxious to have their favorite projects underwritten by private sources. The results of the planning process will form a road map for your foundation officer to follow and to point to when pleas for attention from individuals threaten to alter your course.

Establishing a foundation program in the absence of an academic planning program is putting the cart before the horse. Let me be more specific: Don't ask your foundation officer to fabricate a grant proposal to match a given foundation's guidelines. Have the courage to set your in-house priorities first, and then see which foundations have the same agenda.

4. Have an effective financial sign-off program in place. Foundation grants, while bringing you useful and needed funds, almost always require additional spending. A ripple effect will ensue: The construction of a new building paid for entirely by a foundation grant frees space that must be renovated for its new use; the establishment of new scholarships by a foundation grant requires additional personnel in your financial aid office; the scientific equipment purchased with foundation money has applications that cost more than the equipment itself.

Your treasurer or controller will not be pleased to receive a check for $25,000 if he or she knows it will result in a net loss of funds, and the officer will be especially unhappy if he or she could have communicated that fact before the proposal was made, but did not have the opportunity. A system must be in place, and adhered to without exception, that requires your senior financial official and your provost or senior academic official to approve each foundation proposal during its preparation stage. This step will provide you with their written comments, approval, or objections.

Fight your battles internally, if you have to, *before* you get the grant. Obviously, you don't want to devote a great deal of time to preparing a proposal that will not be acceptable to your senior academic and financial officials. But your academic planning program should prevent that from happening. Individuals in positions to evaluate the full range of your institution's resources and priorities should conduct a thorough review of your proposal's details, its budget, and its impact on other programs, both academic and fiscal. You should not submit any proposal to a foundation without such a review.

The transmittal sheet on page 46 illustrates one method of obtaining the required review and consent. The use of such a form should lend structure to your system, making it easier to utilize and interpret. A foundation program without an effective financial sign-off system will eventually fail, a victim of internal bickering, loss of confidence, and poor financial planning.

5. Be willing and prepared to spend time and money. A foundation program is not an inexpensive way to raise money. Don't imagine that your foundation officer will spend all his or her time sitting behind a desk, writing and mailing proposals and waiting for the checks to come in.

To be effective, your foundation officer must devote a large portion of time to research, travel, and stewardship. He or she must be familiar with the individuals who operate the foundations, and this requires many hours of reading and studying resource materials. A proposal submitted ''cold'' will not be likely to receive attention, so visits must be made to prepare for subsequent funding requests. This cultivation may last for several years before a proposal is given serious review by a foundation.

Building these relationships often involves extensive travel costs for members of your development staff. And once your institution has received an award, you must provide the foundation with progress reports and a final analysis—and this also takes a lot of your foundation officer's time.

Laying the proper groundwork and performing the appropriate follow-up procedures may seem to cost money rather than produce it, yet your foundation program will not succeed unless you are willing and able to expend those costs. Patience is more important in this area of development than in any other area of your program—except estate planning.

Your investment in your foundation program will not be limited to dollars. You will often need to ask your president and chief academic officer to give their valuable time to foundation directors or trustees who have finally agreed, after great effort by your foundation officer, to hear your story. These high-ranking administrators are the appropriate people to deliver your proposal, or to serve as hosts if you are fortunate enough to secure a site visit by foundation personnel. Your top administrators must be able and willing to meet with the visitors and answer their questions about the institution and your proposal.

You will find that fund-raising efforts aimed at foundations are time-consuming and costly, and attempts to cut corners will curtail your success.

There are no guarantees

Meeting the criteria presented here will not guarantee that your foundation program will produce funds for your college or university, but the absence of one or more of these conditions will almost certainly result in disappointing outcomes for your efforts. And these are not the only factors you should consider. The location of your institution is very important. A college located in a generally rural setting, removed geographically from areas where foundations concentrate their attentions, may have much less chance of success in this endeavor than an institution in a metropolitan setting. Many foundations limit their grant making to specific geographic areas, and a sober analysis of those limits is a must before you decide to initiate a foundation program.

On the other hand, your institution's need for the funding is *not* an appropriate consideration, nor is your conviction that your institution is as worthy as others that have received grants. Rather, your decision should focus on your internal readiness, both in program and in attitude, to take the full and best advantage of efforts devoted to fund raising from foundations.

Foundations want to help you. They employ directors who are expected to help you. In my work at Wake Forest, few pleasures have exceeded witnessing the "marriage" of a solid, agreed-upon academic priority and a foundation whose objective it is to meet that very need.

TRANSMITTAL SHEET FOR PROPOSAL – FOUNDATIONS

WAKE FOREST

Department_____ Contact_____

Potential Grantor(s)_____

Purpose of Grant_____
_____

Proposal Includes   Proposal Involves   History

Curriculum   _____   University Funding _____   New Grant   _____
Equipment   _____   Computers   _____   Renewal of Grant   _____
Bricks/Mortar   _____   Supplement of Grant _____
Endowment   _____

Amount Requested_____ Deadline for Proposal Receipt_____
University Commitment_____ Total Project budget_____

I.   ACADEMIC APPROVALS

_____   _____
Department Chairman   Date

_____   _____
Dean   Date

_____   _____
Provost   Date

II.   DEVELOPMENT AND SENIOR ADMINISTRATION APPROVALS

_____   _____
Director, Foundation Relations   Date

_____   _____
Vice President, University Relations   Date

_____   _____
Vice President for Administration and Budget Date

_____   _____
Vice President for Financial Resource Management Date

_____   _____
Vice President for Legal Affairs   Date

_____   _____
Vice President for Student Life and Instructional Date
       Resources

III. PRESIDENT

_____   _____
                                             Date

46

Section 2

Getting Started:
Tools of the Trade

Chapter 5

Understanding Power Structures

James A. Crupi
President
International Leadership Center

Stewart Lytle
Executive Director, Community Leadership Research
International Leadership Center

Academic institutions need to understand and be part of a community's leadership structure. In today's world, knowledge of the leadership structure of a community is a requisite to the effective growth and development of a college or university.

An institution that is an integral part of the community leadership finds fund raising a much simpler task. But just as important as success in fund raising is the need for an institution to bridge the gap between academia and the business, political, and ethnic sectors of the community. The academic institution that is not prepared or qualified to study the community may find itself the unwitting victim of circumstances. Few new programs, activities, marketing or university strategy, however rational or compelling, can afford to ignore the necessity of winning and retaining community support.

At the International Leadership Center, we study leadership in cities, analyzing the power structures that govern a city both formally and informally. Over the past few years we have seen the role of academic institutions increase in community leadership. In many cities, serving on the board of trustees of a major private college or on the development board for a public university is an important step in the community's "rites of passage" to leadership—the process of gaining a seat at the decision-making table. And in some cities the president or chancellor of the local college or university sits at the table when important community decisions are to be made.

Over the next five to 10 years, we expect to see an even greater number of senior college and university administrators among the senior decision makers of communities. For this reason the path to community leadership should not be traveled blindly. Time and energy should be applied to identifying both the individuals and the organizations that make up a community's leadership structure.

This chapter discusses the impact the community power structure can have on academic institutions, how to identify and analyze the power structure of a community, and how to become part of that power structure. Because this book focuses on foundation fund raising, much of our discussion centers on the impact the community power structure has on fund raising.

But fund raising is only one of the many reasons academic administrators need to understand the leadership of the community that surrounds the institution. Once they understand the community power structure, they will be able to build binding relationships with community leaders in the business and political sectors.

Through these relationships, administrators can position the institution advantageously in the community. The institution can gain the support of the business community for a variety of projects including in-kind contributions as well as capital donations. And the institution in turn can influence the direction of the community. Senior administrators who understand the agenda of local and state politicians can anticipate and influence legislation and appropriations. And they can begin building networks of emerging leaders that will ensure the position of the institution in the power structure of the future.

In cities throughout the country, we are witnessing the development of new partnerships that link the business and political sectors with the independent or nonprofit sector that usually centers on a major university. These partnerships are designed to benefit the community by promoting economic development and solving complex social and political problems.

Colleges and universities are increasingly being asked to play the role of economic generator, building small business incubators that utilize the skills and expertise of faculty and staff. The presence of a first-class university is a major magnet when the community attempts to recruit new industry. Consider, for example, the impact of Georgia Tech's engineering expertise on Atlanta's development or the concentration of medical sciences at the University of Texas Health Science Centers in San Antonio, Dallas, and Houston.

Similarly, many communities are looking to academic institutions to solve community problems such as illiteracy and to provide an education for socially disadvantaged youth. The institution that attempts to cope with these complex issues and to provide a meaningful program to resolve them must be able to identify and communicate with the decision makers in the black or Hispanic community. To misunderstand the power structure of the ethnic communities will—at the very least—reduce the effectiveness of the program. At the worst, it can sabotage the program altogether and at the same time create for the institution a lasting credibility problem in the minority community.

Government encroaches on the daily life of a campus in many ways, from funding appropriations to zoning changes to police protection. For example, a neighborhood association in San Antonio opposed Trinity University's attempt to enlarge the campus. The issue of whether Trinity could demolish houses was potentially an issue the San Antonio city council would have ruled on. But Trinity's success in eventually winning support for its master plan was due, in large part, to its understanding of who held power in that association and what their goals were. University officials met with these association leaders to outline the advantages to the neighborhood of the campus expansion. Without this knowledge of the association, Trinity might have been forced to fight it out in a public city council meeting.

Building binding relationships is essential to fund raising. In several cities we have found a direct corollary between institutions with successful capital campaigns and institutions with boards of trustees that include the community power brokers. It is no coincidence that the most influential civic board in Nashville is the Vanderbilt University board of trustees. For decades the most influential individual in the city was the chair of Vanderbilt's board. During the same period, Vanderbilt was enormously successful at fund raising and at controlling its own destiny in Nashville.

What makes a community leader?

How do you define a community leader? A workable, if general, definition of community leadership is "those individuals who can effect or prevent significant change in the community." As this definition indicates, leadership can include having veto power. Unfortunately it is just as important to identify and understand the motivation of leaders who have the power to say "no" to a project as it is to know those who can make things happen. Only then can you understand why certain projects get sidetracked while others succeed. More importantly, you can learn how to circumvent the people with veto power or, better yet, gain their cooperation.

Because only a small percentage of a community's population is actively involved in community decision making, you can use proven research techniques to identify community leaders. But don't make the mistake of assuming that the community's elected public officials are its principal leaders. Although it's important not to discount the power of government, we have found very few politicians who stand on independent power bases. Most mayors, governors, legislators, and city council members are very sensitive to those who hold informal power within the community—those who finance political campaigns and provide jobs to voters. Business leaders, who often work in relative obscurity, have more freedom of decision and action than the government officials they help elect.

Power accrues to those who use their resources effectively. Wealth and position, particularly as the head of a large corporation or bank, are major advantages but by themselves they are not enough. In every community we have studied, we have found people with deep pockets or in high positions who exert little influence on the community.

For example, a wealthy person who is not politically or civicly active may not have much community power. A person may misuse power and alienate other leaders, and thus destroy his or her effectiveness. A corporate president who is not a native of the community and devotes little time to its affairs will have little influence.

At the same time, we see a major rise in influence by leaders of neighborhood associations and ethnic groups. Although these men and women often have little or no wealth, they have been able to use other resources (votes, the courts, the press) effectively.

Community personality

Whether rich or energetic, an individual cannot become a member of the leadership structure unless he or she utilizes the available power resources according to principles of leadership that are acceptable within the "culture" of the community.

Understanding the various factors, personalities, and nuances that make up communities is not easy. If you would learn the secrets of leadership in your community, be warned: It requires a major commitment of time and energy. But the rewards justify the effort. It's not enough to develop a list of names. For most individuals, it takes a minimum of five years to begin to learn who makes the decisions, how the decisions are made, and how to gain access to the decision makers.

To do this analysis, you need the skills of a sociologist, a political scientist, a historian, an economist, a psychologist, and an anthropologist. You must go behind today's power structure and investigate the community's historical and cultural roots. In most communities, these factors help determine who makes decisions and how those decisions are made. Community leaders in most cities are linked together by a body of similar, often unspoken beliefs. Like individual people, each city has its own personality or personalities that determine how it functions.

For example, the cultures or personalities of Nashville and Dallas are more alike than those of other southern and southwestern cities. The strong entrepreneurial culture inherent in those two cities stems from their origin as frontier trading communities. The older, more genteel San Antonio has more in common with Richmond than with other cities in Texas. Thus, in Dallas a business decision is made in a different way and by different types of people than in San Antonio. Dallas is a city of builders and deal makers, while San Antonio's decision-making process is controlled by a bureaucracy heavily influenced by the Hispanic culture and the large military presence there.

The differences in the power structure of the two Texas cities have nothing to do with size—size is often irrelevant to community leadership. It has to do with the differences in culture and history.

In Atlanta, the key decisions are made by bankers. In Houston, attorneys are the key players, while developers make the important community decisions in Dallas. In San Francisco, appointed government commission members have tremendous influence.

An effective community leader understands these cultural or personality traits. The community leadership in Dallas would find a Richmonder not sufficiently aggressive, regardless of what he or she accomplished. The people in San Antonio would perceive a Dallasite as being much too pushy.

Types of power structures

The type of power structure in place in a community determines how open it is to newcomers, how easy it is to get decisions made, and in which directions the community is likely to move for the future.

There are four basic types of power structures: monopolistic; multi-group, non-competitive elite; competitive elite; and democratic pluralism.

Monopolistic power structure. A single person or single group of leaders controls the decision making and community policies. This control is so great that it can stifle conflicts about community direction. The most powerful leaders of the system make most of the decisions, and participation by the rest of the citizens is low. Most people in such a system are either satisfied with it or loathe the consequences of getting involved more than they disagree with the actions and decisions of leadership.

Multi-group, noncompetitive elite structure. This system allows a wider participation in decision making. The leaders, regardless of which group they are in, are generally in agreement about the direction of the community although there may be considerable competition over who gets the rewards of the system, such as fees, contracts, and favorable zoning decisions.

Competitive elite structure. The leaders in this system are often embroiled in major conflicts. The community is in the midst of a power struggle over the kind of city it should be. The groups struggling for power are elite groups (i.e., rival business groups or a middle-class ethnic group against the business sector). Participation by the general public is nonexistent or weak.

Democratic pluralism structure. While we traditionally see this system as the ideal power structure for a democracy, it is very difficult to achieve. Democratic pluralism requires widespread participation in decision making. Citizens participate effectively in the selection of public officials, who govern after listening to the views of a broad base of citizens and volunteer organizations. The system is open to the emergence of new leaders and is constantly changing.

Once you have understood these four different types of power structures, you can begin to analyze leadership in your own community. The seven steps outlined below can help you do this in a relatively systematic manner. But first a few notes of warning:

• Don't think of "power"—at least in this context—as an ugly word. While power is abused all too often by business, by politicians, and by administrators everywhere, both on campus and off, when we refer to "power" here, we mean it in a positive sense, that is, having enough influence to make something happen or, in some cases, to make something *not* happen.

• You'll be surprised at how much information you will accumulate in your research. Organization is critically important. When you conduct research, you'll build extensive files on each major sector of your community (business leaders, political leaders, ethnic leaders, women leaders, key civic organizations, and so forth). You'll need to establish a file on each person, listing name, position, professional association, to whom he or she listens, and in what issues he or she is interested.

• Avoid the temptation to jump to conclusions. Self-acclaimed leaders abound. Upward mobiles without real influence, but with a thirst for it, are easily visible. Less astute community researchers are frequently deceived by those who have high visibility. In many communities, the true power brokers scrupulously avoid the spotlight.

Seven steps to analysis

The process of community research that we have developed employs several sociological approaches, including:

• *reputational analysis:* We interview hundreds of key leaders and knowledgeable persons to gain insight into their perceptions of the market, including the leadership and the critical issues and opportunities the area faces. This allows us to meet individual leaders and analyze their personal leadership styles and agendas.

• *decision-trail analysis:* We analyze key decisions within the community (i.e., expansion of a civic center, construction of a new highway, passage of a bond issue) to determine who holds the power or influence to make the decision.

• *board scan:* We analyze all civic and corporate boards to determine who is involved in area decision making. We identify which organizations are important, particularly as a forum for corporate positioning.

• *issue analysis:* We study the critical issues in the area in order to understand the impact that they may have in the market.

In addition, you may want to add questions that analyze important issues facing the community. At the International Leadership Center, we use a combination of these approaches to dissect the community and produce a highly accurate profile of the power structure.

Using this methodology, we can identify and analyze the power structure of most communities in just six to eight weeks, considerably less than the three to five years it normally takes to penetrate and understand a community. A large, complex community with several centers of power may take longer, but the process is the same, and the degree of accuracy is as high. These are the steps we follow:

Step 1: Review some of the excellent sociological work on the power structures of a community. Studies of community power over the past 30 years have stripped away many of the myths and misinformation about leadership and decision making in cities. These studies will help you gain a personal perspective on how power is structured for decision making. Specifically we recommend Floyd Hunter's

Community Power Structure: A Study of Decision Makers (Chapel Hill, NC: University of North Carolina Press, 1953), Robert Dahl's *Who Governs: Democracy and Power in an American City* (New Haven: Yale University Press, 1961), and Irving Leif and Terry Clark's *Community Power and Decision Making* (Hawthorne, NY: Mouton, 1973).

Step 2: Set specific objectives. In each project, the goals and objectives will vary. But in general the primary objectives of research on a community power structure are to determine:

- who are the most influential persons in community decision making;
- what process do they use to make decisions;
- why do the leaders decide to support or oppose certain projects;
- what are their relationships to other leaders; and
- what organizations (corporate, civic, charitable, or social) have the most influence on community decisions?

Step 3: To answer these questions, ask the people who know. First you must identify the people who know. They may include politicians, executives of civic or charitable organizations, attorneys who are active in the community, and so on. Interview four or five, asking them to name the leaders of the business sector, the political sector, the media, women's groups, ethnic groups, religious organizations, and so forth. Depending on the objectives of your research, there are up to about 25 different sectors in most communities.

After four or five interviews, you will find that you have great insights. In fact, one interview with a knowledgeable person may give you considerable information about the community decision-making process. But don't be tempted to stop there. Several interviews (we do more than 100 per city) will provide cumulative answers that provide insights few others in the community have.

Focus your initial interview on reputation or perceived power. Who is perceived to have the most community power? Who holds the top positions in the largest, wealthiest, or strongest businesses? Who has the top law practice? Who are his or her clients? Whose support do political figures seek? Whose advice is sought by others on business or political issues? Who sits on several major corporation boards? Who owns major real estate holdings? And where are those holdings?

You can do your interviews formally, arranging meetings in which you say, "I'm trying to understand more about the leadership structure of this community." This approach is appropriate if you have recently moved to the city. But college or university administrators who have been in the community for several years would have to ask such questions informally—over lunch for example. If this is the case, the formal interviews should be conducted by a lower-level administrator or by someone outside the university.

Access to leaders in the various sectors of the community is often relatively easy. The person you ask about the leadership of the community is often flattered to be thought knowledgeable about community decisions.

Each of our interviews is conducted on a confidential basis. We do not tape-record any interviews. We take notes and use the aggregate of all the interviews to help us conceptualize the power structure of a community. We tell the interviewee that we will not quote him or her or even tell others in the community whom we are interviewing.

The effect of granting confidentiality is to gain confidence. It also helps reduce bias in the interview. For example, we don't tell the community leader we are interviewing now that our next interview is with a business or political leader. Otherwise, we could never be sure that the interviewee would tell us his or her true feelings about the business leader we would see later.

Step 4: As part of the interviews, ask about powerful organizations such as the chamber of commerce or NAACP. This will give insights into which organizations can help your institution and which hold veto power over community decisions.

The executive director or president of these organizations is usually a fountain of knowledge. He or she has great insights into who is influential in the community, as well as who makes decisions within the organization and what the organization's agenda is.

Step 5: Throughout the process, try to identify key decisions that have had a critical influence on the community. These will vary from city to city. The larger the decision, the greater the probability that the individuals who made that decision will be the most influential people in the city. As in business, community leaders must ration their time effectively. Thus they concentrate their time and energy on what they perceive to be the most important issues.

Identify through media coverage or common knowledge the most outfront person on each decision. He or she can identify others in the process who were closer to the decision. They in turn will lead to those at the core.

Step 6: Collect lists of board members for all the major organizations—art museums, symphony, major banks, corporations with headquarters in the city, key charities like the United Way, country clubs, and private dining clubs. You should analyze all these names and organizations by hand or by computer to determine who shows up the most frequently, how many people are on the same boards, and who sits on the most important boards.

This process identifies who is active in the community, who has money to contribute to organizations, and who has political and civic influence. In most cities these organizations provide training or grooming for community leadership. Their membership, therefore, gives important insights into who are today's leaders and who are likely to be the leaders of tomorrow. Analysis of board lists also reveals who is talking to whom. Although many community decisions are reached at private meetings, a large number of political and business decisions are made as a by-product of a civic or charitable board meeting.

Together all this information provides a comprehensive picture of who makes key decisions, how they make those decisions, who influences whom, who makes things happen, and who holds veto power and why. In addition, it reveals what is most important to the decision makers and which issues interest them the most. This is critically important for the next step in the process.

Step 7: Implement or utilize the knowledge the research has produced. Armed with insights about the leadership of the community, the president of the institution or the vice president for development should launch a comprehensive program to get acquainted with each of the major power brokers. He or she can do this formally through a series of visits or lunches in which the administrator asks for help or asks how the institution can help the community.

The results of the research should enable you to identify which organizations your institution should be involved with. If the power brokers of the community sit on the executive committee of the chamber of commerce, your institution's president should take an active role in that organization. In some communities the most important board is a locally owned bank or a cherished art museum or foundation. Gaining a seat on one of these boards gives you or your president regular and intimate contact with the community leadership.

Here you need to know and understand in detail the issues that are particularly important to the community and to each power broker individually. Knowing where those "hot buttons" are helps you build relationships quickly and gives you insight into where your institution can commit its resources to aid in solving community problems.

Studying the leadership structure of communities is clearly a major undertaking. But once you have done it, it can reap great rewards for the institution and its leadership in increased support for a variety of initiatives. And the institution will be able to make an even greater contribution to the community, which, in return, nurtures and supports the institution.

Chapter 6

Research as the Keystone For Foundation Fund Raising

Linda Williams
Director of Information Resources, Government,
  Corporate, and Foundation Relations
Syracuse University

I f you're actively involved in the business of fund raising, then you know that the profession, like many others today, is becoming more and more information-dependent. As a grant seeker, you need information to decide whom to ask for a grant, what type or form of support to ask for, when to ask, and how much to ask for. As a researcher, you supply the answers to those questions and provide additional useful information that is relevant to fund-raising activities.

Research generates and integrates the information needed to select the best project/prospect matches, devise successful solicitation strategies and contingency plans, and alert institutional fund raisers to changes and trends in the philanthropic environment.

Research's role in fund raising

To appreciate the role research plays in foundation fund raising, examine the fund-raising process itself. At Syracuse University's office of corporate and foundation relations, the process by which fund raisers secure foundation support is twofold:

• *the "inside-out approach":* Development officers find support for the university's priorities and needs from the world beyond the campus—from foundations that have an identified interest in similar projects.

• *the "outside-in approach":* By keeping their eyes and ears open to the goals, missions, and program interests of foundations, development officers identify potential projects that could be brought back to campus and matched with similar university interests and problems.

The goal of both approaches is to secure a grant by getting two groups of people—university faculty, researchers, and administrators, on the one hand, and foundation program officers and representatives, on the other—to work together for their mutual benefit.

In what ways can the two organizations, the donor and the donee, pool their resources and talents so that both parties benefit? The information provided through researching foundations can help answer that question by matching your institution's priorities, projects, programs, and needs with a foundation's priorities, projects, programs, and needs to achieve mutual goals. Furthermore, since researchers keep their eyes on the world in which foundations do business, they can also identify some of those outside opportunities that can be brought inside.

The research process

There are four steps to foundation research:
- collecting and analyzing information;
- synthesizing and packaging it in an attractive and useful format;
- disseminating the information to users; and
- keeping track of the information.

The information you work with falls into two broad categories: (1) internal or in-house data relative to your own institution and (2) external data—facts and figures gathered on potential prospects and the environments in which they operate.

Researchers sift through lots and lots of paper—letters, contact or call reports, newspapers, magazines, annual reports, newsletters, press releases, computer printouts—to select the most useful information for their product's users, the grant seekers. Gathering this internal and external information is absolutely necessary to match interests and to build the base of knowledge that supports foundation fund raising. Since "askers"—those who will ultimately ask for the grants—are the primary users, research contributes indirectly to the bottom line.

Internal information

You should be an expert on your school, college, or university. What are its fund-raising priorities? What are its strongest programs, its teaching strengths? What are the weaker areas? Who are the outstanding faculty and researchers on campus? What image does your institution have? You can't begin to match your institution's needs with a foundation's unless you know the nature and mission of your institution. Because coworkers and colleagues are one of the best sources for this information, you need to maintain frequent formal and informal communication with them.

In gathering in-house data, you may find the following questions useful:

- Is there an interest match? How do the prospect's interests overlap with those of your institution? If a foundation supports science education and your college's school of education trains science teachers, put that foundation's name on your list of potential prospects. Later, you can examine the match more closely to decide if you've made the best choice. Matching interests usually results in a long list of prospects, only a few of which are a truly good fit.

- Is this prospect a past donor? If so, what was supported? The College of Engineering? An endowed chair? The library? What was the form of support? Equipment grants? Matching gift money? Has support increased or decreased? Donors who supported you in the past are likely to continue their support in the future so you need to know who they are and what they funded.

- Who knows whom? Is there a personal contact to the foundation who might act as a champion for your cause? This person's role is not to pressure a prospect, but rather to act as an advocate or leader for your project, provide insider information or advice on the prospect, or perhaps advance or endorse the proposal.

- What is the history of your institution's relationship with the prospect? What type of past relationships were there between people in your institution and people in the foundation? Who was involved? Is the relationship still an active one? If not, what happened? Did someone stop paying attention? Did players change? It's especially important to know if someone at the foundation was unhappy with the institution's representatives or with the institution itself. You need to know where the land mines are buried. Let's hope they were documented.

- What affiliation, if any, does the prospect have to your institution? Do any of the local foundations believe that your institution has made a positive contribution to the community? Which prospects have warm feelings for your institution's mission or research interests? Which foundations limit their grant making to your geographical area?

External information

Answering these questions is half of your research work. To complete the foundation donor profile, you must combine internal data with external data. As you plow through the facts and figures published today on foundations, what are the key bits of information necessary to determine what is happening in the prospect's world? What are the issues, projects, programs, or activities in which the foundation is interested; what are its goals, problems, mission, and philosophy?

You need to document any changes in program areas or funding interests, analyze grant-making patterns, verify names of foundation personnel, and note any recent developments in the news that might have an impact on the prospect's environment.

Remember that your goal in doing this research is not only to figure out why and how a prospect might support your institution, but also to make the best possible project/prospect matches. This makes the most efficient use of the time and energy of everyone involved in the grant-seeking process. It's important not to waste a prospect's time and yours by submitting a proposal that falls outside of foundation guidelines or program interests. If you have questions about a prospect's program area, call and ask. It's better to spend five minutes on the phone than to waste hours preparing and submitting an inappropriate proposal.

Information sources

Several on-line, hard-copy, and human information sources are available to researchers. Numerous publications and information services are offered by organizations such as the Foundation Center, Taft Group, Grantsmanship Center, Public Management Institute, and Council for Advancement and Support of Education (CASE), to name only a few. Each offers directories, books, newsletters, manuals, training seminars, workshops, and reference services in various combinations. Database vendors, such as DIALOG Information Services, offer on-line access to several grants-related databases.

The Foundation Center. I don't believe you can research foundations without the help of the Foundation Center. The Foundation Center publishes the indispensable *Foundation Directory, Source Book Profiles,* and the *Foundation Grants Index.* The directory provides basic information on the nation's four or five thousand largest foundations—those with assets of more than $1 million or whose annual giving exceeds $100,000. The *Source Book Profiles* give more in-depth information and analysis on the top 1,000 foundations, and the *Foundation Grants Index* describes who gave what to whom.

The Foundation Center also has on file the Internal Revenue Service 990-PF (private foundation) forms. These forms list all grants made in a tax year, as well as other financial information. For a smaller foundation, the 990 form may be the only source of information that is readily available to a researcher.

The Foundation Center's Associates Program is a fee-based reference service that gives you telephone access to experts who have a great deal of information at their fingertips. These experts will read a listing of grants from a foundation's IRS 990 form over the phone, send a copy, read any clippings they have, and search computer databases. The Associates Program is a real timesaver, especially if you are researching smaller foundations that are not in the *Foundation Directory.*

The Taft Group. Taft publishes an excellent collection of directories, books, and newsletters. The *Foundation Reporter* is a useful directory that covers the 500 largest foundations, in terms of assets and giving levels. Taft's newsletter, *Foundation Giving Watch,* updates selected foundations, notes trends and news in philanthropy, lists prospects by interest or geographical areas, and devotes a page to "who gave what to whom." Taft packages the information in an easy-to-use, attractive format.

Newspapers, magazines, and trade journals. You can also gather information from the *Wall Street Journal, New York Times, Chronicle of Higher Education,* and local newspapers covering the geographic region in which your foundation prospects are located. Journals focusing on philanthropy and grant making and some of the business journals provide up-to-date information on philanthropic trends, government activities that have an impact on nonprofit institutions, changes in foundation programs or personnel, new foundations, or grants made.

These information sources can often give you an idea of the culture or personality of the foundation prospect and an overview of the environment in which it does business. Not to be forgotten are the newsletters, annual reports, and press releases published by foundations. When they are available, these "must-have" source documents provide one of the most comprehensive pictures of your prospect and are usually free.

On-line sources. With all the data available today in computer databases, it is no longer necessary to gather information manually. Computer-based research, or on-line database searching, can provide you with a great deal of information in a very short time. For example, if you subscribe to DIALOG Information Services, you can access the Foundation Center's databases—the *Foundation Directory,* the *Foundation Grants Index,* and *National Foundations.* Information in these files corresponds to that available in the hard-copy publications. The *National Foundations* database contains records on the smaller foundations that are not included in the *Foundation Directory.*

Using on-line databases enables you to combine selected categories of information and create a targeted list of prospects very quickly. For example, if you searched *Foundation Grants Index* on-line, you could plan a strategy to retrieve a listing of all foundations that provide scholarship support to private colleges or universities located in a specific state or states. You can sort the results in several ways, download the information, or have it printed off-line and mailed to you.

DIALOG also makes available the *Grants* database. In addition to grants of private foundations, this database includes grants made by federal, state, and local government agencies, associations, and organizations, and the subject coverage is quite extensive.

Databases that provide the complete text of documents are becoming more widely available. DIALOG has several files containing the full text of press releases, interviews, and journal and newspaper articles. Another vendor, VU/TEXT, provides the full text of many of the Knight-Ridder newspapers. If you are researching a foundation that is located in an area covered by one of VU/TEXT's or DIALOG's regional files, you can often gather valuable information that is only published locally.

Several vendors offer databases that cover a variety of subjects, information sources, and regions. These on-line tools can enable you to gather more and better information in a very short time. The information helps you identify prospects and target specific interest matches with greater certainty. You can create a more comprehensive picture of the prospect and also save money in your research budget by not purchasing expensive hard-copy resources that you won't use very often. Simply access them on-line.

Information has a price tag, however, and cost is a factor in on-line searching. You need hardware, software, and trained personnel. You need a computer, a modem to connect the computer to a telephone, and, if possible, someone who is an experienced searcher—you are billed for every second you are on-line. When you log off, the computer shows you exactly how much you've spent and how many minutes it took. It's immediately obvious that time is money. However, if time is the one thing that you have less of than anything else, on-line searching will enable you to devote more of your time to prospect analysis than to the labor-intensive activities of prospect identification and data collection.

Libraries and librarians. If you have neither the time nor the desire to learn database searching yourself, cultivate a good reference librarian. Many librarians have been using on-line databases since the early 1970s. They are trained information specialists—finding answers is their job, whether they use a computer database, call an expert, or dig through directories.

A really good librarian will not quit until the user's request is answered completely. These professionals can save you time and provide information you didn't even know existed. Librarians serve a lot of people, however, so give them ample time to work on your requests and be prepared to pay for on-line search costs. If one of the Foundation Center's regional libraries is located nearby, you can take advantage of that resource by telephoning or visiting (see pp. 87-80).

Use the telephone frequently in gathering information. Call the Foundation Center for information. If it's appropriate, call the foundation itself. This is often the fastest way to verify information, such as someone's title. Call trade associations, libraries, chambers of commerce—whoever can provide the most direct answer to your question. Don't write a letter if a phone call will work just as well.

Forms, files, and records

As you collect, synthesize, integrate, and store the information you've gathered on your foundation prospects, it is necessary to organize it logically and update it frequently so that the information retains its usefulness and value. Creating forms and setting up hard-copy and computer files and record-keeping systems are integral to managing your information.

At Syracuse we have established two levels of research. A *level one research profile* provides a snapshot of the prospect and attempts to give fund raisers sufficient material to decide among several possible courses of action, such as:

- determining if a prospect is worth pursuing;
- scheduling a meeting with a university researcher or project director;
- requesting more in-depth research so that we may begin devising a strategy for funding; or
- submitting a letter of inquiry to the foundation.

A level one profile contains facts—address; phone number; philanthropic interests; in-house information relative to the prospect, such as gift history, personal connections or contacts; and any useful attachments, such as the foundation's guidelines.

If we've selected a foundation as a major prospect and decided to cultivate that prospect or submit a proposal, we do a *level two research profile.* In addition to incorporating all the information contained in a level one profile, level two research also includes an in-depth analysis of the foundation's grant making, with emphasis on grants made to competing institutions and to projects similar to the one for which we are seeking funds.

For level two research, we abstract and analyze information gathered from newspapers, press releases, and telephone calls. Key points and changes in financial health, personnel, and programs are also noted.

This level of research attempts to give a complete picture of the foundation prospect and its environment. The development team uses the information to develop appropriate funding strategies and contingency plans, confirm project/prospect matches, and ensure an appropriate investment of staff and resources in seeking the grant.

Tracking the information

Prospect/project tracking systems can be sophisticated or simple. Before you decide what sort of system will work best for you, consider your needs, budget, equipment, level of programming expertise, and the amount of time you and your staff can devote to maintaining the system. You may decide to create a computer system that uses database management, spreadsheet, or word-processing software, or a combination of the three. You may want to maintain hard-copy files as the primary or the back-up system.

As you plan your prospect/project tracking system, determine which of the following data elements you need to include:
- project title;
- academic unit;
- project priority and status;
- project purpose;
- funding target;
- funding strategy;
- project start and end dates;
- steward;
- project director or leader;
- connections to the prospect;
- proposal information;
- past gifts;
- prospect address and phone number;
- comments; and
- date that the record was prepared or updated.

The usefulness of the information you collect in the research process depends on your ability to organize a system so that the data you need can be sorted and manipulated according to criteria that you define.

The value of information in fund raising

Good information is essential to successful fund raising and should be considered a valuable institutional resource. To support development, research seeks to provide and manage much of the information needed to match projects and needs with prospects, to develop successful solicitation strategies, and to compile comprehensive profiles of prospects and their environment.

Research information equips fund raisers to enter the prospect's environment, speaking the prospect's language, and empathizing with the prospect's perspective. Grant seekers who are equipped with good information have done their homework and are prepared to plan collaborations in which mutual goals can be achieved—a win-win situation. They can clearly and intelligently tailor ideas, projects, and plans, and sell them to the right prospects.

The image that well-informed fund raisers present is professional and savvy, and that image reflects on the institutions they represent. As the keystone in foundation fund raising, research's contributions include determining the best project/prospect matches, identifying new opportunities, analyzing potential donors, synthesizing and integrating prospect research findings, building the information base, and, finally, supporting the bottom line.

Chapter 7

Reach Out and Touch Someone: Use Your Telephone For Grant Seeking

Mary Kay Murphy
Director for Development
Georgia Institute of Technology

A s important as a well-written proposal is to foundation fund raising, the proposal is often one of the last steps in a cultivation effort. The telephone, on the other hand, can help you initiate a fund-raising project and keep in touch throughout. It can do the following:

• *Broker projects.* Through your telephone conversations with faculty and the foundation, match the needs of one with the interests of the other.

• *Identify those with funding interests.* Telephone calls at the beginning of a project sort out likely from unlikely foundation prospects. These calls also give clues about the next steps to take in fund raising.

• *Develop name recognition.* When you telephone the foundation program officer, he or she is more likely to remember your name and that of your institution. In this way, you set yourself apart from the hundreds seeking recognition and funding. You also get the names of other foundation contacts you can call later for information and help.

• *Update research information.* You can't be sure that foundation research publications are up-to-date. Telephone calls clarify current funding priorities as well as providing updates on names, titles, telephone numbers, and addresses of corporate and foundation contacts. You can also request annual reports by phone.

• *Pave the way for a proposal.* An unsolicited foundation proposal, like an unsolicited manuscript, has little chance on its own. A telephone call makes it easy for a grant maker to ask for more information. Grant maker and grant seeker play complementary roles: One asks for a preliminary proposal; the other agrees to send the information. Use the telephone to set up this intermediary role. You'll encourage a foundation to invite a proposal.

* *Involve the foundation.* Foundations aren't different from other proprietors. They want to have some role in creating the product they may eventually support. If you telephone the foundation officer on a project, you can get him or her involved. The finished product is often better.

* *Share information.* Call foundation officers to share information about new developments at your institution. They cannot rely on college and university catalogs or other publications for fast-breaking news. It's up to you to keep the officers informed.

* *Save time and money.* Use your telephone instead of traveling. The high costs of travel, food, and lodging have made foraging expensive, especially since a simple telephone call can give you the same type of information. What's more, you'll find that there are benefits to the cutback in open-ended travel. First, you and your institution benefit from more efficient use of your resources, including time and money. Second, your meeting with the foundation officer will be more productive after you've talked by phone and sent a preliminary proposal.

Make it person-to-person

Communication research reveals that two points in a conversation are critical to conveying a message: the first 10 to 15 seconds and the last.

Advancement officers who rely on the telephone as a strategic communication tool have perfected techniques that capitalize on these peak points. Here are some:
* Do your homework before you call.
* Speak to the top officer in the funding area.
* Be positive in your opening remarks.
* Speak in simple terms.
* Project confidence, enthusiasm, and believability.
* Develop a range of voice tones and levels of voice projection.
* Bring only one message to the attention of the listener.
* Talk about potential benefits to the grant maker.

In these days of tight money and increased competition for the foundation dollar, your telephone can give you an edge. Use it wisely, and you'll make the right connection.

Reprinted from CURRENTS, *July/August 1984, p. 29.*

Section 3

The Process of Foundation Fund Raising

Chapter 8

The Winning Strategy: Plan And Cultivate Before Writing Unsolicited Proposals

Sandra A. Glass
Program Officer
W.M. Keck Foundation

Y ou would never run up to an individual major-gift prospect at a first meeting and say, "Please give our institution $1 million." Months, even years, of research, planning, and cultivation go into securing personal gifts. Yet inexperienced foundation fund raisers often mail unsolicited proposals to dozens of foundations they know only from descriptions in a directory.

Just because a foundation's name appears in an index or on a computer printout under the listings "higher education," "capital projects," and "science" does not mean that this foundation will necessarily make a grant to help construct your new physics building. Perhaps the index listings were generated by grants for purchasing scientific equipment or for renovating buildings, and this foundation never supports new construction. Or perhaps the foundation made a one-time exceptional grant to a local college but generally gives all its funds to social services programs. One grant could have triggered the misleading indexing, but it should not lure you into submitting an unsolicited proposal, especially one that begins, "Knowing of your history of making grants for constructing science facilities, we are sure you'll be interested in the special opportunity to help us build Phabulous Physics Hall."

If you are the individual on your campus responsible for writing proposals to foundations, hide your pencil and pen and disconnect your word processor. Curb your desire to draft, edit, and mail unsolicited proposals even if this is supposedly what you have been hired to do. As you work with other members of your academic and development staff on research and cultivation, your goal should be to plan carefully before writing and, if possible, to get the foundations to invite your institution to submit a proposal.

Two-phase processes

Because of the growth in numbers of qualified foundation applicants and because of the inundation of ineligible proposals, a number of professionally staffed foundations have initiated preliminary steps before they invite a formal written proposal. Some foundations require a short letter of inquiry that is evaluated as a preliminary proposal. In this way the foundations are able to screen out ineligible or less qualified projects and to invite those institutions that have submitted the best letters to proceed to the next phase in the application process. Other foundations select a certain number of colleges or universities to submit proposals for a specific grant program, such as faculty development, technological literacy, or minority education. Still others meet with prospective applicants before inviting proposals.

These two-phase processes help us reduce the vast number of proposals so that we can spend more of our staff time working with grant seekers who meet application criteria. The advantage to applicants is that you do not have to spend a great deal of time writing lengthy proposals or assembling supporting documents if your request has no chance for funding. You can concentrate on working on applications to foundations where you will have a better chance of success.

The preliminary letter: Make a good first impression. If the first hurdle is a short letter or preliminary proposal, do not underestimate its importance. You won't get far if you dash off a hurried note saying, "We just want to inform you in our preliminary letter that we have a marvelous idea for revolutionizing the freshman core curriculum here at Dynamic University. We'll tell you all about it when you invite us to submit our proposal."

This letter makes your first impression on the foundation. Even if you have received previous grants or your president has called on the foundation three times, the letter stands alone as it circulates among foundation staff or board members. Following are the elements that build a strong introductory letter:

• In the first paragraph, summarize your project and state the amount you are requesting. Someone at the foundation will probably be recording these statistics, and he or she will appreciate finding the facts and figures quickly.

• Include a brief profile of your institution for those program officers or trustees who might not have heard of you or who know about you only from reading the sports pages.

• Summarize your institution's strengths—faculty, students, alumni achievements. What makes you stand out in the crowd of 3,000 colleges and universities?

• Describe your project clearly and succinctly. Include qualifications of project leaders, goals and purposes, timetable, and estimated budget.

• Discuss the impact of your project both for your institution and beyond your campus.

- Link your project to the foundation. Why should we fund this request this year?
- Thank the foundation for considering your ideas.
- Have the letter signed by your president or chancellor. Or if it more appropriately comes from the faculty member who developed the project, make sure that some presidential or institutional endorsement is also included.

Writing this brief letter forces you to think through your entire program. You can also accept the challenge of helping loquacious faculty members, accustomed to writing 300-page federal grant proposals, condense their ideas into three pages.

Follow directions. Foundations that have made an effort to develop multiphase grant processes generally have published guidelines and procedures for grant seekers. Adhere scrupulously to these directions or you risk being eliminated from the invitation list by a technicality.

- *Meet all deadlines.* In fact, if you send your submission well ahead of the announced deadline, your request will generally receive more careful consideration.
- *Send all required materials.* If, for example, the foundation requests your institution's audited financial statement, send that audit—not a budget or a treasurer's report. If the application procedures require a copy of the Internal Revenue Service's letter attesting to your institution's tax-exempt status, find that letter. Don't send a letter from your administrative vice president saying, "Of course we're tax exempt."
- *Don't send extra items.* Because the purposes of the preliminary stage are to check institutional qualifications and determine the foundation's interest in your project, foundation staff members want to be able to review your materials fairly quickly. Therefore, don't pad your submission with catalogs, alumni magazines, newspaper clippings, or testimonials. If the foundation officers want more information, they will write or phone you.
- *Don't ask for exceptions.* If you can't meet all the foundation's established guidelines, do not ask for requirements to be waived for you. Foundations that can make grants only in Texas or Illinois will not be able to support your college in Florida. Foundations that cannot give scholarships will not make scholarship awards to your students even if they are the most brilliant and deserving in the country. Don't approach foundations if you don't qualify for support. You will just irritate staff members, and you may never be invited to submit a proposal, even if their guidelines change at a later date.

Declinations. There are many reasons for not inviting a first-phase applicant to proceed to the full proposal stage. Some program officers will share these reasons with you; they will tell you, for example, that your college does not fall within geographical, enrollment, or programmatic guidelines. Your project is not a current foundation priority or is not of major interest to the foundation's trustees. Your case was not well stated, or there is no indication that you really need the money.

Try to contact the appropriate foundation program officer to learn why your preliminary request was declined, because the reasons will affect your decision on reapplication. If your institution does not qualify, it would not be advisable to send another request two months later. Instead, wait a year or two or until your status or the foundation's guidelines have changed. If, however, your excellently qualified college happened to submit an inappropriate project, ask if or when you can submit a different and more suitable request. In any case, be sure to thank the foundation for careful consideration.

Joining the in-group. It is disappointing and often hard to understand why your university was not included when the Elitist Foundation invited 30 institutions to submit proposals for its new program for premier engineering schools. Your president, dean, and alumni have been saying for years that you have one of the top programs in the country. Although there may not be much you can do about this rejection in the short run, try to forget your chagrin or bitterness and consider the following suggestions:

• Don't write a nasty letter to foundation staff members. They had certain criteria, which they may or may not publish, for compiling their list of eligible institutions, and you were omitted. They won't be able to add you now, and if you are offensive, you will jeopardize your chances for a future grant.

• Don't make disparaging remarks about the foundation to your educational colleagues or to another foundation. Comments like "The people at that unfair Elitist Foundation couldn't make a good engineering grant if they tried!" have a way of getting back to the foundation staff. Moreover, if you become known as someone who is disgruntled or uncooperative, you may be left off future invitation lists.

• About six months after the initial list for the engineering program has been announced, try to arrange an introductory visit for you and your engineering dean with the appropriate foundation program officer. Be sure to make clear that this is a get-acquainted meeting during which the dean can describe your programs and strengths. Later, if the foundation plans an expansion of its first list of invitees or develops new engineering programs, your university might qualify. Also, ask if you should add the foundation to the mailing list for your engineering newsletter and research quarterly.

• During the next year or two, call the foundation officer occasionally when you have some special news to report. If, for example, one of your Nobel Laureates is speaking in the city where the foundation is located, ask if any representatives of the foundation would like tickets for the lecture. Let the foundation know if your engineers receive a major federal grant for a new research center. Items like this are not forgotten when foundations make new lists of potential invitees.

• Encourage members of the foundation's staff and board of trustees to visit your campus. Site visits give you an opportunity to display the strengths of your academic programs and also provide time for foundation representatives to have substantive discussions with key members of your faculty who can suggest future grant-making programs.

Pre-proposal strategies

Whether a foundation has a preliminary stage or whether your first contact will be the formal proposal, careful preparation will enable you to write a more in-formed and effective proposal. You will be able to anticipate many of the questions foundation staff members may ask before or during the proposal process.

Internal cultivation. Accept the assignment of internal cultivation with all the seriousness you give to external cultivation of prospective donors. Internal cultivation involves gaining a comprehensive knowledge of your own institution and of the specific division or department that is planning to submit the proposal.

• *Know your goals.* This includes the academic goals articulated in your catalog, in your president's annual report, and in your campaign case statement. Also be alert to any new or forthcoming plans that are not yet in print. Be especially certain that you know how the aims of the specific project you are working on mesh with the overall goals of the institution. If you are going to be writing a proposal for equipping a chemistry laboratory, find out how this project will enhance your overall science program. You should understand how purchasing new chemistry equipment will contribute to the plan to have all undergraduates participate in research projects with faculty. How might this program ultimately influence other institutions around the country?

To gain this awareness, you should become involved as early as possible in the academic planning process. Read background materials, go to committee meetings, and take key members of the planning team to lunch. As a result, you will learn how the program evolved and how it became a high priority. Don't hesitate to ask the program planners hard questions—the same questions a foundation staff member might ask you: What are the implications of your new curriculum for student enrollment, faculty development, community relations? Can you justify every item in your budget? What will happen after the initial grant runs out?

• *Know where to find information in your university.* Who can supply the history and original plans of the fine arts building you are trying to renovate? Who can describe the impact of your law school on your community? Who knows the latest percentages for calculating fringe benefits for faculty and staff? Who has your enrollment projections for the next five years?

For some projects, all the information can come from one individual, but it is far more likely that you will need to consult several sources. Get to know the data reservoirs on your campus: assistant deans, registrars, plant directors, and professors emeriti. Ready access to the information channels in your institution will make, proposal writing more interesting as well as more effective.

• *Understand the financial situation.* All development officers, and especially those involved with foundation presentations, should thoroughly understand the institutional financial picture. Many foundations now request audited financial statements, university and departmental budgets, and facts about tuition and endowment. More significantly, we read and study this information because your financial stability and institutional solvency may be crucial elements when we decide whether a grant can be made to your institution.

You should be able to answer the following questions:

1. What are your institution's total assets and liabilities?
2. Is your institution carrying *good* or *bad* debt?

3. What percentage of your institution's total revenue comes from tuition? state allocations? endowment earnings? auxiliary services? gifts and grants?

4. Who manages the investments and expenditures of your institution's endowment?

5. Is tuition going up next year? How much? Why?

If this information is not part of your store of knowledge about your institution, ask your financial officers to arrange one or two special seminars for you and your staff. They should be pleased that those who are responsible for raising funds want to develop some expertise in how the monies are managed and spent.

• *Know who makes major decisions.* If you know where and how decisions are made on your campus, you can eliminate the proposal writer's lament: "I can't finish this proposal on time because *they* haven't decided what *they* want to do." This excuse generally means that you haven't been informed about what the *theys* have decided. Find out how to gain access to the theys on your campus and the best ways to obtain information from them promptly. Never wait until minutes are distributed to find out what went on in a key committee meeting.

The knowledge you gain from internal cultivation and your informed enthusiasm about your institution will enrich and enliven all your proposals.

Contingency planning. Few things are more disheartening than spending months on a proposal only to have it declined. Fortunately, foundation fund raisers generally have several projects in the works at once so that failures are balanced by successes. In addition, if you make some contingency plans before you even write the proposal, you will be able to view foundation declinations as temporary setbacks, not major failures. Consider the following strategies:

• *Prepare for multiple submissions.* It is likely that most of your major projects will need more than one donor. The plan to build the new gymnasium and renovate the field house probably calls for funding from three major individual donors, grants from five foundations, and perhaps smaller gifts from hundreds of alumni. Even though you carefully tailor each proposal according to the guidelines and procedures of the five foundations, you can gather the requisite materials for all five at once. Two of the local foundations, headed by your alumni, may need only minimal documentation because they know you well. The national foundations, however, may require that you supply copies of architects' plans, contracts, or building permits. If you collect all this information as part of your proposal preparation, you will have the materials handy when your president suddenly decides to call on the foundations.

With other projects that are primarily funded by one donor, you should prepare a list of several alternative sources in case the first foundation says "no." When you prepare your request to the foundation that is most likely to support your new education abroad program in Japan, assemble a list of three back-up foundations. Then, if for any reason the first foundation can't help you, you can immediately revise your proposal for the next prospect on your list. Rather than being devastated by the declination, you can immediately move to the next step in your contingency plan.

• *Establish a working timetable.* Review published material from your foundation prospects to determine how long after submitting a proposal you will be notified of their decision. If information is not available from the foundation, call a colleague at another institution who has received a grant from that foundation. Then you can establish a working timetable. For example, if you submit a proposal to Foundation A in January and the normal notification time is about three months, you can have a revised version of that proposal ready for Foundation B in March, just in case A has to decline your request. You don't lose any time between applications.

• *Share contingency plans.* Tell your supervisor and report at staff meetings on your fallback plans. Describe the strategies and timetables you have developed in case of a declination. If your initial proposal is funded, everyone on the staff will celebrate and congratulate you, but, more important, if you are turned down the first time, they will praise your foresight at having other sources to approach.

Personal cultivation. After you finish your planning and information gathering, you have one more preliminary step before you write a proposal: personal cultivation and self-assessment. What is your own role in this program? How can you help implement all phases of this fund-raising project?

As a writer, you are at once a creator, a synthesizer, a fund raiser, and an educator. Your part in attaining the overall goals of your institution is an important one. You can help promote communication among the constituencies at your institution. You can speed up project planning and help bring grantors and grantees together. By taking a close look at your own role in each project, you can increase the likelihood that the proposal you write will be funded.

Adapted from an article published in CASE CURRENTS, *May 1980, pp. 29-31.*

Chapter 9

From Prospect Research to Foundation Grant

Mary Kay Murphy
Director for Development
Georgia Institute of Technology

B efore significant fund raising can take place, the staff must identify and evaluate those persons, foundations, corporations, and organizations from which it reasonably can expect to receive support. "Blue-sky" prospect identification is dangerous....

Such research includes collecting information on which to base sound determinations about the right prospects for the project (amount and purpose), as well as the right time to solicit from those prospects.[1]

The case for prospect research on foundations

Should your institution do prospect research on foundations? At first glance at the relevant figures, you may think that your efforts would be better spent on individual prospects. In 1987, individuals gave 82 percent of the $93.68 billion total philanthropic gifts. Foundations contributed only 6.81 percent, while corporations contributed 4.80 percent. Bequests accounted for the remaining 6.39 percent of philanthropic contributions in 1987.

Education received 11.57 percent or $10.84 billion of all philanthropic support in 1987, second only to religion. While total giving increased, the rate of growth slowed from the previous year. The 7.91 percent growth was less than half the 19.91 percent growth from 1985 to 1986. While individuals contributed 51.8 percent to education in 1986-87, corporations and foundations were not far behind at 39.1 percent. Religious and other groups accounted for 9.1 percent of the remaining contributions to higher education in 1986-87.

In 1987, foundations gave about one-fifth of their gifts to education.

Goals of a prospect research program

Your institution's foundation prospect research program should have several goals, including the following:

• to research your institution, identifying academic and other programs that relate to funding interests of foundations;

• to research foundations to identify and rank those that have supported your institution in the past; and to identify and rank new foundation prospects that could support it in the future; and

• to identify, analyze, and manage the information developed through foundation research and route it to the appropriate faculty, staff, and trustees of your institution.

Research the institution

Prospect research begins by identifying programs at your institution that relate to funding interests of foundations so that the development officer can make a match between a foundation's priorities and an institution's programs. Thus, effective institutional research produces information on the following:

• your college, university, or independent school's mission statement, philosophy of education, history, enrollment profile, library holdings, and physical plant;

• your institution's long-range plan for its future;

• budget information for at least three years, including sources of support and disbursement of funds;

• compliance with provisions of not-for-profit, civil rights, employment, and handicapped students' legislation at state and federal levels;

• the alumni body and its recent history of fund-raising activities;

• academic programs and their importance to your institution and its priorities;

• research specialties and strengths of your institution's faculty;

• innovations and new directions for operation of your institution; and

• cost-effectiveness of programs offered at your institution, especially the program being proposed to the prospect.

Armed with information on the institution, you can now move on to identify past and potential sources of foundation support.

Research the foundation: Building a research library

For this stage in the research process, you need space, materials, budget, and time. Identifying and ranking the institution's past foundation supporters and its top 50 to 100 new prospects is no small task, and it is never complete. As the institution develops new program specialties and foundations identify new guidelines and priorities, you will drop some prospects and add others.

Space. You'll need storage space in the office research library for data developed in foundation research. Whether you use computer programs or freestanding vertical files, easy access is the key. If you are in the process of building your foundation research library, buy materials in whatever combination of hard-cover, photocopies, and microfiche will allow speedy, convenient, and easy access to that information.

Materials. Specialized research materials on private foundations are important in an office reference library. There are three main types:

• directories such as the *Foundation Directory* and the *Taft Directory of Nonprofit Organizations,* which list vital information made public by the foundations;

• annual reports;

• IRS 990 forms, which, since 1969, have been required by law of all foundations; the 990 discloses market value of assets, names of trustees, and recipients and size of annual awards.

You need to know what types of awards a foundation makes or doesn't make. Directories and annual reports will note the types of awards made by the foundation. Among the nearly 30 types of awards are the following: conferences/lectures, endowment, research, scholarships, equipment, and unrestricted gifts.

Be sure to note which type of foundation you are researching. Over time, foundations have developed interests based on the philanthropic views of those who incorporated the foundation or those who serve as its trustees or professional staff members. There are four basic types of foundations:

• general purpose (large endowment, broad interests, professional staff);

• family (interests of family members);

• corporate (conduit for corporate giving interests); and

• community (support for community programs).

A fifth type, the privately operating foundation, does not make awards but initiates projects for funding on its own.

You can extend your library with materials available at regional collections of the Foundation Center (see the list at the end of this chapter). These collections are housed in public libraries in each of the 50 states as well as Puerto Rico and Mexico. IRS 990 reports, annual reports, news releases, newsletters, and periodicals are available in photocopies or microfiche on local, regional, and national foundations. You can consolidate the services offered by the Foundation Center by enrolling in its Associates Program for an annual fee. To find out more about this service, call the Center's toll-free number, (800) 424-9836.

Monthly publications such as *Foundation News* and *Foundation Giving Watch* provide updates on giving trends and identify possible new prospects. These publications complement specialized publications used for foundation research.

In addition to printed books, publications, and periodicals, don't overlook computerized research services. For a fee (in addition to the annual membership fee), the Foundation Center will do computerized database searches of foundation grant information for members of its Associates program.

You can also use the computer to compile research from public records on foundations and to facilitate record-keeping and report making.

Budget and time. While budgets vary from institution to institution—as do personal preferences for research materials and methods—every institution needs convenient, accessible, and thorough research on foundation prospects. If your institution puts a high priority on foundation funding, it must be prepared to allocate the money and the staff time to create and maintain an effective prospect research program.

Forms, files, formats

The information that results from prospect research must be in usable form. You will need forms, files, and formats so that you can fulfill the primary purpose of prospect research—sharing the information with fund-raising staff, faculty, top administrators, the president, and trustees. Figure 1 is an evaluation form we use at Georgia Tech to record information on a prospect and its relationship with the institution, especially past giving, research contacts, and other forms of support.

For a foundation prospect, you can use the evaluation form to record the following information:
- specific contacts between the prospect and your institution;
- distribution limits of awards;
- the foundation's operating procedures;
- key alumni or other contacts at the foundation;
- foundation officers;
- past awards to your institution; and
- financial information on the foundation, including market value of assets, disbursements, and recipients and size of awards.

Use the evaluation form as the basis for the data collected for each foundation prospect and include—in freestanding vertical files—other material, such as data on IRS 990 forms, newspaper clippings, annual reports, correspondence, and proposals submitted.

Develop word-processing and computer formats to summarize this data and to rank prospects. You can rank prospect by size of assets or by match with institution program, institutional readiness to solicit a gift or present a proposal, or any other relevant criterion.

Developing forms, files, and formats will help you collect, organize, and communicate research on your institution's top 50 to 100 foundation prospects.

Understanding research information

The information you collect in your research efforts may be overwhelming or even incomprehensible if you do not decode, analyze, and interpret it.

To decode foundation information, you must be able to identify trends in support of institutions (such as funding public or out-of-state institutions, research, or scientific projects), increases or decreases in the size of gifts, growth or decline

Figure 1: Foundation Evaluation Form

Date: _____

Foundation name:
Address:
Phone:

Chief executive officer:
Title:
Secretary:
Other key contacts:

Geographic link to Georgia Tech:

Assets of foundation (FY ____):

Total grants:
Range of grants:
Average grant:
Annual report available:

Record of activities within Georgia Tech:
Co-op program:
Continuing education:
Research volume:
Other (CLP, CAP, etc.):
Summary of educational grant:

Areas of interest related to activities at Georgia Tech:

Gifts to other institutions:

Date	Amount	Institution

Record of gifts to Georgia Tech:

Date	Amount	Purpose

Georgia Tech Cultivation Record (mailings, correspondence, personal contacts, responses, etc.):

Date   Nature of communication

Miscellaneous information and remarks:

of foundation assets over time, and extensions of support to emerging and unannounced new program areas. You also need to determine the relationships of award recipients to people within a foundation, staff, board, or donor family. The observant researcher knows that the rule, "people give to people," applies to foundation giving as well as to individual gifts and bequests.

Key information in the foundation IRS 990 includes the market value of assets, officers of the foundation, range and size of awards, and types and locations of institutions receiving awards.

Grid management of research information

One of the major goals of prospect research is to identify a finite number of prospects on which to conduct in-depth research. You do this by eliminating foundations with priorities or interests that do not match institutional goals.

A grid can help you in this important step. After conducting research on your institution, list its priority needs in order of importance. Then conduct initial research on foundations that fund these priorities. Table 1 on the next page shows the grid format.

For this initial phase of prospect research, you will need to use directories indexed by types of institutional need, compilations of types of awards such as COM-SEARCH Printouts, and periodic listings of types of awards and institutions that received awards. These are published in sources such as *Philanthropic Digest, Chronicle of Higher Education, Chronicle of Philanthropy,* and *Foundation Grants Index.*

Initial research will eliminate a large number of prospects that will not be interested or able to fund your institution's programs. When a match is not possible, the prudent researcher immediately moves on to the next prospect.

Be sure to include geographical constraints in your grid. Foundations may consider location when they make funding decisions. General purpose foundations, for the most part, make national awards, but family and community foundations make awards within geographic limits.

Does your institution have special ties with any foundations, such as shared research interests? Include any such ties in the grid format.

Using grid management can help you refine your research effort and identify key foundation prospects on which to conduct in-depth research.

The rolling calendar

As the primary means of transmitting information from an institution to a potential funding source, the written proposal is a crucial document. It's not only the wording of the proposal that is vital to its success, but its timing. A late proposal may not only fail to receive funding but may damage your institution's image as a responsible organization. A rolling calendar can help you organize information

Table 1: Foundation Prospects Related to Institutional Need

Foundation Priority

	Robotics program	Endowed chair	Scholarships	Fellowships	Computers	Laboratory equipment
ABC Foundation	✖	✖				
First Trust		✖				✖
Concrete Foundation					✖	
United Foundation						✖
J.P. Ross			✖			
Smith Foundation						✖
Pauline Foundation				✖		
Will Trust	✖					✖
Rich Foundation			✖			
Still Foundation						✖
Jones Foundation		✖				✖
Morton Foundation			✖	✖	✖	
D&R Fund		✖				✖
CBA Trust						✖
S.D. Goodfellow	✖			✖		
L&J Fund						✖

Institutional Need

about deadlines, content, format, and the names of the foundation officers who should receive the proposal.

Simple in format, the rolling calendar helps you plan how much time you— and everyone else involved—need to research, coordinate, write, and present a proposal for funding consideration. Figure 2 on the next page shows a sample rolling calendar. Include information on your institution's top 50 to 100 foundation prospects and monitor it carefully so that each prospect is moved through the research-to-proposal stage at the appropriate times.

Sharing and routing research information

Unless prospect research is shared with the right people at the right time, it won't result in effective fund-raising action. The researcher who accumulates and interprets the information begins the action, but it is continued by the development officer or faculty member who writes the proposal or the trustee who calls on the prospect or speaks in favor of the project to decision makers at the funding source.

One way to share prospect research information is through a peer review process—a committee of faculty and key administrators who meet regularly to review the information. This should not be a one-way process, however; the committee can provide the researcher with information on new academic and research initiatives and can serve as a clearinghouse, making sure that funding requests are prepared in an orderly fashion. The committee can rate or rank foundation prospects "A," "B," or "C." "A" prospects are those where cultivation and solicitation activities should result in submission of a proposal during the next six months; "B" prospects, within a year; and "C" prospects, within two years.

Work with development officers and faculty to create one-page summaries of your institution's academic, research, fellowship, scholarship, and equipment needs. These summaries, compiled into one volume, constitute your institution's "Programs for Private Support." You can then develop a grid management format based on these needs and use it to identify a finite number of key foundation funding prospects.

In addition, researchers, key development staff, and faculty members can prepare strategy papers to share and route pertinent information regarding foundation prospects.

Before you submit a proposal to a foundation, you should identify the alumni or trustees who are decision makers within the foundation or who have personal contact with the decision makers. Their support can be helpful but be cautious if you use these internal contacts to advocate your institution's proposal. Attempts to unduly influence the funding decision can damage your proposal's chances and even affect your institution's reputation.

Once the proposal has been funded (or rejected), the prospect researcher often has major responsibilities for recording gift information in appropriate files and formats for use in later solicitations.

Figure 2: Board Meetings and Proposal Deadlines for Major State Foundations

Foundation	Officer	Board meetings	Deadline	Number of copies of proposal required
1. Jones Foundation ($3,094,241)	Emma Gaillard	Annually	December	Letter/one copy
2. United Foundation ($8,700,762)	Thomas Hunt	Quarterly	15 December, March, June, September	Letter/one copy
3. J.P. Ross ($10,745,369)	Laura Robey	Quarterly	January, March, June, September	Letter/two copies
4. Stores Foundation ($80,690,200)	Brian Irvine	Quarterly	End of month before Jan., April, July, Oct.	Letter/one copy
5. L&J Fund ($330,334)	Katherine Darter	Semiannually	September	Letter/one copy
6. Morton Foundation ($1,356,800)	Sharon Sheppard	Semiannually	July, January	Form request
7. Karen and David Brown ($2,742,207)	Jefferson Stevens	NA	NA	NA
8. Pauline Foundation ($4,693,693)	Sarah McNamara	Quarterly	January, April, July, October	Grant application letter
9. S.D. Goodfellow ($16,033,113)	Robert Eaton	Semiannually April and November	January, September	Letter/one copy

Tracking prospect development

You'll need a monitoring system to coordinate prospect research through the proposal submission phase. At Georgia Tech we use an action-oriented flow chart (Figure 3) that keeps paperwork to a minimum. You can use such a chart to do monthly summaries, adding new projects as they appear.

Figure 3: Phase I—Initial Research to Proposal Submission

Foundation	Initial research	Telephone contact	Foundation visit	Follow-up letter	Faculty contact	Faculty meeting	Letter of inquiry	Request for full proposal	Proposal submitted

We use the flow chart to monitor a project through the nine sequential or nearly sequential steps of Phase I—initial research to proposal submission.

1. Activation of initial research phase—by faculty, development staff, or prospect researcher.

2. Telephone contact—by prospect researcher, faculty, or development staff to verify current giving information.

3. Foundation visit—by faculty or development staff.

4. Follow-up letter—by faculty or development staff.

5. Faculty contact—scheduled by faculty or development staff.

6. Faculty meeting with funding source—follows initial contact.

7. Letter of inquiry—sent instead of faculty or development staff visit.

8. Request for full proposal—previous steps have paved the way for the funding source to invite a full proposal to be submitted. No proposals are sent unsolicited.

9. Proposal submitted—follow-through activities planned if project is not funded. New cultivation activities possible if project is funded.

The flow chart in Figure 4 tracks the project through Phase II from funding to recognition activities, including acknowledgement letter, press releases, progress reports, final reports, and recognition activities.

Summary

Prospect research on foundations is a major factor in the success of an educational institution's fund-raising program. Commitment to an organized prospect research effort correlates with an increase in foundation support. Thus, enlightened self-interest suggests that educational institutions have much to gain from an organized, thorough, and continuous program of foundation prospect research.

Note

[1] Thomas E. Broce, *Fund Raising: The Guide to Raising Money from Private Sources,* 2d ed. rev. (Norman, OK: University of Oklahoma Press, 1986), pp. 23-24.

Figure 4: Phase II—Funding Through Recognition

Date proposal funded	Acknowledge-ment letter	Press release	Progress report #1	Progress report #2	Final report	Recognition activity

THE FOUNDATION CENTER COOPERATING COLLECTIONS NETWORK

The Foundation Center is an independent national service organization established by foundations to provide an authoritative source of information on private philanthropic giving. In fulfilling its mission, The Center disseminates information on private giving through public service programs, publications and through a national network of library reference collections for free public use. The New York, Washington, DC, Cleveland and San Francisco reference collections operated by The Foundation Center offer a wide variety of services and comprehensive collections of information on foundations and grants. The Cooperating Collections are libraries, community foundations and other nonprofit agencies that provide a core collection of Foundation Center publications and a variety of supplementary materials and services in subject areas useful to grantseekers.

Over 100 of the network members have sets of private foundation information returns (IRS Form 990-PF) for their states or regions which are available for public use. A complete set of U.S. foundation returns can be found at the New York and Washington, DC offices of The Foundation Center. The Cleveland and San Francisco offices contain IRS returns for those foundations in the midwestern and western states, respectively.

Because the collections vary in their hours, materials and services, IT IS RECOMMENDED THAT YOU CALL EACH COLLECTION IN ADVANCE. To check on new locations or current information, call toll-free 1-800-424-9836.

Those collections marked with a bullet (●) have sets of private foundation information returns (IRS Form 990-PF) for their states or regions, available for public reference.

Reference collections operated by The Foundation Center are in **boldface**.

ALABAMA

● Birmingham Public Library
2100 Park Place
Birmingham 35203
205-226-3600

Huntsville–Madison County
Public Library
108 Fountain Circle
P.O. Box 443
Huntsville 35804
205-532-5940

University of South Alabama
Library Building
Reference Department
Mobile 36688
205-460-7025

● Auburn University at
Montgomery Library
Montgomery 36193-0401
205-271-9649

ALASKA

● University of Alaska,
Anchorage Library
3211 Providence Drive
Anchorage 99508
907-786-1848

ARIZONA

● Phoenix Public Library Business
and Sciences Department
12 East McDowell Road
Phoenix 85004
602-262-4636

● Tucson Public Library
Main Library
200 South Sixth Avenue
Tucson 85701
602-791-4393

ARKANSAS

● Westark Community College
Library
Grand Avenue at Waldron Road
Fort Smith 72913
501-785-7000

● Little Rock Public Library
Reference Department
700 Louisiana Street
Little Rock 72201
501-370-5950

CALIFORNIA

● California Community
Foundation Funding Information
Center
3580 Wilshire Blvd., Suite 1660
Los Angeles 90010
213-413-4042

● Community Foundation for
Monterey County
420 Pacific Street
Monterey 93940
408-375-9712

California Community
Foundation
4050 Metropolitan Drive #300
Orange 92668
714-937-9077

Riverside Public Library
3581 7th Street
Riverside 92501
714-782-5201

California State Library
Reference Services, Rm. 309
914 Capital Mall
Sacramento 95814
916-322-4570

● San Diego Community
Foundation
525 "B" Street, Suite 410
San Diego 92101
619-239-8815

● **The Foundation Center**
312 Sutter Street, Room 312
San Francisco 94108
415-397-0902

● Grantsmanship Resource Center
Junior League of San Jose, Inc.
Community Foundation of Santa
Clara County
1762 Technology Dr., Suite 225
San Jose 95110
408-452-8181

● Orange County Community
Developmental Council
1695 MacArthur Blvd.
Costa Mesa 92626
714-540-9293

● Peninsula Community
Foundation
1204 Burlingame Avenue
Burlingame 94011-0627
415-342-2505

● Santa Barbara Public Library
Reference Section
40 East Anapamu
P.O. Box 1019
Santa Barbara 93102
805-962-7653

Santa Monica Public Library
1343 Sixth Street
Santa Monica 90401-1603
213-458-8603

Tuolomne County Library
465 S. Washington Street
Sonora 95370
209-533-5707

COLORADO

Pikes Peak Library District
20 North Cascade Avenue
Colorado Springs 80901
303-473-2780

● Denver Public Library
Sociology Division
1357 Broadway
Denver 80203
303-571-2190

CONNECTICUT

Danbury Public Library
170 Main Street
Danbury 06810
203-797-4527

● Hartford Public Library
Reference Department
500 Main Street
Hartford 06103
203-525-9121

D.A.T.A.
30 Arbor Street
Hartford 06106
203-232-6619

D.A.T.A.
25 Science Park
Suite 502
New Haven 06511
203-786-5225

DELAWARE

● Hugh Morris Library
University of Delaware
Newark 19717-5267
302-451-2965

● Santa Barbara Public Library
DISTRICT OF COLUMBIA

● **The Foundation Center**
1001 Connecticut Avenue, NW
Washington 20036
202-331-1400

FLORIDA

Volusia County Public Library
City Island
Daytona Beach 32014
904-252-8374

● Jacksonville Public Library
Business, Science, and Industry
Department
122 North Ocean Street
Jacksonville 32202
904-633-3926

● Miami–Dade Public Library
Humanities Department
101 W. Flagler St.
Miami 33132
305-375-2665

● Orange County Library System
101 E. Central Blvd.
Orlando 32801
305-425-4694

Selby Public Library
1001 Boulevard of the Arts
Sarasota 33577
813-366-7303

● Leon County Public Library
Community Funding Resources
Center
1940 North Monroe Street
Tallahassee 32303
904-487-2665

Palm Beach County Community
Foundation
324 Datura Street, Suite 340
West Palm Beach 33401
305-659-6800

GEORGIA

● Atlanta–Fulton Public Library
Ivan Allen Department
1 Margaret Mitchell Square
Atlanta 30303
404-688-4636

HAWAII

● Thomas Hale Hamilton Library
General Reference
University of Hawaii
2550 The Mall
Honolulu 96822
808-948-7214

The Hawaiian Foundation
Resource Room
130 Merchant Street
Bancorp Tower, Suite 901
Honolulu 96813
808-538-4540

IDAHO

● Caldwell Public Library
1010 Dearborn Street
Caldwell 83605
208-459-3242

ILLINOIS

Belleville Public Library
121 East Washington Street
Belleville 62220
618-234-0441

DuPage Township
300 Briarcliff Road
Bolingbrook 60439
312-759-1317

● Donors Forum of Chicago
53 W. Jackson Blvd., Rm. 430
Chicago 60604
312-431-0265

● Evanston Public Library
1703 Orrington Avenue
Evanston 60201
312-866-0305

● Sangamon State University
Library
Shepherd Road
Springfield 62708
217-786-6633

INDIANA

Allen County Public Library
900 Webster Street
Fort Wayne 46802
219-424-7241

Indiana University Northwest
Library
3400 Broadway
Gary 46408
219-980-6580

● Indianapolis-Marion County
Public Library
40 East St. Clair Street
Indianapolis 46204
317-269-1733

IOWA

● Public Library of Des Moines
100 Locust Street
Des Moines 50308
515-283-4259

KANSAS

● Topeka Public Library
Adult Services Department
1515 West Tenth Street
Topeka 66604
913-233-2040

● Wichita Public Library
223 South Main
Wichita 67202
316-262-0611

KENTUCKY

Western Kentucky University
Division of Library Services
Helm-Cravens Library
Bowling Green 42101
502-745-3951

● Louisville Free Public Library
Fourth and York Streets
Louisville 40203
502-561-8600

LOUISIANA

● East Baton Rouge Parish Library
Centroplex Library
120 St. Louis Street
Baton Rouge 70821
504-389-4960

● New Orleans Public Library
Business and Science Division
219 Loyola Avenue
New Orleans 70140
504-596-2583

● Shreve Memorial Library
424 Texas Street
Shreveport 71101
318-226-5894

MAINE

● University of Southern Maine
Office of Sponsored Research
96 Falmouth Street
Portland 04103
207-780-4411

MARYLAND

● Enoch Pratt Free Library
Social Science and History
Department
400 Cathedral Street
Baltimore 21201
301-396-5320

MASSACHUSETTS

● Associated Grantmakers of
Massachusetts
294 Washington Street
Suite 501
Boston 02108
617-426-2608

● Boston Public Library
Copley Square
Boston 02117
617-536-5400

Walpole Public Library
Common Street
Walpole 02081
617-668-5497 ext. 340

● Western Massachusetts Funding
Resource Center
Campaign for Human
Development
Chancery Annex
73 Chestnut Street
Springfield 01103
413-732-3175 ext. 67

● Grants Resource Center
Worcester Public Library
Salem Square
Worcester 01608
617-799-1655

MICHIGAN

● Alpena County Library
211 North First Avenue
Alpena 49707
517-356-6188

University of Michigan–Ann
Arbor
Reference Department
209 Hatcher Graduate Library
Ann Arbor 48109-1205
313-764-1149

● Henry Ford Centennial Library
16301 Michigan Avenue
Dearborn 48126
313-943-2337

● Purdy Library
Wayne State University
Detroit 48202
313-577-4040

● Michigan State University
Libraries
Reference Library
East Lansing 48824
517-353-8818

● Farmington Community Library
32737 West 12 Mile Road
Farmington Hills 48018
313-553-0300

● University of Michigan–Flint
Library
Reference Department
Flint 48503
313-762-3408

● Grand Rapids Public Library
Business Dept.
60 Library Plaza
Grand Rapids 49503
616-456-3600

● Michigan Technological
University Library
Highway U.S. 41
Houghton 49931
906-487-2507

MINNESOTA

● Duluth Public Library
520 Superior Street
Duluth 55802
218-723-3802

● Southwest State University
Library
Marshall 56258
507-537-7278

● Minneapolis Public Library
Sociology Department
300 Nicollet Mall
Minneapolis 55401
612●372-6555

Rochester Public Library
Broadway at First Street, SE
Rochester 55901
507-285-8002

Saint Paul Public Library
90 West Fourth Street
Saint Paul 55102
612-292-6311

MISSISSIPPI

Jackson Metropolitan Library
301 North State Street
Jackson 39201
601-944-1120

MISSOURI

● Clearinghouse for Midcontinent
Foundations
P.O. Box 22680
Univ. of Missouri, Kansas City
Law School, Suite 1-300
52nd Street and Oak
Kansas City 64113
816-276-1176

● Kansas City Public Library
311 East 12th Street
Kansas City 64106
816-221-2685

● Metropolitan Association for
Philanthropy, Inc.
5585 Pershing Avenue
Suite 150
St. Louis 63112
314-361-3900

● Springfield–Greene County
Library
397 East Central Street
Springfield 65801
417-866-4636

MONTANA

● Eastern Montana College Library
Reference Department
1500 N. 30th Street
Billings 59101-0298
406-657-2262

● Montana State Library
Reference Department
1515 E. 6th Avenue
Helena 59620
406-444-3004

NEBRASKA

● University of Nebraska, Lincoln
106 Love Library
Lincoln 68588-0410
402-472-2848

● W. Dale Clark Library
Social Sciences Department
215 South 15th Street
Omaha 68102
402-444-4826

NEVADA

● Las Vegas-Clark County Library
District
1401 East Flamingo Road
Las Vegas 89119
702-733-7810

● Washoe County Library
301 South Center Street
Reno 89505
702-785-4012

NEW HAMPSHIRE

● The New Hampshire Charitable
Fund
One South Street
Concord 03301
603-225-6641

Littleton Public Library
109 Main Street
Littleton 03561
603-444-5741

NEW JERSEY

Cumberland County Library
800 E. Commerce Street
Bridgeton 08302
609-453-2216

The Support Center
17 Academy Street, Suite 1101
Newark 07102
201-643-5774

County College of Morris
Masten Learning Resource
Center
Route 10 and Center Grove Rd.
Randolph 07869
201-361-5000 ext. 470

● New Jersey State Library
Governmental Reference
185 West State Street
Trenton 08625
609-292-6220

NEW MEXICO

Albuquerque Community
Foundation
6400 Uptown Boulevard N.E.
Suite 500-W
Albuquerque 87110
505-883-6240

● New Mexico State Library
325 Don Gaspar Street
Santa Fe 87503
505-827-3824

NEW YORK

● New York State Library
Cultural Education Center
Humanities Section
Empire State Plaza
Albany 12230
518-474-7645

Bronx Reference Center
New York Public Library
2556 Bainbridge Avenue
Bronx 10458
212-220-6575

Brooklyn in Touch
101 Willoughby Street
Room 1508
Brooklyn 11201
718-237-9300

● Buffalo and Erie County Public
Library
Lafayette Square
Buffalo 14203
716-856-7525

Huntington Public Library
338 Main Street
Huntington 11743
516-427-5165

● Levittown Public Library
Reference Department
One Bluegrass Lane
Levittown 11756
516-731-5728

● The Foundation Center
79 Fifth Avenue
New York 10003
212-620-4230

SUNY/College at Old Westbury
Library
223 Store Hill Road
Old Westbury 11568
516-876-3156

● Plattsburgh Public Library
Adult Services Department
15 Oak Street
Plattsburgh 12901
518-563-0921

Adriance Memorial Library
93 Market Street
Poughkeepsie 12601
914-485-3445

Queens Borough Public Library
89-11 Merrick Boulevard
Jamaica 11432
718-990-0700

● Rochester Public Library
Business and Social Sciences
Division
115 South Avenue
Rochester 14604
716-428-7328

Staten Island Council on the Arts
One Edgewater Plaza Rm. 311
Staten Island 10305
718-447-4485

● Onondaga County Public Library
at the Galleries
447 S. Salina Street
Syracuse 13202-2494
315-448-4636

● White Plains Public Library
100 Martine Avenue
White Plains 10601
914-682-4488

● Suffolk Cooperative Library
System
627 North Sunrise Service Road
Bellport 11713
516-286-1600

NORTH CAROLINA

● The Duke Endowment
200 S. Tryon Street, Ste. 1100
Charlotte 28202
704-376-0291

Durham County Library
300 N. Roxboro Street
Durham 27701
919-683-2626

● North Carolina State Library
109 East Jones Street
Raleigh 27611
919-733-3270

● The Winston-Salem Foundation
229 First Union National Bank
Building
Winston-Salem 27101
919-725-2382

NORTH DAKOTA

Western Dakota Grants Resource
Center
Bismarck Junior College Library
Bismarck 58501
701-224-5450

● The Library
North Dakota State University
Fargo 58105
701-237-8876

OHIO

● Public Library of Cincinnati and
Hamilton County
Education Department
800 Vine Street
Cincinnati 45202
513-369-6940

● The Foundation Center
Kent H. Smith Library
1442 Hanna Building
1422 Euclid Avenue
Cleveland 44115
216-861-1933

The Public Library of Columbus
and Franklin County
Main Library
96 S. Grant Avenue
Columbus 43215
614-222-7180

● Dayton and Montgomery County
Public Library
Grants Information Center
215 E. Third Street
Dayton 45402-2103
513-227-9500 ext. 211

● Toledo–Lucas County Public
Library
Social Science Department
325 Michigan Street
Toledo 43624
419-255-7055 ext. 221

Ohio University–Zanesville
Community Education and
Development
1425 Newark Road
Zanesville 43701
614-453-0762

Stark County District Library
715 Market Avenue North
Canton 44702-1080
216-452-0665

OKLAHOMA

● Oklahoma City University Library
NW 23rd at North Blackwelder
Oklahoma City 73106
405-521-5072

● Tulsa City–County Library System
400 Civic Center
Tulsa 74103
918-592-7944

OREGON

● Library Association of Portland
Government Documents Room
801 S.W. Tenth Avenue
Portland 97205
503-223-7201

Oregon State Library
State Library Building
Salem 97310
503-378-4274

PENNSYLVANIA

Northampton County Area
Community College
Learning Resources Center
3835 Green Pond Road
Bethlehem 18017
215-865-5358

● Erie County Public Library
3 South Perry Square
Erie 16501
814-452-2333 ext. 54

● Dauphin County Library System
Central Library
101 Walnut Street
Harrisburg 17101
717-234-4961

Lancaster County Public Library
125 North Duke Street
Lancaster 17602
717-394-2651

● The Free Library of Philadelphia
Logan Square
Philadelphia 19103
215-686-5423

● Hillman Library
University of Pittsburgh
Pittsburgh 15260
412-624-4423

Economic Development Council
of Northeastern Pennsylvania
1151 Oak Street
Pittston 18640
717-655-5581

James V. Brown Library
12 E. 4th Street
Williamsport 17701
717-326-0536

RHODE ISLAND

● Providence Public Library
Reference Department
150 Empire Street
Providence 02903
401-521-7722

SOUTH CAROLINA

● Charleston County Public Library
404 King Street
Charleston 29403
803-723-1645

● South Carolina State Library
Reader Services Department
1500 Senate Street
Columbia 29201
803-734-8666

SOUTH DAKOTA

● South Dakota State Library
State Library Building
800 North Illinois Street
Pierre 57501
605-773-3131

Sioux Falls Area Foundation
404 Boyce Greeley Building
321 South Phillips Avenue
Sioux Falls 57102-0781
605-336-7055

TENNESSEE

● Knoxville-Knox County Public
Library
500 West Church Avenue
Knoxville 37902
615-523-0781

● Memphis Shelby County Public
Library
1850 Peabody Avenue
Memphis 38104
901-725-8876

- Public Library of Nashville and
  Davidson County
  8th Avenue, North and Union
  Street
  Nashville 37203
  615-244-4700

TEXAS

Amarillo Area Foundation
1000 Polk
P.O. Box 25569
Amarillo 79105-269
806-376-4521

- The Hogg Foundation for Mental
  Health
  The University of Texas
  Austin 78712
  512-471-5041

- Corpus Christi State University
  Library
  6300 Ocean Drive
  Corpus Christi 78412
  512-991-6810

- El Paso Community Foundation
  El Paso National Bank Building
  Suite 1616
  El Paso 79901
  915-533-4020

- Funding Information Center
  Texas Christian University Library
  Ft. Worth 76129
  817-921-7664

- Houston Public Library
  Bibliographic & Information
  Center
  500 McKinney Avenue
  Houston 77002
  713-236-1313

- Lubbock Area Foundation
  502 Commerce Bank Building
  Lubbock 79401
  806-762-8061

- Funding Information Library
  507 Brooklyn
  San Antonio 78215
  512-227-4333

- Dallas Public Library
  Grants Information Service
  1515 Young Street
  Dallas 75201
  214-670-1487

- Pan American University
  Learning Resource Center
  1201 W. University Drive
  Edinburg 78539
  512-381-3304

UTAH

- Salt Lake City Public Library
  Business and Science
  Department
  209 East Fifth South
  Salt Lake City 84111
  801-363-5733

VERMONT

- State of Vermont Department of
  Libraries
  Reference Services Unit
  111 State Street
  Montpelier 05602
  802-828-3261

VIRGINIA

- Grants Resources Collection
  Hampton Public Library
  4207 Victoria Blvd.
  Hampton 23669
  804-727-6234

- Richmond Public Library
  Business, Science, & Technology
  Department
  101 East Franklin Street
  Richmond 23219
  804-780-8223

WASHINGTON

- Seattle Public Library
  1000 Fourth Avenue
  Seattle 98104
  206-386-4620

- Spokane Public Library
  Funding Information Center
  West 906 Main Avenue
  Spokane 99201
  509-838-3364

WEST VIRGINIA

- Kanawha County Public Library
  123 Capital Street
  Charleston 25301
  304-343-4646

WISCONSIN

- Marquette University Memorial
  Library
  1415 West Wisconsin Avenue
  Milwaukee 53233
  414-224-1515

- University of Wisconsin–Madison
  Memorial Library
  728 State Street
  Madison 53706
  608-262-3647

WYOMING

- Laramie County Community
  College Library
  1400 East College Drive
  Cheyenne 82007
  307-634-5853

AUSTRALIA

Victorian Community Foundation
94 Queen Street
Melbourne Vic 3000
607-5922

CANADA

Canadian Center for Philanthropy
74 Victoria Street
Suite 920
Toronto, Ontario M5C 2A5
416-368-1138

ENGLAND

Charities Aid Foundation
18 Doughty Street
London W1N 2 PL
01-831-7798

JAPAN

Foundation Center Library
of Japan
Elements Shinjuku Bldg. 3F
2-1-14 Shinjuku, Shinjuku-ku
Tokyo
03-350-1857

MEXICO

Biblioteca Benjamin Franklin
Londres 16
Mexico City 6, D.F.
525-591-0244

PUERTO RICO

Universidad Del Sagrado
Corazon
M.M.T. Guevarra Library
Correo Calle Loiza
Santurce 00914
809-728-1515 ext. 357

VIRGIN ISLANDS

University of the Virgin Islands
Library
Saint Thomas
U.S. Virgin Islands 00802
809-776-9200 ext. 1487

THE FOUNDATION CENTER AFFILIATES PROGRAM

As participants in the cooperating collection network, affiliates are libraries or nonprofit agencies that provide fundraising information or other funding-related technical assistance in their communities. Affiliates agree to provide free public access to a basic collection of Foundation Center publications during a regular schedule of hours, offering free funding research guidance to all visitors. Many also provide a variety of special services for local nonprofit organizations using staff or volunteers to prepare special materials, organize workshops, or conduct library orientations.

The affiliates program began in 1981 to continue the expansion of The Foundation Center's funding information network of 90 funding information collections. Since its inception, over 80 organizations have been designated Foundation Center affiliates. Affiliate collections have been established in a wide variety of host organizations, including public and university libraries, technical assistance agencies, and community foundations. The Center maintains strong ties with its affiliates through regular news bulletins, the provision of supporting materials, the sponsorship of regional meetings, and by referring the many nonprofits that call or write to The Foundation Center to the affiliate nearest them.

The Foundation Center welcomes inquiries from agencies interested in providing this type of public information service. If you are interested in establishing a funding information library for the use of nonprofit agencies in your area or in learning more about the program, we would like to hear from you.

The first step is for the director of your organization to write to Zeke Kilbride, Network Coordinator, explaining why the collection is needed and how the responsibilities of network participation would be met. The Center will contact you to review the details of the relationship. If your agency is designated an affiliate, you will then be entitled to purchase a core collection of Foundation Center materials at a 20% discount rate (annual cost of approx. $500). Center staff will be happy to assist in identifying supplementary titles for funding information libraries. A core collection, which must be maintained from year to year, consists of current editions to the following publications (subject to change):

Corporate Giving Directory
The Foundation Directory
The Foundation Directory Supplement
The Foundation Grants Index
The Foundation Grants Index Bimonthly

Source Book Profiles
The National Data Book
Foundation Fundamentals
Foundation Grants to Individuals

For more information, please write to: Zeke Kilbride, The Foundation Center, 79 Fifth Avenue, New York, NY 10003.

9/88

Chapter 10

Planned Obsolescence: The Path to Successful Foundation Relations

Kenneth Spritz
Director, Foundation and Corporate Relations
Dartmouth College

T he idealized courtship and mating ritual between a college and a foundation appears so reasonable and realizable in the realm of the imagination.... A draft proposal (in nearly final form!) for a new and exciting program arrives on your desk from a member of the faculty; a foundation (to which a stewardship report was recently sent on a prior successful grant) springs to mind as a prospect for support of this program; you telephone the appropriate program officer (who immediately takes your call) to inform her of this new project, and she asks you to come in with the faculty member for a meeting, which you are able to arrange on all three calendars with little difficulty. Of course, the meeting goes exceptionally well; a proposal is requested, submitted, and three months later—funded in full, with no matching requirements!

This scenario is repeated time and again, and life for the foundation development officer becomes "the glory and the freshness of a dream."

The reality of experience, unfortunately, all too quickly recalls another line from Wordsworth's "Ode (Intimations of Immortality from Recollections of Early Childhood)": "The things which I have seen I now can see no more."

In truth, what you all too often experience includes draft proposals that are poorly conceived or outside the priorities of the institution, projects that bring to mind no foundations to which they can be submitted (or only foundations with which no prior relationships exist), or a request by a program officer or secretary at a foundation to "send something in writing"—again and again—with no encouragement forthcoming for either a formal submission or a personal meeting. The capricious-ness of the territory in which we work causes the "reality" of foundation relations to mesh but rarely with the point of it all: the common pursuit of a higher pur-pose shared by the constituents we serve on our campuses, the foundation per-sonnel with whom we relate, and ourselves.

Seeking a balanced perspective

Each of us constantly strives to achieve a balanced perspective in our working en-vironment between the "worst case" and that rarely achieved "ideal." Success can-not be measured solely through grants approved or payment schedules—that way lies the mentality of the "carpetbagger," striving for short-term accomplishments over the more fundamentally significant relationships through which grant suc-cess can be achieved *and* sustained.

It is, indeed, debilitating when you continually suffer under the strain of "cri-sis management" during the course of days, weeks, or months spent either "cor-recting" well-meaning (but ill-advised) initiatives taken by others, or establishing and policing policies meant to control (and thereby limit) foundation approaches that could prove damaging in the future. I am fortunate to work at a college where a clearly structured and outlined set of policies and procedures for foundation and corporation relations are generally respected and adhered to by all constituents on campus. Because of this, "trouble-shooting" or "damage control" takes up com-paratively little of my time or that of my staff and associates.

Each campus, however, is structured in a different manner with different histor-ical precedents and current methods of operation that, in turn, determine the degree to which a foundation relations officer can expect to take proactive initia-tives as a leader as opposed to the reactive measures of a manager. The more you are drawn into a management mode, the less likely you are to allow vision to run free and risks to be taken. Without risk, significant financial gains for the institu-tion are exceedingly difficult to realize.

Unfortunately, most of us, to a greater or lesser degree, grapple with this dichoto-my on a daily basis: How can I spend less time doing what it seems I must do to "protect" the institution (and my job in it!) in order to spend more time doing that which will truly advance the institution's mission and give me the greatest sense of satisfaction (i.e., raising money in a creative manner for a worthy cause)?

It doesn't make your dilemma any easier that you know your success will not be evaluated on the basis of how well-organized or "controlled" foundation rela-tions appears to be on your campus, but rather on how much money you raise—a result directly proportional to the number of quality proposals that are matched with foundations prepared to receive them in a welcoming manner!

Establishing a partnership to achieve mutual goals

In the September/October 1987 *AGB Reports,* George W. Johnson, president of George Mason University, discusses "Creating a Model University-Business Partnership" and proposes that "to participate in community building one must pursue an agenda which transcends self-interest."[1] Johnson is making the point that, while it is essential to understand the inherent dangers of tipping the scales toward initiatives that skew the relationship toward the corporate interests at the expense of the institution, it is, nevertheless, the university's responsibility to take the broader view—not always an option for the business partner in the development relationship—in seeking mutuality of purpose and effect.

Through the maintenance of a clear institutional vision and a judicious balancing of corporate/university interests, the model that Johnson outlines works most effectively.

What seems to be lost in those institutions that totally separate foundation relations from corporate relations (and less overtly for those of us who merge the two in name if not in practice) is the parallel application of this model's basic principle to foundation relations: Our role as foundation development officers should be the establishment of a community joining our campus with the interests of a foundation in a manner that establishes as equal a partnership as possible between the two parties. A development officer who succeeds in doing this should find that his or her contribution to the maintenance and growth of that relationship becomes decreasingly important.

The Charles A. Dana Foundation is supporting a number of collaborative programs that assist a disciplinary area of study for a broad number of institutions through the sponsorship of programs on one campus. Dartmouth is host to a Dana Collaborative project in language instruction. Although I was involved extensively in the initial negotiations, my direct contact with foundation staff has decreased significantly as the program receives funding and begins implementation. This is as it should be: My contribution to the success or failure of the effort will be slight, and not only do I feel confident in the ability of my administrative and faculty colleagues to meet their own expectations and those of the Dana Foundation, but I know that they will call on me if they need my assistance.

Obsolescence: A job well done

By far the most difficult adjustment you can make in your professional life is the acceptance that through a job well done, your currently defined job has been made obsolete: Your presence is no longer required for the work to continue. How often have you participated in a meeting between scientists from your faculty and foundation program officers (or their counterparts on the corporate side) where you listen to lively and engaged conversation to which you have next to nothing to contribute? Why do you stay?

Hard as it may be to acknowledge obsolescence as success, the foundation development officer has, at this point, given a child away to matrimony and (as any parent knows) must accept the role of senior adviser—to be heard from when requested or (infrequently) when extraordinary circumstances require his or her intervention. Unlike the father of the bride, however, the foundation officer should feel no sense of loss but only joy at the release of campus relationships to those most directly affected. He or she may now focus on creating new relationships.

A consultant with whom I recently worked characterized a group of development professionals (with no derogatory implications intended) as "hired guns." Indeed, it is the pursuit of the quarry that tends to provide the greatest challenge and the greatest satisfaction to the development professional. Too many times have I heard senior colleagues decry the fact that their professional development has been achieved at the expense of what they do best: spending time in-house and "on the road" in a continual effort to raise funds.

Underlying this perception is the inability to accept (or perhaps even to acknowledge) that very often the greatest success in development is achieved when a development officer creates the opportunities for others (including faculty, administration, and volunteers) to raise money for him or her. Clearly this flies in the face of the "hired gun" mentality (which does have its place in development and is an essential response to "crisis-based" development). Still, as a successful development officer, you must possess the ability to recognize when you have achieved the desired state of "planned obsolescence" in the furtherance of the relations between your campus and a foundation.

"Matchmaking": Creating opportunities for others

As a foundation relations professional, you must establish and maintain excellent communications between yourself and the faculties, administrators, and funding agencies with whom your business must be conducted. These relations must be based upon honesty and trust, without which they are destined to unravel. To accept the rightness of the role of "matchmaker" is difficult when you are used to front-line action as a development officer. However, your best work is often accomplished as you persuade potential partners—who are wary of each other but sense a strong mutual attraction—to give each other a chance. And while they chat over a shared soda or beer, you should slip away into the twilight to allow nature and the eleemosynary spirit to take their course.

All sorts of people have experienced success as foundation, corporate, or capital giving development officers. This will undoubtedly continue to be true as long as there exists such a widely divergent universe of colleges and universities seeking funds during various stages of their advancement. However, to approach that "ideal" state where unions between funding agencies and your institution are made repeatedly and easily requires an ability to perceive the limits of your own usefulness and to trust the capabilities and instincts of your colleagues and the institution to which you all contribute.

You may find it hard to accept the idea that a faculty member should be allowed to raise funds when you can do it "better." However, it takes true maturation to recognize that although a member of your faculty may not be as proficient as you in your line of work (at least in your opinion), trusting that faculty member to raise the funds for his or her own work allows you to create new opportunities that others are not as well equipped to pursue.

We should all cultivate the ability to consider objectively whether our involvement in a particular solicitation—writing a memo, attending a meeting, making a phone call—is truly the best use of our time.

I constantly ask myself to consider the question: "Am I doing what I should be doing (given the choices available to me) to raise the most money I can for my institution?" Lately, I'm finding myself answering in the negative about half the time. And rather than being angry or discouraged that the prospect or relationship I've worked so hard to develop stands the risk of being set adrift by a dean or a member of the faculty, I'm pleased that I've created a new possibility where none existed before in a manner that provides me the freedom to continue to do what I seem to do best. And that, in the words of Wordsworth, is "the glory and the freshness of a dream."

Note

[1] George W. Johnson, "Creating a Model University-Business Partnership." *AGB Reports,* September/October 1987, p. 21.

Chapter 11

The Faculty and the President: Vital Resources In Grant Seeking

Linda Hayes Gerber
Director of Foundation Relations
Duke University

> *How much greater our vital resources are than we had supposed.*
> —William James

Many a foundation development officer could quote William James as he or she thanks the president and the faculty for the major role each has played in winning a foundation grant. All too often, although we know what a valuable resource these people are, we tend to forget that their aid is right at our finger tips. The faculty and administration can probably do more than any other group to help in our efforts to secure foundation support, and one of our major tasks is to develop this vital resource and use it effectively.

You can help this group help you in several ways:

• by educating them so they will understand how foundations operate and what each foundation's specific program interests are;

• by assisting them in their efforts to generate support for their projects and programs; and

• by coordinating their activities so that your institution makes the strongest case and presents the most attractive ideas for the foundation's consideration.

Keep these objectives in mind at every stage of the solicitation process.

Cultivation

You can probably divide the foundations you are cultivating into two groups: those with which you are seeking to establish a relationship, and those with which you already have a relationship that you wish to continue. For foundations in the first group, your job is to try to find the appropriate match—the right project, the best idea, the most effective representative of your institution. For those in the second group, the key phrase is, "Always keep the door open"—that is, always work at strengthening existing ties.

Although your institution may not be receiving funds from Foundation X at present, maybe you did in the past or you hope to in the future. In any case, if you or a member of your faculty has a good contact at a foundation, it's up to you to make certain the relationship is constantly nurtured whether or not the foundation is currently supporting a project at your institution. Encourage Professor Smith, whose project was funded in 1983, to send a copy of his latest book or an annual progress report on his program. He should do this even if the terms of his grant don't require it and even if he has no grant from the foundation at present. Program officers like to see not only the accomplishments of a current grant but also the ripple effects of past grants.

In some cases, it is easier for faculty members and administrators to cultivate foundation program officers than it is for you to do so. Your faculty can discuss ideas; they can explore new foundation initiatives; they can talk about the work of their colleagues and explore the foundation's possible interest. Not that *you* can't do these things. But a faculty member may be viewed as having more credibility in these areas than you do. Foundation officers often perceive faculty as "idea-oriented" and you, a development officer, as "dollar-oriented."

You can make other kinds of foundation contacts on your own, however. Some program officers will be willing to talk to you about new directions in which the foundation is moving and to discuss faculty ideas you think might be of interest. In short, you learn by experience and hard work to recognize those situations where you can make the contact and those where someone else at your institution can do it more effectively.

Cultivating foundations is different from cultivating individuals (and sometimes corporations). An individual may enjoy attending a football game, a reception to recognize major donors, or a general informational program weekend ("Come visit Podunk University for the weekend and see the exciting things we have to offer!"). But these kinds of activities may not appeal to foundation program officers. It's much more likely that foundation staff will agree to visit your campus for one of the following purposes:

• to evaluate a project the foundation has already funded;

• to conduct a site visit for a project currently under consideration for foundation funding; and

• to explore new opportunities for possible future support.

When foundation officers come to campus, the good development officer attempts to arrange a visit that accomplishes all of these objectives.

The extent of your involvement in such a visit depends on the situation. When Professor Jones invites a program officer from the Ford Foundation to see the project the foundation has been funding for three years, she probably will not require your assistance in planning or carrying out the visit. On the other hand, when your president invites the president of a foundation (and perhaps several of the staff) to come to your campus for a day-long visit, you will probably need to make all the arrangements, provide briefing materials, set up appointments, and do everything you can to make certain that (1) your institution puts its best foot forward, and (2) the foundation people see what they came to see and leave with a positive impression of your institution.

Setting up the appointment

While a campus visit is probably the ideal contact between your institution and the foundation, it isn't always possible. The next best option is a visit to the foundation by someone from your institution (president, faculty member, development officer, or an institutional "team").

When you are planning appointments with foundation officers, make every effort to use the most appropriate person to schedule the visit. If Professor Wilson has previously received funding from the Carnegie Corporation's international program and he wants to talk with the people there, he should schedule the visit. If he has no experience with a particular foundation he thinks might be interested in his work, then you can call to arrange the appointment, offer to accompany him, and agree to serve as the institutional liaison during initial discussions. If your president is to make a foundation visit, he or she may ask you to arrange an appointment with the foundation president.

The particular situation should determine who makes the foundation call. In the case of a president-to-president communication (when your president meets with the foundation president), the two may prefer to meet alone. But there may be times when your presence can be beneficial. The general rule of thumb is: Look at the individual situation and send in the person or the team who can make the strongest case—the president alone, the president with a colleague, the development officer alone, the development officer with the faculty member, and so on.

Making calls

You've spoken on the telephone with the appropriate foundation officer, and now you and the president or you and Professor Brown have an appointment scheduled with Mrs. Gray at the ABC Foundation. What should you do next?

At this point, your task is to see that you and your team are properly prepared for the visit. You should prepare a succinct briefing paper for all participants that contains the following:
- details about the appointment (time and place);

- a biographical paragraph about each person with whom you are meeting;
- a brief history of the foundation, its current program interests, and the history of your institution's relationship with the foundation (e.g., projects the foundation has supported in the past, contacts at the foundation);
- subjects for discussion and purpose of the visit (e.g., you want to express thanks to the foundation for past support, present new ideas for the foundation's consideration, explore new directions or initiatives of the foundation, present information about new programs on your campus); and
- summary of *no more than three things* that you want your faculty member or president to come away with (e.g., information about new initiatives at the foundation, information about its interest in a specific program, a general plan or strategy for dealing with the foundation in the next six to eight months).

If you are making the visit with another person, you should meet with him or her a few minutes prior to the actual call to review the materials listed above, to plan your final strategy for the meeting, and to decide who will raise each of the major points to be discussed.

Your role in a team visit is to keep the conversation flowing and to see that the objectives of the visit are accomplished. Before you leave the meeting, ask yourself the following questions:

- Have we asked all the questions we intended to ask, and have we come away with some answers?
- Do I know what the proper follow-up to this visit will be (write a letter of inquiry, send additional information, arrange for a campus visit, and so on) and who is responsible for doing it?
- Have we used this visit to our best advantage?
- Have we come away with some useful information? (Perhaps something we didn't know before or something not on the agenda but arising from our discussions with foundation staff.)

Even if your visit reveals that the foundation is not interested in the work of Professor Wilson (which was what you previously thought), perhaps you have learned that the foundation might consider Professor Fisher's new project. Maybe you have learned that one of the foundation's board members serves on another board with one of your alumni or that the foundation's interest in criminal justice will continue for only two more years. In short, every foundation call represents an opportunity for you to learn more about that foundation and how your institution can relate to it.

Writing or editing proposals

Once you've arranged the appointment, made the visit, and learned that the foundation is interested in seeing a proposal from your institution, you reach the development officer's dilemma: to write or not to write. Should *you* write the proposal or should the faculty member in charge of the project do it? There are several clues that may make this decision easier for you.

First, read the excellent article that appeared in the January 14, 1987 *Chronicle of Higher Education.* "Writing Proposals Grows More Exacting as the Competition for Grants Heats Up" is a perceptive review of proposal writing, containing comments by several foundation officers, including Sandra Glass from Keck, who, among others, specifically addresses this issue. Glass notes that she prefers the proposal be written by faculty and deans, the people who are going to implement the work, not professional writers. Echoing these thoughts, the president of a major national foundation once told a colleague of mine, "I can spot a proposal written by a development officer a mile away!" Comments such as these should make this decision an easy one.

Encourage faculty members to present their own case. They know their project or program much better than you do. And their enthusiasm for something in which they believe so strongly will be apparent to any reader. Your role should be that of an editor, offering suggestions about organization, structure, content, grammar, and spelling. But the ideas, the language, the style—these should come from the faculty member or the project director.

You can expand your editorial role by offering to review the proposal as if you were the foundation officer. Raise the questions that he or she will raise. Point out to the faculty member the points that must be covered in the proposal:

- What are the goals and objectives of the project?
- Why should the foundation fund such a project and why at your institution?
- How will the faculty member evaluate the work when it is completed?
- Who will support the project once foundation monies are no longer available?

The better these questions are answered, the better the chance of success.

While the faculty member originating the project is usually the one who should prepare the proposal, there are at least two situations where you may need to write the formal request:

1. The institution is requesting funds from a corporate foundation. Corporate foundations are extremely different from private foundations. They are more likely to make a grant that will "do" something for them ("This concert has been made possible by the XYZ Corporate Foundation") or that relates to their products or services. This is a marketing problem. The institution's idea or project must be "sold" to the corporate foundation, and this is a task that you can probably do better than the faculty member.

2. The institution is requesting funds for an interdisciplinary project or program in which several departments are involved. If you don't write this proposal, it may become a "proposal by committee"—a document doomed to fail because of lack of unity.

In both these cases and any others that may arise, you should be careful to use the thoughts and ideas of the faculty and to avoid that language and style that can be "spotted a mile away."

Educating the faculty

Part of your responsibility in dealing with faculty and administrators is not only to assist them in their grant seeking, but also to educate them to the realities of the world of funding. For example, are foundations the best source of support for the work they wish to undertake? Would federal sources be a more likely target? If foundation support is possible, which are the most likely prospects? Once foundation prospects have been identified, what steps should be taken next?

One way to help faculty deal with questions like these is to hold a workshop once or twice a year. This can serve two purposes: While your faculty is learning about foundations, you are learning more about them and their respective interests and research efforts.

A foundation workshop should cover the following subjects:

- how the grant-seeking process works at your institution (e.g., where to begin, what clearances are required, etc.);
- types and characteristics of foundations;
- foundation attitudes, current interests, and trends;
- resources and services provided by your office; and
- how to write a letter of inquiry, arrange an appointment, structure a formal proposal, and so on.

You can supplement your presentation with handouts that provide an overview of the four types (independent, company-sponsored, operating, community) of foundations (see the excellent chart in the *Foundation Directory,* 11th edition, p. vi), a bibliography of the reference materials available in your office (see the bibliography at the end of this book for a list of foundation research materials), an outline of how to structure a proposal (style, questions to be addressed when the proposal is being written, subjects that must be covered, materials to be included), and a few well-written pieces on proposal writing.

If organizing and conducting a workshop isn't possible, you can visit new department chairs and administrators who may not be aware of the resources and services your office provides. This offers tremendous possibilities both for you and for the new chair. He or she can share with you the names of faculty members engaging in exciting new research or programmatic initiatives. You can provide information about those foundations who might have a strong interest in the department's particular subject. For example, when visiting the chair of your department of economics, you would certainly want to mention the work of the Alfred P. Sloan Foundation and the Russell Sage Foundation.

Faculty who are well-educated about foundations—who they are, how they operate, where their interests lie—will be better able to attract foundation support. Therefore, anything you can do to increase knowledge regarding this important constituency will make your overall fund-raising job easier.

Providing leadership

Finally, you will want your faculty, members of the administration, and your president to assume a leadership role where foundations are concerned. Their leadership can be demonstrated in a number of ways, which are outlined below, and you can help by encouraging them, particularly the president and the deans, to accept primary responsibility for three or four key foundations.

You may not want your president to spend his or her time concentrating on small foundations such as the Smith Family Foundation, which has assets of $1.5 million and grants of less than $100,000 a year, the largest of which is $5,000. But there can be exceptions to that rule. For example, if a small foundation located in your city or region has provided frequent, albeit small, dollar support for your college or university, maybe the president *does* need to continue to be the point person. This is particularly true if his or her contact, John Johnson, makes gifts not only through the foundation but through his corporation or out of his own pocket.

Another exception: Perhaps your president *wants* to be the door-opener for most foundations. If so, then you need to work within that framework. It is more likely, however, that your chief administrator will want to accept responsibility for major foundations or those where his or her involvement can have the greatest effect. Your president should probably be the contact person for a foundation in the following cases:

• The subjects to be discussed include the overall picture of your institution, its priorities for the future, and a review of several ideas or programs that might be of interest to the foundation.

• The request is a major priority. Big dollars and comprehensive programs are involved.

• The president has strong contacts at the foundation.

For example, your president probably should assume the leadership role with President William Bowen at Andrew Mellon, but maybe you or the dean of arts and sciences or the chair of the history department is the appropriate person to make follow-up calls with Mellon program officers James Morris, David Saltonstall, and Clair List.

Once the contact person has been selected and has agreed to make the key calls, be sure to follow up with him or her regularly. Can you find out in a five-minute phone call what happened at the last meeting? Will the president or the faculty member keep you apprised of the salient points of the conversation so you can record them for your files, share the information with others, and act on it? What needs to be done for follow-up and who will do it?

Your president, members of the administration, and your faculty can also provide leadership through their important contacts. They can help you recruit other people who can assist in your grant-seeking efforts—alumni and friends who may be able to speak on your behalf, open a door, help arrange an appointment at a foundation, or endorse a request you have submitted. It's up to you to do everything you can to find out who your administrators and faculty know and how you can make use of this information.

Conclusion

The people at your institution—your faculty, staff, and administrators—constitute your most valuable and, as William James said, your most "vital resource." As a development officer, one of your primary objectives should be to recognize the wealth of talent on your own campus and to utilize it to the fullest. If you are successful in building a team of key people who work well together, not only will you increase the support you receive from foundations, but, more importantly, you will be able to assist in strengthening the overall growth and development of your institution.

Chapter 12

Writing the Proposal

Mary Kay Murphy
Director for Development
Georgia Institute of Technology

Writing successful foundation grants is not like writing other types of fund-raising appeals such as those to individuals, corporations, and state and federal funding agencies. These eight ground rules point up the differences:

1. Dealing with foundations is much more personal work than dealing with federal or state funding sources.

2. Foundations make awards in areas of priority. Research and confirm the foundation's interest in a proposed area of activity *before* you submit your proposal.

3. Telephone calls, staff visits, and board member contact are types of personal communication initiated with foundations *before* a proposal is submitted. Collaboration on a proposal with a foundation is an essential method of achieving successful funding. Thus, it is important to involve the foundation officer *before* a completed proposal is submitted.

4. A foundation may request that a proposal be submitted in one of several different forms:

- a letter of intent;
- an abstract;
- as a response to the foundation's request for a proposal (RFP)—this doesn't happen very often in foundation fund raising;
- a full proposal.

It's important to follow foundation guidelines carefully in the preparation, timing, and submission of your proposal.

5. Do not send the same proposal to a large number of foundations unless you have a strong rationale for doing so. In that case, inform all the foundations that you are submitting multiple proposals.

6. Leadership is a must in successful foundation proposals. Identify a volunteer

of influence and enlist him or her to support your proposal with key decision makers in the foundation.

7. Follow-up is an important part of foundation proposal writing. If your proposal is funded, conveying acknowledgement and thanks is very important. If your proposal is not funded, determine from the foundation officer its areas of weakness and find out if you can revise and resubmit.

8. Long-term funding relations with foundations are possible and desirable. The proposal is not an end in itself but a means of beginning or continuing a long-term affiliation with a foundation.

Before writing the proposal: Finding the best prospect

Proposal writing for foundations is not an assembly line activity. Careful screening must precede plans for writing a letter of intent, a preliminary proposal, or a full proposal.

Finding the best prospect for foundation fund raising means that you don't waste your time and money on inappropriate proposals to uninterested prospects. Of the 25,000 foundations in the country, fewer than 500 are likely to be major funding prospects for your project. Of that number, further screening should produce a list of your institution's top 50 to 100 prospects.

You'll need several types of information to guide your institution in the decision to submit a letter of intent, a preliminary proposal, and—if invited—a full proposal to a particular prospect.

In the screening process, consider the following variables:
- geographic limits on awards made;
- restrictions on the types of awards made;
- restrictions on the types of institutions to be funded;
- current and future program priorities (few foundations make awards outside of program priority areas);
- types of awards *not* made;
- range of awards made, including high, low, and average awards;
- time limits on support made;
- key individuals involved in funding decisions, including staff and board;
- deadlines for receipt of funding requests;
- format for funding requests, including budget information and indirect cost allowances.

Unless the foundation indicates otherwise, the best method to gather and verify this information is through direct contact with the foundation—a telephone call or a personal visit. You can also consult the annual report of the foundation, the entry on that organization in a foundation directory, its IRS 990 report, and information contained in newsletters, periodicals, and other publications.

After you have evaluated the fit between the information gathered on a foundation prospect and your institution's profile and priorities, if you decide that the match is a good one, you are ready to proceed to the next step.

Determining what information the proposal should contain

Few successful foundation fund raisers would suggest that once you have identified a possible funding source, you can immediately submit a complete proposal. We call this "blind submission" and justifiably so.

Instead, you will need to gather information that will shape the developing document, including:

- priorities of the funding source to be cited in the proposal;
- other information such as your institution's tax-exempt statement and statement of compliance with federal nondiscriminatory legislation;
- the appropriate format for writing the proposal (letter of intent, abstract, preliminary proposal, or full proposal);
- timetable for preparation and submission of the proposal as specified by the foundation or in time for review prior to the quarterly or annual meeting of the foundation's board of trustees; and
- suggestions and comments after a preliminary review of the proposal by foundation representatives prior to its formal submission.

After you gather this information, bear in mind that the contents of your proposal should be determined in part by which of the following stages in your relationship with the foundation you have reached:

1. *Ratification of informal agreements on a project made during preceding months of meetings and telephone calls.* (Your institution is well-known by the funding source and those serving on review panels.)

2. *Follow-up to informal telephone calls made to elicit current information on foundation priorities and proposal format.* (Your institution is not well-known by the funding source or review panels.)

3. *Initial contact between potential funding source and new applicant.* (Your proposal carries the considerable responsibility of introducing the institution, its personnel, and the project to the foundation. Further, the proposal alone must create a favorable impression as well as secure financial support. Institution is not well-known by the funding source or the review panels.)

While foundation funding sources do not adhere to a single format, your proposal should contain several standard elements, no matter how much previous contact there has been between the foundation and the institution. These elements help produce a logical flow of ideas and an orderly method of linking one part of the proposal to the next:

- *Title page.* This should include the title of project, name of institution, amount requested, date of application, and signatures of approving officials.

- *Introduction and summary.* State the reasons for your project and why this particular funding source should be interested in it. State the amount of the request and the time limit of the project.

- *Statement of need and opportunity for investment.* State the need for your project and its significance. Identify the people who will benefit. Describe their geographic location and characteristics. Provide background information on the need if such information is relevant. If your institution is a public college or university, note how funds will be used for needs that the state cannot support. (Do *not* request funds to replace monies not made available by the state.)

After describing the need, relate it to the program priorities of the foundation. Describe the opportunity for the foundation to invest in an interest related to its priorities. Note the ways in which your project presents an opportunity for the foundation to fulfill its goals. If possible, describe the impact of the foundation's gift on the success of the project.

Note the credentials that your institution and your project directors hold. Describe their abilities to develop this project. Relate the project to the mission of your institution. Describe your institution's history, funding sources, and previous contact with the foundation.

List other foundations pledged to support this project. Note your institution's 501(c)(3) status and include a copy of the IRS Letter of Tax Exemption.

• *Objectives.* Identify the results expected from the project. State objectives in attainable, practical, and measurable terms. Relate objectives—outcomes of the proposal—to needs stated previously. If there is more than one objective, list the most important objectives first.

• *Methods and procedures.* Methods are the manner in which you approach accomplishment of objectives. Relate your methods to your objectives and describe clearly the steps that will be taken to accomplish each objective. Create confidence in the approach you describe by noting other possible options, results from other approaches, and limits that you foresee from your approach.

Describe methods in chronological order. Relate the timetable of your methods to the overall project.

Identify methods for each objective in the project. Relate the objectives to the need for the project.

• *Evaluation.* Do not overlook the importance of identifying a means of evaluation. Describe the steps that will be taken to determine if the project accomplished its objectives. It is important to describe any adjustments to the project that you anticipate may become necessary. Describe the measurement of the achievement of objectives in quantifiable terms.

Provide evaluative criteria for each objective. Include objective criteria, names of expert evaluators, and descriptions of evaluation techniques.

Develop an evaluation system to be put into effect at the beginning of the project. This will help ensure that objective measurements of progress and results over time can be quantified.

• *Resources and personnel.* Describe any unique equipment or facilities available at your institution. Note in-kind contributions made by your institution to the quality or life of the proposal.

Identify the personnel who will work on the project. Note their background and credentials, especially as these relate to the expected success of the project.

Include an organization chart if the staffing is complex. Provide biographical sketches of key staff members. Include resources or vitae in an addendum if appropriate.

• *Budget.* Describe costs of the project. Divide costs into categories such as personnel and non-personnel. Provide figures for indirect costs and be prepared to negotiate with the foundation about inclusion of these costs as a legitimate budget item. Include a budget item for each objective, method, and evaluation item listed or implied in the body of the proposal.

• *Addendum.* Cross-check this item before you submit the final proposal. Include information that would have interrupted the flow of ideas in the main body of the proposal but that you believe foundation staff and board members should have, such as your institution's annual report, faculty or staff vitae, IRS tax-exempt letter, newspaper clippings, list of previous foundation support, and a timeline and flow chart for project activities.

• *Cover letter and signature approval sheet.* Write the cover letter with great care. Note the key elements of the proposal. Link foundation priorities with project objectives. Include amount requested, statement of institutional and project personnel credentials, and title of project.

Note if the proposal is the follow-up to a personal meeting or the response to an invitation to submit a proposal.

Prepare the cover letter for the signature of your institution's highest ranking official. Note that the project has a high institutional priority and refer to the signature approval sheet that demonstrates this.

For the convenience of foundation staff, provide telephone numbers of key project personnel.

Understanding what information to exchange for the foundation's support

While there are several appropriate formats to present the standard elements of a foundation proposal, research indicates that the message most likely to achieve foundation support does the following:
• captures the foundation's attention;
• gains comprehension on the part of the foundation of the project you propose;
• brings forth a favorable attitude;
• is memorable; and
• triggers action—favorable action.

As you attempt to present a message that does all of these things, remember these fundamentals of foundations today:

1. *Foundations support projects that fit their priorities.* Capture a foundation officer's attention by relating your proposal's intent to the foundation's priorities.

2. *Foundations seek signs of competence in the operation and management of those organizations they choose to support.* Demonstrate your institution's management and fiscal competence and invite the foundation to invest in the sound, businesslike opportunity your proposal offers.

3. *Foundations seek results.* Demonstrate to the foundation the favorable results of joining in support of your institution and its priority project.

4. *Foundations seek to share the risk.* Create a memorable message by showing

which other individuals, corporations, and foundations have invested in your institution. Note the benefit that will accrue to the foundation if it shares the investment with others.

5. *Foundations make gifts to people they know and trust.* Trigger favorable action on the part of the foundation by detailing in your proposal what the foundation knows about your institution and why the foundation trusts your institution.

The successful proposal presents persuasive information in a clear, concise, readable, and appropriate style, free of cumbersome words and cluttered ideas.

The business of the proposal is to request money for a significant project, in the most appropriate approach and setting, by a scholarly and well-managed institution. There are three appropriate formats to present such a request, and foundation guidelines will probably specify which of these three you should use:

The two-page letter or letter of intent. Many foundations require a brief, two-page proposal or letter of intent before they will grant a personal meeting with an applicant. If you are approaching a foundation with this requirement, take great care in putting the standard elements of a proposal into a straightforward business letter format. The following outline may help:

• *Paragraph one.* State why you are seeking funding; include a one-phrase description of your project's purpose. Note the relationship between the foundation's priorities and your proposal's intent.

• *Paragraph two.* In one or two sentences, state the need for the project and the opportunity to invest. If possible, document the need in numbers.

• *Paragraph three.* In two or more sentences, outline the objectives and the measurable methods of your project. Include a sentence on plans for evaluation.

• *Paragraph four.* In two or more sentences, note the unique features of your institution's facilities and personnel.

• *Paragraph five.* In two sentences, list the budget totals. Note that this figure appears to be within the range of the foundation's awards.

• *Paragraph six.* In one sentence, close the letter with a request for a specific follow-up action. Letter proposals should never be mass-produced and mass-distributed. An original, personalized two-page letter of intent should be sent to each potential funder who requires it.

Begin and end the letter by asking the foundation officer for an appointment to discuss the project in person. Include information on all contacts your institution has had with the foundation in the past—on the telephone, through the mail, or in person.

The preliminary proposal. Frequently, foundations will invite a preliminary proposal from individuals or from a select group of institutions. The foundation will provide the guidelines for the information to be submitted for preliminary review. It will also provide to those institutions not eliminated by the screening process an invitation and standard format for a full proposal.

The preliminary proposal should contain the standard elements of the foundation proposal, but the foundation guidelines may suggest a specific order or method of presentation. Follow these suggestions as you prepare the preliminary proposal:

- *Read all forms and instructions provided by the foundation for submitting a preliminary proposal.* When you submit the preliminary proposal, be sure that all documents are provided in the order and format requested.
- *Signal the reviewer as to the important parts of the proposal.* Use key phrases, underlining, and subheadings. Guide the reviewer's eye to the key parts of the proposal.
- *Adopt the language of the funding agency and its reviewers.* Explain all technical terms, abbreviations, and acronyms.
- *Write clearly and concisely.* Edit the proposal and ask peers to read, review, and edit it.
- *Present key parts of the proposal in conspicuous parts of the document.* Do not bury important ideas in flowery prose or cluttered text.

The full proposal. In the best interests of cost-effectiveness and efficient use of faculty and staff time, successful development officers reserve submission of a full proposal for those occasions when they are invited to do so by a serious foundation prospect.

Full proposals require internal coordination, idea development, and administrative approval. The judicious development officer will carefully choose those funding opportunities that call for a full-blown, full-scale effort to produce a full proposal.

Summary

The business of foundation fund raising requires deftness and adroitness in the art of writing proposals. Foundation proposal writers must develop finesse in collecting pertinent information before the proposal is written. Further, they must develop skill in determining what information—and in what form and format—will persuade the foundation to contribute. Finally, the writers must become adept at understanding what information is in the control of the institution that can be exchanged and, in turn, lead to a foundation's support.

And lastly, remember what business we are in. As "Bear" Bryant, the late football coach of the University of Alabama, used to tell his team season after season, "That's enough theory for today. Let's get out there on that field and practice."

Chapter 13

Small Can Be Beautiful: How to Win Grants from Regional, Community, and Family Foundations

Betsy van Patten
Assistant to the President and
Secretary to the Board of Trustees
Mills College

T he wife of historian and author Henry Adams once wrote of him, "It's not that he bites off more than he can chaw, but he chaws more than he bites off." In proposal writing, as in books, writers should strive to avoid this bad habit.

Proposals are most likely to succeed when they are based on solid, well-conceived ideas. In my experience, a continuing process of long-range planning is the best way to come up with workable ideas that will convince small foundations of your projects' merits. Planning will help you identify your institution's top priorities and achieve a consensus on them.

Mills has had such a system since 1981, and I'm sure it has contributed to our successful record of foundation fund raising in recent years.

Targeting the foundation

You need to approach foundation research with lists that reflect two perspectives:
1. *Projects that the institution has set as top priorities for funding.* Your job here

is to find the most likely funding sources for each.

2. *Regional, community, and family foundation prospects that you want to approach.* You should select these because of your institution's past relationship with them; good ties through trustees, volunteers, parents, or alumni; or a good match between their interests and the needs of your institution.

The challenge is matching up the two lists. This is particularly important in a campaign in which you need multiple funding sources for each project and you could approach many foundations for one of several projects. It's essential to set up a system for monitoring these lists—and for juggling them as you begin to see where the money is needed most.

Making the approach

After matching a foundation with an institutional priority, your next step should be to find out just how to structure your approach.

To do that:

• get a copy of the foundation's guidelines or check another reference source that has that information, and

• find out what contacts you already have or can develop with the foundation (such as trustees, alumni, parents, staff, volunteers) to get more accurate information about the foundation.

You want to know where the real power lies in the foundation and how that source of power makes decisions. For example, in a small family foundation, the board itself may see all proposals and make all decisions. Here, because the staff simply acts as a conduit, personal contacts are especially important.

It's best to pursue the likeliest prospects first. Not only will successful proposals build momentum for your campaign, but a record of success for individual projects will also be a powerful recommendation to foundations farther afield. Each approach will be time-consuming if you do it right, so stick to your "best shots" as long as possible. Top fund-raising priorities require generic proposals that you can tailor to individual foundations without completely rewriting them. But blanket approaches and broadcast appeals are a waste of time. They also give your institution a bad reputation in foundation circles.

Keep the challenge gift in mind as a way to fund large projects demanding multiple donors. Few foundations today will agree to a long-term commitment or to full funding of a project. As a result, both challenge grants and joint funding are much favored.

One strategy that has worked well for us is, where possible, to approach the foundation on two levels: staff to staff and trustee to trustee. The development staff stays in touch with the professional foundation staff while, at the same time, an appropriate trustee, alumnus, parent, or friend talks to his or her contact among the foundation's directors. (I should mention, by the way, that some foundations actively discourage contact with individual trustees, and you should respect this preference.)

The object of these approaches is primarily information-gathering. (In fact, this is often a good time to check whether your choice of a project for that foundation was a good one and to make some changes if not.) But it doesn't hurt to "warm up" the foundation also. Throughout this process, keep your volunteer contacts posted on progress by sending them copies of the proposal and follow-up letters.

The cultivation process should continue even after you've submitted the proposal. Pass along to foundation personnel any published materials (yours or something clipped from a newspaper or magazine) related to the project or the problem being addressed. Let them know about other grants you've received for the project, especially challenge grant opportunities that would give their grant more impact.

Do all you can to encourage a site visit. This is your chance to give the foundation a better picture of the project itself and to create a favorable impression of your institution. This can be a critical factor in your success. You will want to present the institution as a place where creative and important things are happening. Thus it's a good idea to have a carefully planned site-visit agenda involving faculty, students, and top college staff.

Writing the proposal

When the time is right (or as right as you can make it), go in with a full proposal. If your timing is off, you may be turned down or forced to wait a specific period of time before you can try again.

Here are some general principles of proposal writing.

1. Be as brief as possible while still getting across the case for the institution and the particular project.

2. Use language that is clear, easy to read, free of jargon and typos, and readily understandable to a lay reader—one who is not an expert in the field. Also strive for a clear and convincing flow of ideas from one section to the next.

3. Furnish necessary background. Don't assume that the foundation knows a great deal about your institution or the need you are addressing.

4. Allow plenty of time for each stage of the proposal preparation—planning the project, constructing the proposal, and getting it on paper. Also leave time for internal clearance. After all, a funding approach is a team process, and everyone involved—faculty, staff, administration, and even trustees in some cases—must be kept well-informed at all stages and feel comfortable with the approach.

5. Involve actual project personnel in your approach whenever possible—both in the cultivation and in the actual writing. You cannot possibly know the details of the project as well as they do. Also, they are likely to be your most convincing advocates because they have the highest stake in the success of the project.

6. Remember that many foundations make their judgments not so much on the specific project as on their confidence in the institution. They evaluate its financial stability, its educational excellence, its leadership, and its ability to carry out the project successfully and responsibly.

Following up after the grant

First, of course, be sure to acknowledge the grant promptly and graciously. If possible, send letters from more than one person—for example, the president plus the project director or a vice president. If you want to prepare a press release, check the copy with the foundation beforehand. And be sure to let the contacts who helped you obtain the grant know of your success and how grateful you are for their assistance.

It is essential that you follow all instructions the foundation gives you concerning handling of the funds and reporting. (You'll find out that your work is just beginning in some cases!) You'll also need to keep foundation personnel informed of any changes in plans or in personnel for the project. Send reports on progress, articles written about the project, and any other information about the institution that might be helpful. When major grants come in for the project from other funding sources, you've got a good opportunity to provide an update.

In sum, do everything you can to keep the door open for the next "ask" down the road.

Reprinted from CURRENTS, *July/August 1984, pp. 24-26.*

Chapter 14

Positioning the Private Research University for Foundation Grants

Deborah W. Callard
Executive Director
Fund for Johns Hopkins Medicine

F oundation giving has historically favored private institutions and continues to, as reflected in the 1985-86 figures of the Council for Aid to Education, which show that 70 percent of foundation support to higher education was to private institutions. Although public institutions are beginning to challenge this bias, over the years the development of major independent research universities has been closely intertwined with the growth and influence of the major foundations.

Foundation grants currently provide up to one-quarter of the voluntary support to graduate institutions in this country and are, therefore, a very significant source of support. You don't need a crystal ball to predict that foundation support will continue to be of importance to major research universities in the future.

In recent years, however, foundations have begun to reflect a greater social consciousness and have become more proactive in their program development and grant making. At the same time, research universities are experiencing extraordinary needs for new and renewed physical facilities. This has resulted in a mismatch between foundation grant making and the priority needs of the research university. The foundation relations officer at the research university must be sensitive to this apparent conflict and understand its impact when he or she is attempting to match foundation program interests with university needs.

Foundation relations has become a major program specialty in virtually all development offices and particularly in those of the research universities. In the last decade, three factors have caused university foundation relations programs to become more professional and sophisticated in their management:

- foundation programs have become better defined;
- information about foundations has become better publicized and more accessible; and
- competition for grants has increased.

Because research universities usually include multiple schools or academic divisions relating to a variety of disciplines such as the humanities, medicine, engineering, law, business, international affairs, and education, a university may qualify for support from the same foundation in several of its program areas. Foundation relations offices, therefore, are focal points for keeping faculty and administrators informed about foundation programs and for coordinating their approaches to this grant-making constituency.

While there are approximately 22,000 grant-making foundations in this country, only a small percentage of these have the assets, programmatic interests, and geographical focus relevant to major research universities. Out of the total population of foundations in 1982, about 1,000 of them accounted for 87 percent of the total assets of the foundation community.

The foundation "birthrate" has been steady or declining for a number of years, and foundation assets did not increase in real terms between 1962 and 1982. Although the mid-eighties saw foundation assets soar (the W.K. Kellogg Foundation assets, for example, were up 60 percent in 1985), the October 1987 collapse of the stock market no doubt eroded most of these gains.

In summary, the foundation constituency is stable in number; it represents a predictable source of support for various programs; foundation areas of interest shift but do not, as a rule, change dramatically; and foundation assets fluctuate with the stock market.

Foundations: A long-term investment

Because the number of foundations is not increasing, most universities recognize that current foundation donors are their best prospects and, as such, deserve special treatment over the long term. This makes good communication skills, credibility, and competence essential to the development officer responsible for foundation relations. He or she must stay well-informed about foundation programs, staff changes, and asset management, as well as the status of current foundation grants to the university.

While foundation guidelines and annual reports provide basic information and proposal guidelines, personal meetings with foundation program officers are a vital part of any successful foundation relations program. Personal contact is an integral step to establishing a relationship with a foundation. However, because foundation officers are besieged by university representatives seeking visits, the development officer should request an interview primarily to introduce himself or herself or to accompany faculty or administrative officers of the university. The telephone can provide ongoing access to clarify guidelines and develop proposals.

Credibility is essential to any foundation relations officer. The days of "take the money and run" are long over. Every development officer who works with foundations should strive to develop a relationship of trust and open communication.

It is important that the development officer not only accurately represent the university to each foundation but also, and equally important, that he or she accurately represent each foundation to the fund seekers in the university. The development officer provides the bridge between a foundation and the university as a friend of mine once learned when she was being interviewed for a position at a research university. After a pleasant lunch and a good deal of discussion about how the candidate would present the university to the foundation, the interviewer said, "But I haven't heard you talk about how you represent each foundation to your university." This crucial point, all too often overlooked in foundation relations, is basic to long-term success.

Both the university's foundation relations officer and the foundation's program officer are dealing with money that belongs to a third party—the foundation. Consequently, the development officer must maintain a high level of professionalism in seeking grants and in the stewardship of those grants during the period of years for which they run and long afterward.

Foundation relations is like a game of tennis: It is not the overhead smashes or the service aces that win the match; it is how few unforced errors are made. A mistake in communication with a foundation can be costly. Trust may be lost or damaged, and the foundation may decline to entertain another proposal from the institution in the future.

Recent trends in foundation programs

The Tax Law of 1969 had a pervasive effect on foundation giving and policy: It tended to inhibit innovation and risk taking in foundation grant making; it strengthened the tendency to make grants to well-established institutions; and it brought to light the inadequate public reporting practices of most foundations.

Historically, foundation grant making, while based on the common interests of the university and the foundation, was actually a result of university initiatives taken to meet institutional or faculty needs. Grant making was not, by and large, driven by foundation requests for proposals about issues of public concern, but rather by foundation responses to faculty entrepreneurship or to the expressed priorities of educational institutions.

In the last five years, however, there appears to have been a shift that is reflected in the increased numbers of established foundations that, separately and sometimes collaboratively, invite proposals that address such issues as the homeless, health promotion, faculty development, and adolescent pregnancy. Often these programs, which seek to solve a broad range of human problems, require collaboration between educational institutions, social agencies, and public organizations.

For university staff and development officers, program development and management that involve interdisciplinary or interorganizational collaboration can be time-consuming, complex, and frustrating. The jury is still out on the effectiveness of these initiatives—many of them are still in progress or just getting started.

One such program stands out in my experience as a clear success. The grant supports a program at a research university in which two science professors from liberal arts colleges spend a year in one of the university's research laboratories, retooling and updating their knowledge and skills. They then return to their teaching careers at their home institutions.

This program is a success because it benefits all four participating organizations—the colleges, the university, and the foundation that provides the funding. The university gains the services of two enthusiastic, knowledgeable researchers for a year; the liberal arts colleges gain refreshed and recommitted faculty; and the foundation has used its funds to benefit research at one institution and teaching at two others.

The challenge grant is an example of creative leveraging by foundations. The challenge grant is not a new phenomenon but it continues to find new applications, and it can be very persuasive in an institution's efforts to gain further funding. For example, a challenge grant can provide a means to increase both the participation of alumni and their dollar commitments; it can stimulate corporate and other foundation support; it can create a campaign aura—a sense of drama and excitement at meeting the conditions of the challenge.

On the other hand, the challenge grant can result in additional costs for mailings and extra staff time; it can also be a source of great anxiety if it looks as if the institution may not be able to meet the conditions. In this case, the foundation relations officer can reap the benefit of having established a relationship of credibility and trust with the foundation. Foundation program officers who manage challenge grants will be sympathetic if the facts are persuasive and they know a good faith effort is being made.

A challenge grant takes its toll on development staff: It requires good groundwork, constant monitoring, and the ability to bring into play alternative plans for meeting the challenge, if necessary. Again, a tennis analogy fits here: It's important to "keep the ball in play." That is, the foundation relations officer should guard against miscommunication by maintaining a timely and candid dialogue with foundation representatives.

University priorities

As some of the largest foundations become more proactive, they are developing programs that reflect deep concern about such important social issues as the underclass, the homeless, teenage pregnancy, and the environment. In the past five years, increasing numbers of foundation programs have also addressed health (health policy, reform of medical education, alcoholism, care for the aging) and educational issues (strengthening the humanities, providing opportunities for faculty development, increasing minority opportunities in medicine). Through these new programs, foundations are expressing the concerns of their trustees and/or staff.

Unfortunately these concerns do not always coincide with an institution's most pressing needs. If we were to ask the presidents of our research universities to identify the greatest need on their campuses today, the answer would probably be new construction and the refitting and equipping of research laboratories. Just at a time when foundations are developing invited programs that address important social, health, and educational issues, universities are finding their campuses in critical need of renovation, modernization, and expanded physical facilities.

Foundations are offering increasingly restricted programmatic support to universities, and in only a very few cases are they coupling this with the capital or endowment funding to keep the substructure of the institution sound. Compounding this problem are several other factors that make university capital needs an ever more pressing problem:

- the shift in federal funding from support of physical facilities at universities;
- the escalating costs of construction; and
- the reluctance of major individual donors to give dollars for construction.

The process by which an institution identifies its priorities differs from institution to institution, but some common elements are present in all. The primary mission of the research university is research and teaching. Inspired by this mission, university administrators seek funding for space needs and for faculty and student programs; additionally, individual investigators must secure funding for their research either from public or private sources. To do this successfully requires an enterprising and entrepreneurial spirit on the part of the grant seeker, and this spirit is central to ensuring the continuing quality of the university.

But this entrepreneurial spirit must be subjected to more important institutional considerations through the orderly process of setting institutional priorities. For example, every project should be submitted to departmental review and approval, along with institutional review of such issues as indirect costs, the use of human subjects, and the availability of space.

The funding feasibility of a proposal idea must also be an important consideration; a project for which it will be difficult to find private money will require a proportionately greater percentage of the development officer's time. Unless such a project is a high-priority one, time might be better spent on other needs of the institution. University priorities are also affected by opportunities that are unexpectedly presented by scientific discovery or by a disease epidemic such as AIDS, already identified as a worldwide health emergency.

Furthermore, priority setting is also affected by the need to recruit and retain faculty who will maintain the standard of excellence necessary to a major research university.

Thus, we see that the priority-setting process at research universities is beset by tugs and pulls in several directions. To play an effective role in the process, the development officer must understand all of these factors. Credibility and good communications skills help him or her walk the fine line between faculty initiatives and the institutional priority-setting process. Mutual respect between the development officer, faculty, department heads, and deans is essential. Above all, however, the development officer must never be in the position of helping a faculty member submit a grant proposal for which there is no approved priority.

A mismatch: Foundation trends and university needs

How does a development officer negotiate the terrain when there is such a mismatch between foundation initiatives and university needs? The answer is: with great care. The development officer will continue to spend a lot of time raising foundation program money for universities because this support is the funding lifeline of individual investigators. However, in seeking money for individual faculty initiatives, he or she may in fact be compounding the space problems of the university and spending valuable time to find support for a project that is not an institutional priority.

The easy answer to this dilemma, from the university's point of view, would be for more foundations to recognize the problem and to institute programs to fund construction and renovation. The Kresge Foundation is one of the few foundations that does fund physical needs; Kresge uses the challenge grant to great effect as leverage to encourage the support of alumni and other prospects for renovation and new construction. Unfortunately, the Kresge Foundation is the exception and not the rule.

The widening gulf between the program orientation of the big foundations and the physical needs of universities forces us to consider the following question: What does a university do when a foundation invites a proposal in a program area in which the institution has expertise but cannot consider a priority? Does the university endanger its long-term relationship with the foundation if it declines the invitation?

If the present trend in foundation program development continues, and if space needs on university campuses are not met in other ways, universities will have to weigh very carefully the merits of applying for grants in areas that are not a high institutional priority. The foundation relations officer needs to plan ahead for this eventuality and consider its implications for his or her credibility and effectiveness, both on the home campus and with foundation staff.

Summary

Positioning the research university for foundation grants will continue to be an important investment for private institutions of higher learning. Because current foundation donors are a university's best foundation prospects, the development officer should appreciate the long-term nature of foundation relations. Foundations will remain one of the most significant funding sources for university investigators whose careers depend on grant support. The faculty investigator is, after all, the key to the teaching and research mission of the university.

Given the apparently divergent paths of foundation program development and emerging university priorities, the development officer has an ever more challenging task of responding to faculty initiatives and, at the same time, abiding by approved institutional priorities. With renovated and new facilities highest on the list of needs for research universities, these institutions must weigh their responses to foundation RFPs with great care, recognizing that maintaining a healthy substructure—both physical and academic—may be more to the institution's interest than implementing new programs. Successful foundation/university matches rest on the mutual benefits of collaboration.

Over the long term, then, we must recognize that foundation trends will ebb and flow just as university needs will. But whatever happens to be of paramount importance to each, the major foundations and the private research universities still share common goals that are basic to their separate missions: the development of new knowledge, the alleviation of human suffering, and the improvement of the quality of life for all.

Reference Sources

"Foundations Face Growing Worry: Giving Away Money Fast Enough." *Wall Street Journal,* November 11, 1986, Highlights Section 2.

Harris, James T., and Bezilla, Michael. "Point of View: Excellence or Elitism: Foundations Must Decide." *Chronicle of Higher Education,* October 21, 1987, p. A-52.

Nielsen, Waldemar A. *The Big Foundations.* New York: Columbia University Press, 1972.

Nielsen, Waldemar A. *The Golden Donors: A New Anatomy of the Great Foundations.* New York: Truman Talley Books, E.P. Dutton, 1985.

Odendahl, Teresa J., ed. *America's Wealthy and the Future of Foundations,* New York: The Foundation Center, 1987.

Section 4

The Grant Maker's Perspective

Chapter 15

Making Foundation Calls Effective

Craig Kennedy
President
The Joyce Foundation

F rom my position as a foundation president, I have many opportunities to observe what I consider to be appropriate and inappropriate requests for visits with foundation officers and staff members. Thus, the following observations:

• Not all requests will result in a call on a foundation program officer. Many foundations require a preliminary letter of inquiry or proposal before they will schedule a visit.

• A successful visit consists of three phases: (1) preparation; (2) during the meeting; and (3) follow-up.

Preparation for the foundation visit

The most important element is the initial planning phase. The more time you spend in preparation, the better the visit is likely to be. Consider these points as you prepare for the foundation visit:

1. *Do you have the right foundation?* Is this foundation the right one for your project? Does your institution fit within the foundation's programmatic and geographic guidelines? If not, do not request a meeting. Unless you believe that your project can result in a grant, you are wasting your time and your institution's resources.

2. *Do you have ideas to discuss?* Why do you want this meeting? Do you have a proposal or funding idea to discuss? Remember that appointments are hard to get. Program officers often do not appreciate "friendly" chats that lack focus or

clear purpose. Do everything you can to make a meeting count when you are fortunate enough to get one scheduled.

3. *Do you have the right person at the foundation?* The foundation president is not always the best person to visit. The role for the staff varies from foundation to foundation. Conduct careful research up-front about the best person to see; ask the foundation for guidance if you are not sure who should be contacted.

4. *Do you have the right team?* To make a foundation visit effective, the right person must be a part of your institution's team. The most frequently asked question about a planned visit is, "Should I bring my president?" The answer is "yes" if he or she wants to be a part of the visit, and "no" if he or she doesn't. If you do bring the president, make sure he or she has been briefed on your institution's relationship with the foundation and on the foundation's interests.

Who else should be on the call? Include a key faculty member or dean whose expertise is critical to the success of the visit. But don't pack the meeting with silent observers; invite only those who have a clear role in the meeting.

5. *Are you prepared for this meeting?* Three specific areas of research are crucial to the success of a foundation visit. First, you should conduct a careful study of the history of grants from the foundation to your institution. What happened with these grants? Were there any problems? What were the benefits coming from the grants to your institution?

Second, you must know basic data on your school, college, or university. What is the operating budget? What is the financial profile? What are the trends in enrollment? What percent of your alumni give to the annual fund and how much do they give? From what states or regions of the country does your institution recruit students? What is the percentage of minority recruitment, attendance, and graduation?

Third, you must have an understanding of the foundation's guidelines. Before the visit, request a copy of the foundation's annual report. If no report is printed, review the IRS 990 reports for information on assets, officers, and grant recipients and amounts. Have a clear idea of how the foundation's priorities are selected in its actual grant making.

6. *Are others on your campus pursuing a grant with the foundation?* Is such a pursuit appropriate? A complex campus is not necessarily a large campus. Your role in the process is that of coordinator of all efforts on your campus having to do with the foundation. Make sure you know this information before you request or make the foundation call.

7. *Have you properly prepared the foundation for the meeting?* Prepare a carefully thought out two-page letter prior to the meeting. Get assistance in the writing of this letter from the appropriate faculty members or administrators on your campus. It should be a sharply focused document that relates to the foundation's guidelines and the project you will discuss at the meeting. Have the president and the others who will make the visit with you review this document before the meeting. Then send it to the top-ranking foundation person who will attend the meeting. He or she should receive the letter about a week before the visit.

Do not bring a completed proposal with you to the meeting. If the foundation invites you to submit a proposal, you can send it as a follow-up to the meeting.

8. *If you do not go on the call.* If for any reason you are not a part of the team that visits the foundation, make sure that you coordinate all the campus efforts and that you brief the team about previous foundation gifts, basic fund-raising information, and foundation priorities well before they leave campus. Ask for and diplomatically insist upon a follow-up report after the call is made.

During the meeting

Here are five guidelines to conducting a purposeful, businesslike, and orderly meeting with a foundation officer:

1. *Get to the point.* Don't consider the meeting as a way to make friends with the foundation officer. It is an opportunity to spark a foundation officer's interest and lay the groundwork for submitting a successful proposal. Have your ideas ready. Throw them out for discussion. Remember to have a role for each person on your team during the meeting. For example, the president can talk about the institution's long-range plans. The dean or faculty member can discuss basic information about fund raising, the budget, and financial matters related to your institution.

2. *Present ideas as real projects.* Carefully think out and present ideas and data related to the project you want to discuss. If there have been previous grants from the foundation to your institution, discuss these and their results. Do not present a long list of "needs" and then ask the donor to pick one. Do not allude to or suggest numerous nebulous things needing support. Rather, specify two or three possible projects that you believe best represent your institution's priorities and conform to the foundation's guidelines.

3. *Ask questions.* Clarify points as they are raised. Query the foundation officer about points that were unclear before your visit. Ask the foundation officer about aspects of the funding process that need clarification.

4. *Listen and speak to everyone at the meeting.* The protocol of a foundation visit, like that for any other type of business call, requires that your team members speak to each member of the foundation staff. Do not direct questions to only one member of the staff. Include any and all members of the host group in conversation and in questions. Do not exclude anyone during the meeting. Snubbing someone in this way will come back to hurt you and your institution.

5. *Clarify before you conclude your visit.* At this point in the meeting, it is important to ask specific questions and to take notes on the answers given by the foundation officer. Is a proposal to be submitted? When? Is a campus visit warranted first? Should you prepare a proposal related to one of the two or three ideas discussed? If so, for what amount? Who in the foundation will be the contact person? Who on the campus will coordinate the work and communicate with the foundation? When do the trustees meet? What format should the proposal follow?

Your meeting concluded, you and your team members return home. Now you must take the follow-up steps that result in a strong proposal.

Follow-up

There are three possible outcomes from a foundation visit—"maybe," "yes," and "no." If your visit resulted in a "maybe" response, once you are back on campus, you can call the foundation officer and ask for clarification. If the answer was "yes," and you were invited to submit a proposal, do so promptly. If you were discouraged from sending a proposal, do not send one. If you persist, your actions could hurt other initiatives from your institution. Trust the foundation officer who discouraged you, and do not pursue this avenue.

Three keys to effective calls

In summary, there are three important aspects of making effective foundation calls. First, you must make an up-front commitment to research to discover the right foundation for your institution, the right ideas to discuss, the right people to bring, and the right foundation people to meet on the visit. Second, when you get to the meeting, get down to business and present your ideas in a direct, orderly, purposeful method. Third, the key to successful fund raising is to use this meeting with foundation representatives to move your institution's project from planning to the point of being funded.

Through persistence on your part as a foundation officer and discretion in knowing when to influence and when not to influence the foundations from which you are seeking funds, you can be the person on your campus who ensures that all foundation calls are effective calls. Remember, the key element is "Do It Right."

Chapter 16

Networking: Relationships Among Foundations

Sandra A. Glass
Program Officer
W.M. Keck Foundation

You rarely ask one foundation to fund the total cost of a major project. Whether you are building a theater, computerizing your administrative records, or starting a business administration program, you usually seek funding from several foundations, as well as from individuals, corporations, and perhaps from federal and state sources. Because we in the foundation world receive far more deserving requests than can possibly be funded, we are always looking for ways to stretch our dollars and, therefore, you must look for more grant-making sources.

"Challenge grants," "cost sharing," "matching funds," and "partnerships" are oft-heard phrases over our desks. Your excellent university has a high-priority project of renovating Old Science Hall, and you've made a strong case for need and timeliness. You have an alumnus who has pledged half the total cost. Our foundation can't, unfortunately, fund all the remaining cost of modernization, but we can cover the renovation of two laboratories, if you can provide a solid plan for raising the balance of funds for the project.

Should you go to several other foundations to try to put together a comprehensive package? Should you approach the foundations one at a time or all at once? Should you ask our foundation for help in opening the door to other foundations, or would that be presumptuous? Is one foundation ever willing to help a deserving grant seeker approach other grant makers?

Foundation networks

It's important to realize that foundations have developed both formal and informal networks. Foundation staff members and directors see each other frequently, and it is natural for us to discuss matters of mutual interest. In addition to national professional organizations like the Council on Foundations and Independent Sector, with their annual conventions, there are over 20 regional associations of grant makers, whose members include private, corporate, community, and operating foundations. Some of the larger and more active groups across the country include the Southeastern Council of Foundations, the Donors Forum of Chicago, the Minnesota Council on Foundations, and the Southern California Association for Philanthropy.

Members of these foundation consortia meet regularly to hear guest speakers, to encourage staff development, and to share common problems. We frequently explore educational issues, as well as items of community concern and pressing social issues. Provocative topics challenge foundation staff members to reassess their approaches to grant making: "Foundation scholarship programs: excellence or access?" "Should foundations make grants for endowments?" "Can foundations help build bridges between high schools and colleges?"

Not only do these meetings help foundation program officers become more knowledgeable about timely topics, they also provide us with many opportunities for informal exchange of ideas and news. Before or after speeches or panel discussions, we talk with colleagues about grant-making techniques and often share information on current activities: "I heard that you made a grant to Urban University last year. Did they use the money well?" "Did you know that County College's enrollment has dropped by 20 percent? Are they having budget difficulties?" "What did you think of the proposal that the new president of Prestige University sent to all 10 of us?" You can assume that your proposal, visit, or statements to one foundation are well-known to several others, especially within your city or region.

We also telephone foundation colleagues in other regions if we have a mutual interest in a project or if we have questions about an institution or a program that is well-known to another grant maker. When I receive a request from a first-time applicant in another part of the country, in order to obtain background information, I may telephone a program officer at a foundation that has made several grants to that college. Just as I might check with a program officer at the National Science Foundation about the scientific abilities of a researcher, I would also call a staff member of a private foundation to learn about a university's strengths. I would ask whether the institution is well-managed and if faculty and staff performed well and reported regularly on past grants. Comments are generally frank and confidential. These types of references are especially useful if I am unable to make a site visit to the applicant's campus.

All of these contacts—both structured and informal—indicate that a great deal of information circulates about grant seekers through established foundation networks. If your institution has misused an award or has not reported to the foundation on expenditures of funds, you will find it difficult to establish credibility with other foundations in the network. On the other hand, these personal exchanges among foundation staff can be beneficial to you if you have done a good job with past grants. You will have a solid reputation and can count on a high-quality professional reference.

How to make networking work for you

Once you are aware that foundation networks exist and that you are working with sophisticated professional staff, you no longer assume that every proposal you send out is reviewed in isolation. Now you can begin to plan strategies for using these networks.

If our foundation cannot fund your request because your project does not meet our criteria, we may be able to open doors for you at other foundations in our region or network. How should you broach the issue? First, try to avoid the obvious question: "Do you know of any other foundations to which I can submit this proposal?" This question implies that you haven't done your research homework. Moreover, we foundation staffers—busy with our own programs—do not necessarily have current information on what other foundations are funding. If your request is for building an athletic complex, which we cannot support, I would probably not know other regional grant makers interested in that type of program. In addition, we are cautious about referring grant seekers to our colleagues. No one wants to have the reputation of foisting incompetents off on friends, and we hesitate before sending even very good applicants to other foundations. We don't want to take advantage of our colleagues' good natures.

But foundations are, by their very nature, in business to help grant seekers, and the right approaches and questions can secure valuable assistance with other grant makers. Several long-term approaches are important to create an atmosphere in which one foundation will be happy to assist you with others:

Be cooperative. You want to gain a reputation for following directions and for adhering to a foundation's grant policies. If you are applying to a foundation that has a proposal deadline, don't wait until the last two days to submit your proposal. Or, worse yet, don't phone and ask for an extension or any other exception to established procedures. If you have agreed to send a grant report in July, don't put it off until September. If you are dedicating your music building and would like donors to attend the program, don't wait until a week before the event to invite foundation representatives. Be a cooperative professional who understands that busy foundation program officers established their procedures in order to have more time to help you with your proposals and grants. Your cooperation will not be forgotten.

Carry out appropriate public relations. Ask us directly what type of public relations our foundations prefer. Do we want articles about our grants in newspapers and alumni magazines, or do we want to keep a low profile? Should buildings be named for us, or should that honor go to an individual donor? Do we want to attend luncheons and football games on your campus, or would we

131

rather have a card for your library? Would we like to receive regular copies of your president's annual report and your engineering newsletter, or are we so inundated with reading matter that these would just be discarded? Because foundations' attitudes vary so greatly in the matter of public relations, we'll appreciate your efforts to comply with our preferences.

Have something to offer. Be alert to ways in which you can help foundations. Before you visit us, spend some time thinking about ways in which ideas or innovative plans from your university might be of help to us as we begin to develop new programs. What experts on your faculty might be especially qualified consultants? Perhaps your sociology professor is an expert on the urban homeless and your dean of physical science has just written a book on the technological revolution, and we are interested in these areas. Both are willing to speak at foundation programs or talk with program officers and trustees. Without requesting a grant or even relating these offers of expert assistance to any proposals you are planning, you can demonstrate that your institution has a great deal to offer the foundation community. We may also be able to refer you to several other foundations in our city that could benefit from your help.

If we foundation staffers believe that you represent a premier institution, we are much more likely to recommend you to our colleagues. We know that you are the type of perceptive and cooperative professional whom our associates will enjoy meeting.

Ask the right questions. If you are a credible professional, program officers will be more willing to help you gain access to other foundations. The following questions, which you can ask either in person or by telephone, reveal that you've done your research homework and are someone a foundation staff member will benefit from meeting.

1. *"Our president has an appointment with the Dogooder Foundation in New York next month. Do you think that describing our success with your grant might be helpful?"* Depending on the situation, the program officer might make one of three responses:

• "No, I understand that Dogooder has stopped making grants to universities and colleges."

• "Please feel free to do so; I haven't kept up on Dogooder's grant-making priorities, but it can't hurt to mention our grant."

• "By all means, and please tell Dogooder's Education Program Officer Jim Helpful to call me if you need a reference."

2. *"I've read that the Worldwide Foundation is developing a new program to support international education. Do you think Worldwide might help with our Asian Studies Program?"* Responses might include:

• "Your college may be too small to qualify for grants from Worldwide, but it won't hurt to try to contact the foundation and ask for the new guidelines that have just been published."

• "I haven't heard about that program, but Worldwide's Grants Officer Betty Bright is very receptive to letters from grant seekers. Why don't you write to her about your project and tell her you talked to me?"

- "I'm going to see Betty at a foundation seminar next Thursday. I'll tell her about your good work with our grant and that you'll be writing to her."

3. *"We've just published a monograph describing current research projects of all our science faculty members. We don't want to mail it to every foundation in the directory. Do you know two or three foundation staff members who might like a copy?"* A program officer might answer:

- "Be sure to send me a copy."
- "I think that Ann Astronomer and Carl Chemical Engineer would like copies."
- "You might send these five foundations a short note asking them if they'd like your publication. Tell them I gave you their names."

All of these questions are graceful attempts to gain access to additional foundations. Honest answers from someone who trusts your judgment and professional good taste can help you enter the foundations network.

Multiple submissions: Ethical? Advisable?

You have a major institutional project to construct a new business administration building, renovate a wing of the medical school, or computerize all library systems. You need to raise all the money within the next 18 months, and you do not know one donor capable of funding the total project. Should you simultaneously approach seven foundations, as well as three corporations and five individuals, for the same project? Can you submit multiple applications?

The answer is "yes, certainly," if you have a clear idea of your goals and plans and if you communicate these ideas clearly to all potential donors. But keep in mind these considerations:

1. *Always be completely honest with grant makers.* Tell all the foundations about your fund-raising plans—where and when you are submitting proposals and how much you are requesting from each potential donor. Foundations rarely object to project cost-sharing if you give them advance notice. Grants officers may ask, "How much have you raised to date?" or "When will you hear from the other foundations?" or "What portion of the project will be named in honor of our foundation?" If you answer these questions clearly and directly, most foundations will encourage you to proceed with your plan for multiple submissions.

Don't, however, ask two prospects to support the same project at the same time. For example, don't ask two foundations for the $1 million needed to endow a chair in macroeconomics or the $250,000 it will take to refurbish the freshman dining hall. If two foundation officers learn that you have asked each of them to fund the same project, you may lose the support of both. Don't approach the second foundation until you have received a declination from the first. If the first foundation informs you that it can fund only part of the project, then you can approach the second for the balance of the funding.

While proposals are pending, keep the foundations posted on your fund-raising progress. Success with one foundation may stimulate other givers. And, most important, if you reach your overall goal and you have all the money for your project in hand or pledged, be sure to notify all foundations where you still have proposals pending. Offer to withdraw the request. Often the program officer will permit you to redirect the proposal, perhaps toward an endowment fund for building maintenance or to a contingency fund for cost overruns. If, however, you do have to withdraw the proposal, you will gain a great deal of credibility for your honesty, and you may even receive a larger grant next time you submit a proposal.

2. *Personalize each submission.* Rather than mailing identical proposals to all 10 foundations on your prospect list, tailor each submission to the recipient. One of the least effective types of proposals is the one that was obviously written for some other foundation—or for some generic grant-making entity. We don't have to be detectives to spot phrases that were not designed for us: "appreciating your extensive funding of music education...." (when we've never made any grants for music); "grateful for your long-time support of our college...." (when we've never had any contact with your institution); or "as you recall from your visit to our campus...." (when we haven't even been in your state).

Worst of all are the errors caused by "wordprocessoritis," such as not changing the name of one foundation when you resubmit the same proposal to another foundation. When two program officers meet and one says to the other, "Did you receive a proposal from Shotgun University last week?" the response should not be, "Yes, and it had *your* name on it."

Although the basic request to several foundations can be the same and you will probably want to include the same background information on your institution with all the proposals, be sure that you spend time crafting each submission as if it were not merely your most important proposal, but your only one.

3. *Have good reasons for submissions.* Don't send out multiple proposals just because you have a vague idea that you might get more money if you try several foundations. Have a sound plan that you can share with donors. If, for example, you need $2.5 million to renovate your humanities building, you might plan to approach 10 foundations for grants of $250,000 each. Or if one donor has already pledged $1 million toward the project, you can ask the 10 foundations for $150,000. Or you might ask 18 donors for grants of $85,000 because this is the approximate cost of remodeling and furnishing one classroom.

You might also ask the staff members if their foundations make challenge grants or are willing to match other donors' challenges. If one of your trustees has challenged donors to a scholarship fund by promising to match every dollar contributed during the next year, some foundations might view this as an excellent opportunity to make a grant that leverages other dollars. Other foundations, however, would rather create their own challenges to your alumni than contribute to a project invented by someone else.

Beware of telling a foundation that you would be delighted to accept its challenge if you don't think you can fulfill it within the requisite time or if you already have two or three other challenge grant goals to meet. And don't abandon your own fund-raising priorities to accept a foundation challenge. For example, if a foundation offers to give you $100,000 for a political science curriculum development fund, provided that you will match its dollars three-to-one from alumni contributions, your answer should be "no" if you really want your alumni to make unrestricted contributions to the annual fund. By discussing your goals and needs frankly with foundations, you may miss out on some one-time grants, but you will fare much better when seeking long-term support.

Multi-institutional projects

When our foundation's annual report lists a grant that was made to two cooperating universities or to a college consortium, I am often asked whether foundations prefer to make multi-institutional grants. My unequivocal answer is, "Not if you're just getting together with someone else in order to impress a foundation." Don't invent an artificial or unworkable two-college curricular project or a faculty development program just because you think a foundation will get excited about your cooperation. Experienced program officers will quickly see through your plan and ask whether faculty members at both institutions actually designed the curriculum, whether both administrations endorse it, and whether it has been approved by both boards of trustees.

Genuine multi-institutional cooperation can, of course, be an excellent way to maximize resources and enrich academic programs. Sharing facilities, equipment, or faculty can provide both academic and economic benefits. Formal or informal educational networking can be an institutional asset and can capture the attention of foundation officers who are also accustomed to networking. Well-established university and college consortia have little difficulty gaining access to foundations because they often represent hundreds of faculty and thousands of students. There are over 90 of these higher education associations in the country. If, however, your college does not have formal ties to other institutions in your region, ask yourself these networking questions when you are preparing foundation proposals:

• Are we asking the foundation to supply us with equipment, programs, or services that are already in place and working well at other universities in our region? Do all three colleges in our town need to develop new child-care centers? How many neighboring university hospitals need to perform open-heart surgery?

• Are we requesting funds for facilities or projects because we are unwilling to travel a few blocks or a few miles to our sister institution? Do we both need a fully equipped television studio? Should both our libraries collect works of twelfth-century Scandinavian poets? Might our graduate students benefit from intercollegiate seminars in microbiology?

Cooperation is certainly an institutional decision, but foundations with funds in short supply cannot be blamed for favoring grantees who make good use of their resources.

If your institution, College A, decides to work with Colleges B and C in submitting a request to a foundation, here are some suggestions that may expedite your procedures and also reinforce harmonious relationships with the foundation:

1. *Have a series of planning meetings with representatives of all three colleges long before you approach the foundation.* Make sure goals, concepts, and details

of program and budget are clear to everyone.

2. *Gain administrative support from all parties.* It is embarrassing to telephone a foundation, after submitting a proposal, with an apology: "I'm sorry we have to redo our request because the president of College B, who was out of town last week, didn't like our plans."

3. *Make sure all group members agree on the list of foundations you are going to solicit for the project.* Often foundations that support the group effort will not make grants simultaneously to the individual colleges or universities in that group, even if the projects are completely different. If the Ecumenical Foundation supports both international education and financial aid, your three cooperating colleges may not easily agree on a joint proposal. While all three colleges agree, in theory, that your joint education abroad program in Tibet is a high priority, it may not be as important to College C as support for freshman scholarships.

4. *Have one group meeting with the foundation representatives to discuss concepts; then designate one institution as the lead college.* Select one development officer from that college to serve as liaison with the foundation. He or she will continue negotiations, draft the proposal, and keep the other participants informed about the ongoing discussions. We foundation officers don't relish receiving phone calls from A, B, and C each week, especially when it becomes evident that each of the three colleges has a slightly different conception of the project. If the grant is made to the group, one college should assume responsibility for administering grant funds and submitting requisite reports to the foundation.

You should also realize that planning and preparing a multi-institutional proposal may take a great deal longer than writing a proposal for a single institution. Conferring, gaining approvals, revising, and revising again can double or triple your normal timeline. Start early so that the foundation does not think your joint efforts are rushed or poorly organized. If you can produce a successful multi-institutional program, the foundation will appreciate your joint endeavors, and your results will be worth the extra time and effort.

Conclusion

Networking among grant makers or grant seekers—more often informal than formal—has become a customary and acceptable part of foundation fund raising. Recognizing and discussing these processes openly with us can help overcome your misconceptions about proposal reviews and open and closed foundation doors. The more we foundation professionals understand about college and university networks, the more we will be able to help you with both individual and multi-institutional programs. Professional communication, combined with credibility and trust, will benefit both grant makers and grant seekers and lead to more grants more skillfully made.

Chapter 17

From the Other Side of the Desk: Characteristics of a Successful Application

Alfred H. Taylor, Jr.
Chairman of the Board
The Kresge Foundation

T he Kresge Foundation typically reviews approximately 1,000 proposals each year. The applying organizations are seeking challenge grants in support of building construction or renovation projects or the acquisition of major capital equipment. From this foundation's perspective, there are a number of characteristics that successful proposals have in common.

Prior contact. It is important for an applicant to be familiar with the established guidelines of the foundation, guidelines that are available in its statement of policies and application procedures.[1] While not a requirement, should an applicant desire an appointment or a conference call, it is urged that such a discussion occur *prior* to submitting a proposal.

Financial stability. The foundation is interested in an organization's general financial condition, including its ability to operate within a balanced budget. A careful examination of the organization's most recent audit assists the foundation in this regard. Knowledge of recent operating results provides guidance about an organization's future prospects. Moreover, a review of an organization's finances gives the foundation information about its assets, its liabilities, and the funding sources used to meet its various expenditures.

Demand for an organization's services. The foundation is interested in the level of demand for an organization's services. A review of usage data over several years enables the foundation to determine how fully an organization's services are being utilized. If a hospital, the number of admissions, occupancy rate, and average length of stay are reviewed. If a college or university, enrollment figures are tracked, including numbers of applications and retention data. If a cultural organization, attendance figures and data on educational programs will be reviewed. It should be emphasized that the foundation does not expect that demand for services will increase year after year. The purpose of the review, however, is to determine that there is sufficient demand and, when applicable, to be informed of the steps being taken to address factors that bear adversely on the level of that demand.

Effective leadership. This includes information about the quality and continuity of an organization's administrative leadership and governance. There is interest in the composition of boards of directors including the identification of their outside affiliations. There is also interest in knowing the extent to which volunteers play active roles in an organization. One way, of course, that the foundation learns about leadership is through periodic meetings with senior representatives of potential applicant organizations. When necessary, due usually to a lack of prior knowledge of an organization, the foundation may also obtain assessment from others about the leadership and program quality of the organization.

Well-defined projects. The foundation is interested in knowing that a project has been developed at least to the point that reasonably accurate cost estimates as well as a specific timetable have been determined for the project. There is a preference for project-specific applications rather than being offered a list of projects from which to choose. The foundation prefers that an organization determine its highest priority with respect to consideration by the foundation. In this connection, the foundation has no preference as to type of project or as to construction of new facilities or renovation of existing buildings.

Whatever project is presented in an application, its impact on the institution's operating budget should be identified as well as the specific plan for meeting any increase in operating costs.

A compelling fund-raising strategy. Kresge grants are made on a challenge basis. Typically, a successful applicant will have obtained early leadership gifts. It then approaches the foundation with a request for a challenge grant to assist in the raising of the balance of the funds to complete the project. In this process, the foundation hopes to help expand the base of support for an organization. There is *no* formula or specific matching requirement; the challenge relates to whatever fund-raising balance remains to assure full funding of a project. A well-defined fund-raising strategy, incorporating the requested challenge grant, is a critical component of an organization's application. The strategy is often broadly based as in a general campaign, but other times, and appropriately so, it is more narrowly focused, with a more limited number of prospects involved.

Over the years, the foundation has contributed unwittingly to the impression that most of the funding for a project must be committed before the organization applies to the foundation. While initial funding is essential, the foundation accepts the prevailing view of its applicants that the stimulation of a challenge grant usually can be greater if it occurs somewhat earlier in a fund-raising effort.

A review of the foundation's annual report will provide some guidance with respect to the appropriate amount of a request. While there is a tendency for a request to be for more than what is expected, an excessive request may, by its sheer size, preclude favorable consideration of the proposal.

Accreditation and/or licensure reports. Most organizations are periodically reviewed for ongoing accreditation and/or licensure. The foundation is interested in reviewing the most recent reports of such examinations and, when appropriate, of learning about the steps taken to address specific areas of concern outlined in such reports. Moreover, these reports often highlight the cooperative efforts of the applying organizations with other organizations regarding both the avoidance of unnecessary duplication of services and the beneficial sharing of resources.

Proposal format. There is no single, correct way to prepare a proposal. The Kresge Foundation prefers a concise proposal but one that addresses fully the threshold requirements outlined in its statement of procedures. Supporting documents should be included as appropriate. However, rather than being given complete feasibility study reports or long-range planning documents, the foundation prefers to be advised of such efforts in summary form.

Timing of the proposal. For many years the foundation accepted proposals for consideration only during the first six weeks of the year. As of December 1, 1985, however, it began accepting proposals at any time of the year, with the resultant announcement of new commitments throughout the year. This change in procedure enables an organization to determine when, in its own judgment, is the best time to apply. Also under this new procedure, the response time has been shortened to approximately five months, occasionally less.

It must be emphasized that even though all of these characteristics may be well documented in an application, there still remains the intense competition in selecting organizations to receive grants. Many worthwhile proposals have to be declined. In those instances, and if requested, the foundation's staff will discuss those factors that contributed to a declination. It will also assure a declined applicant that it may reapply to the foundation the following year, or subsequently, toward the same or a different project.

Highlights from an Information Workshop sponsored by the Southeast Council on Foundations in Atlanta, Georgia, on January 27, 1986.

Note

[1] In January 1988, the Kresge Foundation announced a *Science Initiative*, a special companion program to its traditional bricks and mortar grants. Details are contained in a pamphlet entitled *The Kresge Foundation—Science Initiative.*

Chapter 18

Community Foundations: Expanding Sources of Local Philanthropy

Alicia Philipp
Executive Director
Metropolitan Atlanta Community Foundation

W ithout a lot of fanfare, the community foundation "movement" has emerged in recent years as the growth industry of American philanthropy. According to *Giving USA,* more than 300 community foundations now manage combined assets of $3.3 billion. They range in size from small organizations with a few thousand dollars to the New York Community Trust with assets of half a billion dollars. Quite a phenomenon when you consider that it was only 75 years ago that a banker named Frederick Goff spearheaded the establishment of the Cleveland Foundation.

What is a community foundation?

While it's hard to come up with a definition that covers all community foundations, they do have some common features:
* *Geographical focus.* Most community foundations restrict their activities to particular metropolitan areas, although some (like the Oregon Community Foundation and the Rhode Island Foundation) operate statewide.
* *Public charity status.* This legal classification requires that a significant portion of the foundation's support comes from a relatively large number of donors. Public charity status also gives donors maximum deductibility for their contributions. Many people have established funds within community foundations because

141

it is a far less expensive way to become involved with professionally managed philanthropy than to create a private foundation.

• *Representative nature of the board.* Whether board members are appointed by public officials (e.g., judges, mayors) or private groups (chambers of commerce, bar associations, medical societies) or are self-perpetuating, these boards seek to reflect the demographics of their community populations. (In some cases, boards also appoint distribution committees to assist them with grant-making decisions.) The style of each community foundation is strongly influenced by this board leadership. In fact, because community foundations are public organizations and therefore highly accountable, it could even be said that their boards play a stronger role in establishing policy and setting the directions for program activity than do the boards of many other foundations.

In some ways, community foundations function as philanthropic brokers or clearinghouses. They raise funds from the private sector, manage them, and redistribute them to eligible nonprofit organizations and even, in some cases, to individuals and local government agencies. Especially during recent times, some community foundations have also extended their roles to become catalysts for the discussion and resolution of community issues and problems.

Whose money?

Every community foundation has built its assets in a way that reflects its own history and leadership and those of the community. A number of community foundations (especially the oldest ones like Cleveland and Hartford) have high percentages of *unrestricted* or *discretionary funds* available for disbursement. Others (like Baltimore) have raised these kinds of monies with special capital campaigns. Donors to community foundations range from men and women who annually contribute a few thousand dollars to the very rich who may give or bequeath millions of dollars, either in unrestricted funds or for special purposes.

As a general rule, contributors make their gifts from accumulated assets rather than from their income. However, some community foundations—El Paso is a striking example—work hard to encourage what its executive director refers to as "populist philanthropy," contributions of even very small amounts from people with limited financial resources. This promotes a community-wide sense of ownership in the foundation.

Many community foundations that experienced significant growth during the 1980s (like Atlanta), as well as some of the largest ones (New York, for example), have a large portion of their assets in *donor-advised funds*. These funds permit living donors to participate actively in philanthropic decisions by recommending to community foundation boards the areas of need they want their resources to address. In these situations, the community foundation, knowing the donor's charitable interests, can suggest projects for funding. Sometimes the foundation, by drawing upon several donor-advised funds, can put together a package of support for a local nonprofit organization.

There are times when a community foundation may expand upon this concept more directly. Because of its knowledge of the local scene and particular needs, it may establish *field-of-interest funds* and publicize the opportunity for donors to pool their resources to address these needs. For example, community foundations have responded in this fashion to the needs of the homeless. Several of them have also created field-of-interest funds to support programs specifically targeted for women—a group that historically has received relatively low levels of support from the philanthropic community. Often these field-of-interest funds have specially appointed advisory committees that assist with both fund raising and grant-making decisions.

Community foundations also manage *designated funds,* the income of which is earmarked for particular beneficiaries. This service is especially helpful for donors who want to designate specific recipients, but prefer not to turn over investment responsibilities to them. In this way they have the satisfaction of knowing that the funds will be managed well in perpetuity on behalf of their chosen charities.

Increasingly, community foundations are also offering to manage endowment portfolios for nonprofit organizations. At a very low cost, these institutions and agencies receive the benefit of professional investment counsel—a feature that can be a strong selling point to their own donors who are further reassured by the community foundation's credibility. United Way organizations in some communities, for instance, have placed their endowments in community foundations.

Who benefits?

There is scarcely a charitable need that hasn't received support from some kind of community foundation fund. Contributions have gone to established institutions like symphonies and museums, but they have also supported emerging agencies and organizations. Recently, for example, some community foundations have been in the forefront of providing assistance to programs that address the needs of AIDS sufferers.

One of the most important services that community foundations offer the nonprofit sector is to assist new and/or controversial projects and programs to gain legitimacy and credibility in the eyes of other donors. It is not unusual for a community foundation to make the first major grant to some emerging venture—an endorsement that can send a positive signal to other funding sources.

Catalysts for positive change

The men and women who created community foundations envisioned a greater role for them than that of processing local philanthropy. Balanced as they are between donors and community needs, these unique foundations can also play a catalytic part in promoting discussion and action on behalf of particular problems. This sort of activity may involve as simple a step as convening a meeting of concerned leaders to explore cooperative solutions to a major community need. It may also lead to a large-scale and more formal effort like the Corporate Special Projects Fund of the New York Community Trust that now receives the support of several corporations for the joint funding of pressing community problems.

Indeed, the only limitations on "proactive" leadership by a community foundation are the energy of its personnel and its financial resources. Community foundations have sponsored grantsmanship seminars for nonprofit organizations, offered management suggestions to grant applicants, and assisted them with board development by recommending candidates.

In some cases, community foundations function almost like real estate developers. The Winston-Salem Foundation is one of the organizations that actually holds title to the buildings occupied by not-for-profit groups and then leases them back at virtually no cost to the "tenants." This arrangement is very attractive to donors who want to contribute to the bricks-and-mortar needs of an arts group or social service agency, but also want to ensure that the property will remain in the public trust should the nonprofit cease to exist.

Approaching community foundations

At the risk of sounding immodest, those of us in this unique sector of the philanthropic universe doubt whether there is any grant-making organization that is more accessible than a community foundation and its staff. Anyone who has labored in the fund-raising vineyards knows the difficulties that can surround an approach to a government agency, a private or corporate foundation, or a wealthy individual.

By contrast, and as implied by its name, a community foundation is "in business" to serve the public—and that "public" is very broadly defined. For anyone with a great new project, an idea whose time has come, or simply a question about possible sources of support, the community foundation is an excellent way station on the fund-raising pilgrimage. A review of the annual reports of most community foundations will attest to this accessibility.

The community foundation board and staff members I know pride themselves on their knowledge about the local scene and readily make themselves available for appointments. They can offer suggestions about other local philanthropy; they can volunteer information about projects similar to the one for which the visitor is seeking support; they can even provide practical suggestions about fund-raising steps and strategies.

It has also been my experience that community foundations do not place unreasonable or excessive demands for paperwork upon grant seekers. Most community foundations strive to keep both application and reporting procedures simple, and it is not unusual for them to help would-be grant recipients to put together the strongest possible proposal for support.

An excellent first step for any grant seeker is to request a copy of a community foundation's annual report. This document will quickly reveal the kinds (and financial ranges) of grants made by the foundation as well as such important information as the deadlines for proposals.

After studying this information and *before* submitting a proposal, the grant seeker should call, write, or visit the director or a staff member of the foundation to explore whether there is a "fit" between the foundation's interests and the project for which he or she is seeking funding. Although board members make the final decision about grants from unrestricted assets, staff members can be helpful guides and even advocates for a project they understand and believe to be important. They can also bring together grant seekers and the contributors to donor-advised funds.

For further information about community foundations

The Council on Foundations maintains current data on the location and asset size of most community foundations and keeps a library of annual reports and other background information. The Council is located at 1828 L St. NW, Washington, DC 20036, (202) 466-6512.

Chapter 19

Grant Accountability and Long-term Relationships with Foundations

Richard R. Johnson
Director for Research
Exxon Education Foundation

M ost "how-to-do-it" advice for development officers focuses on getting grants, not on what to do once the grant is in hand. And yet, when you consider the long-term relationship between the institution and the foundation that provided the grant, how a grant is managed may be crucial in determining whether the institution will ever receive another grant from that foundation. A careful examination of the responsibilities assumed by an institution in accepting a grant from a foundation suggests a special stewardship role for the development officer.

Foundations make many types of grants, but this chapter focuses on "project" grants—grant support for a focused, special activity to be completed in a specified period of time. A "general support" grant, on the other hand, is more like a contribution from a major, individual donor; it is not limited to support for a specified activity and it may not specify a date by which the funds must be used.

On occasion, however, you may find that treating a general support grant like a project grant has certain advantages. You may be able to increase the interest and involvement of the donor (whether individual or foundation) by assigning general support funding to an institutional activity of interest to the donor and by reporting back to the donor on accomplishments under the grant. In this way, the general support grant can be managed like a project grant to promote a longer-term relationship with the donor by demonstrating how well the funds were used. This is the theme of this chapter: Good grant management can build long-term donor relationships.

Responding to a grant notification

A timely reply should be made upon receiving notification from a foundation of grant funding. Such a reply serves several purposes. In the case of a project that has been developed and negotiated in the proposal process at lower echelons in the institution, having the president sign the reply letter is a way of getting him or her "on board" in relation to the project. And the function of the reply for the foundation addressed is more than merely that of the "thanking" letter sent to an individual donor.

You would never forget to send a "thanking" letter to an individual donor who has made a major gift or even a routine donation to the annual fund. To forget would be neither polite nor politic. Such a letter serves several purposes:
- it acknowledges receipt of the gift;
- it serves as the donor's receipt for tax purposes;
- it expresses the institution's gratitude; and
- it may pave the way for a further solicitation.

While your follow-up to a foundation serves some of these same purposes, there are differences.

Thanking letters are appropriate for small foundations that are fundamentally mechanisms for an individual's giving, or that are managed by an individual who functions in place of the donor with broad discretionary powers. This rule of thumb recognizes the fact that the decision making was basically that of an individual, who can be thanked for choosing to support your institution. Furthermore, because such a foundation probably makes relatively few grants and thus receives relatively few "thank-you's," your letter will be meaningful.

The general rule is, however, do not send a thanking letter to a large "professional" foundation. Thanking letters are inappropriate in this case for several reasons:

1. When the grant review process is complex, you cannot single out a person to be thanked. The typical solution is to send the thanking letter to the CEO of the foundation. But consider a parallel, hypothetical case: What if all the graduating seniors at your institution sent a thanking letter to the president? How meaningful would any single letter be?

2. When a foundation has made many grants, it's unlikely that anyone is keeping track of who sends thanking letters and who does not. Some large foundations receive literally thousands of thanking letters in a single year. And most of these are clearly the product of a word-processor. If your thanking letter is part of this form-letter, paper blizzard, how effective will it be?

3. When a foundation prides itself on making grants on the basis of merit after careful review, an overly effusive thanking letter may suggest that the grant was not really deserved. When such a letter is sent to the CEO, it could embarrass foundation staff by implying that your institution received preference in the review process.

But any rule of thumb must be tempered by Lars Aallyn's ninth law of communication: "People considerations preempt structural communication rules."

Some people like to be thanked. If you know who they are, thank them. In other cases, a staff member, the foundation CEO, or a foundation board member who has done something special for the institution should be recognized appropriately. Under these exceptional circumstances, you can thank the person by personal letter, a phone call, or a letter to his or her superior mentioning briefly the concrete actions that were both helpful *and appropriate* within the operating context of the foundation.

Thanking should almost never take the form of recognition plaques, certificates, statues, or trophies. Imagine the space any large foundation would have to allocate to all the ornaments it would quickly collect.

The appropriate response to a "professional" foundation is via an acknowledgement letter that will accomplish some of the functions served by the thanking letter. This letter should:

1. *confirm the fact that the grant letter (and check) was received;*

2. *indicate explicit agreement with any special conditions or stipulations the foundation has stated in the grant letter;*

3. *communicate any new developments at the institution relevant to the funded project.* For example, if you are acknowledging a grant that requires matching funding, mentioning money already in hand, pledges, and even planned solicitations, shows your intent to meet the challenge.

You also want the foundation to see that the project is getting off to a strong start. Include in the acknowledgement letter information that demonstrates that the institution takes the project seriously and that the project is likely to be successful—indicate new personnel hired for the project, parallel efforts in other aspects of the institution's program that will complement the work, and so on.

4. *raise any issues that need to be considered early as the project gets underway.* If the funding was delayed, you may need to suggest a new calendar; if personnel have changed, you may need to nominate a new project director; and so on.

5. *introduce the institutional contact person for the grant.* Grants made to colleges and universities are typically linked to a particular faculty member or administrator who will be the project director. But often it is useful to have someone else serve as an additional contact with the foundation to represent the institution. For example, a foundation wishing to discuss a grant it has made could have difficulty reaching a faculty member away from his or her office. The institution also has a wider and longer-term interest in the grant than the project director may have. For these reasons it is a good idea to provide the name of another contact person (e.g., vice president for development, director of corporate and foundation relations, the grants and contracts administrator) so that the foundation will have a second, institution-level contact for the grant.

6. *provide a subtle "thank-you" from one organization to another.* The thank-you in an acknowledgement letter is clearly subordinate to the other functions of the letter. For example, the letter might say that the institution is "pleased to be working with" the foundation or it might emphasize how important the task to be undertaken is (i.e., how astute the foundation is to be funding it). In short, the acknowledgement letter is as far as you can get from an expression of gratitude

for a handout.

The acknowledgement letter can establish and define the tone for continuing communication with the foundation. Where the typical, word-processed thanking letter "closes the loop" by expressing gratitude at a completed transaction, your acknowledgement letter opens a line of communication with the foundation.

Who should write and sign the acknowledgement letter? The development office should almost always be responsible for drafting the acknowledgement letter. The exception to this structural rule may occur when the signatory (e.g., the president) knows the addressee personally (remember Aallyn's ninth law of communication: "People considerations preempt structural communication rules"). In this case, he or she may wish to write the letter.

Who should sign the letter? To paraphrase an old saying, "Rank doth have its functions." If the acknowledgement letter were merely a receipt for a check received, you could send a computer-generated ticket to the foundation (and this has been done!), signed by a senior clerk in the business office. But since the letter is intended to open a channel of communication for the institution as well as for the project, it should almost always be signed by a high-level administrator (unless, for example, the project director is a Nobel Laureate or an otherwise prestigious "name"). When the high-level person signs for the institution, he or she acknowledges the importance of the project and the commitment of the institution to it.

However, "high-level administrator" does not necessarily mean the president of your institution. A project may more properly belong under the wing of a dean of the school responsible for it. Another project may call for commitment at the level of the vice president for academic affairs. What is significant is that, for grants important to your institution, you communicate to the foundation an appropriate institutional level of commitment beyond the intentions of the project director to carry out the work described in his or her proposal.

But once again, be aware of people considerations. Some foundations always like to see "top-level" (presidential) involvement. Some presidents like to write to foundation executives. Know what is appropriate in each case.

Setting up the project

While the central responsibility for management of foundation-funded projects should fall on the development office, you should strive to keep an extremely low profile as you perform this function. A faculty member or administrator will undoubtedly resent it if the development office asserts managerial responsibility for "his" or "her" project. The project director is likely to believe that:

• he or she got the grant, not the development office;

• he or she can manage the project very well without interference from the development office;

• the development office, in getting involved in the project, may complicate or mess things up;

• the development office is getting involved to try to cut in on a "special relationship" he or she has with the foundation.

In order to manage without seeming to manage, you should follow these rules:

1. Never use the word "management." Talk about "providing institutional support" instead.

2. Show how useful you can be by setting up a separate institutional account for the project director, running the necessary interference in the business office (e.g., clarifying any limitations on expenditure to the institution's controller, dealing with overhead charges, and so on).

3. Clarify to the project director any limits (from the institution's or foundation's perspective) on types of expenditures or project activities, and offer to help in negotiations if any changes or exceptions are needed.

4. Set up a calendar for the project director showing when various activities described in the proposal are to be completed and when reports are due (and keep a copy for yourself).

5. Tell the project director that the development office will handle fiscal reporting (with copies to him or her) and will remind the project director when various reports are due. Later you may also help with editing and word-processing of project reports if called upon.

6. Set up a project file in the development office that contains:
• a copy of the proposal;
• copies of related official correspondence with the foundation;
• notes on important, project-related telephone calls; and
• notes on any special relationships or requirements.

This file should *not* contain materials produced as part of the project. Collecting all the output of the project is not cost-effective for the development office and would unduly harass the project director.

Reporting, communicating, and negotiating

While some may see the development officer merely as a money raiser, the true development role is far broader. In considering the long-term needs of the institution in relation to its external constituencies, the development officer is mainly a communicator and often an ombudsman. This role is exemplified in the way in which ongoing project reporting should be handled.

Generally, the reports for a foundation are not expected to come from the development office. The project director is responsible for the narrative reports on project activities, and the business office should be the source of fiscal reports on project expenditures. Thus, while you are responsible for the management of the project, you must depend upon the actions of others. Your role is like that of the conductor of an orchestra. While the sounds come from the actions of the musicians, the conductor must bring the disparate elements together to make music.

Fiscal reports. While the business office can be expected to produce standard account reports, these may amount to only the raw material out of which an expenditure report is constructed. The functional expenditure categories in the grant proposal may not match the standard account reporting categories of the business office. One way to deal with this problem is to negotiate with the business office, when the grant is received and the account is set up, to use the foundation's reporting categories.

In other cases, the standard, institutional budget categories will have to be translated into the grant line-item expenditures for each fiscal report. You may have to assume significant responsibility for doing this. The best solution to this problem is to deal with this issue before the proposal is submitted by tailoring the proposal budget to the institutional expenditure categories.

Narrative reports. The problem you are most likely to encounter is getting the project director to meet deadlines for narrative reports on grant-funded activities. The project director is often so busy carrying out the project (as well as other responsibilities at the institution) that he or she finds it hard to take the time to write a report of what has been accomplished.

One way to deal with this is to offer to help edit the report; the project director may respond with notes and documents that can be pulled together to make up the report or at least a rough draft. Reading the rough draft may inspire the project director to add to it or even rewrite it to correct errors. In this way, by prodding and facilitating, you can produce—or cause to be produced—a timely report to the foundation.

Communication, however, goes beyond meeting the foundation's standard reporting requirements. Some foundations are quite relaxed about formal reporting deadlines. If such is the case, you should set up internal, institutional deadlines so that timely reports are sent even when they are not required. This creates an image (and the reality) of businesslike, responsible management of grants. This does not mean that you should bury the foundation under a paper blizzard. Rather, you should consider what may be of interest to the foundation beyond the required reporting and see that such information is passed along.

In regard to what and how much to send, remember Aallyn's fourth law of communication:

> Everything else being equal, the probability that any piece of information in a message will be received and understood is inversely proportional to the length of the total message. That is, if someone is expected to find a needle in a haystack, it is a good idea not to have piled on too much hay.

Send interesting items, but choose what you send judiciously.

The following items (often omitted from standard project reports) could be of particular interest to foundations:

• newspaper clippings (including the student newspaper!) related to the project, especially if they indicate the foundation's support. (Don't forget that foundations, too, are interested in their public image.)

• reports on other funding that the project has attracted since the foundation provided the grant. (This both confirms the judgment of the foundation about the worth of the project and shows that the foundation is a "leader" in getting funding to a worthwhile effort.)

• information about other events on campus that are relevant to the foundation-supported project and show the project's impact in a wider context. This strategy of communication, providing project-relevant though not required information, can create a context for future funding of other institutional activities.

Some information is too important to be held until the next project report is due. For example, you should inform the foundation immediately:

• if the project director moves to another campus or must be replaced for some other reason;

• if expenditures on a project need to be changed significantly from the budget submitted in the proposal or if expenditures on the project are running far ahead of the expected level and projections suggest a cost overrun. Do not wait for the money to run out before discussing the problem with the foundation.

In some of these communications, you will be in the middle, serving as a negotiator between project director and foundation, or between project director and institution. When expenditure plans on a project do not match the typical institutional mode, you may need to negotiate with institutional officers for more flexibility. Conversely, you may need to interpret the institution's priorities to the project director and show him or her how project goals can be accomplished within the institutional context. You serve as communicator and ombudsman—between institution and foundation, project director and foundation, and between project director and institution—clarifying goals, clearing up misunderstandings, and seeking mutually acceptable means to achieve common ends.

It is clear that your role as a development officer is one that goes far beyond merely "getting the money." In considering the longer-term interests of the institution that employs you, you should work to build long-term relationships with foundations. Any one grant received by the institution is not only a success story in relation to funds secured, it is also the occasion for building a stronger relationship with the foundation by managing that grant successfully.

Chapter 20

Smoothing the Process Between Grant Seeking And Grant Making

Joel J. Orosz
Executive Assistant
W.K. Kellogg Foundation

Peter R. Ellis
Program Director
W.K. Kellogg Foundation

T he development of a successful relationship between grant maker and grant seeker follows the age-old pattern of courtship—an introduction, a conversation, and the discovery of a mutual attraction leading to commitment. At the same time, as in a courtship, there is ample opportunity for breakup or strain based upon miscommunications, misperceptions, or downright incompatibility. In this chapter, we offer both grant seeker and grant maker some suggestions on how to avoid mistakes on the perilous road to commitment.

Common mistakes by grant seekers

The first mistake that some grant seekers make is to fail to read the foundation's grant-making guidelines before preparing a proposal. If the foundation says that it does not give to capital campaigns, buy equipment, or give to institutions in foreign nations, you can be confident that a request to fund a computer system for the use of Oxford University's capital campaign will be declined.

Many grant seekers do read foundation guidelines but not very carefully. A quick glance at a foundation's brochure may tell you that it is interested in health, but this does not necessarily mean it will fund your programs in otolaryngology and x-ray technology.

In short, foundations generally have specific priorities within broad fields of interest; a careful reading of their materials, particularly the list of active projects, will usually reveal what those priorities are. Beginning your proposal with "Knowing that you are interested in health...." is a tip-off that you have not done your homework. On the other hand, an opening that reads "Knowing of your specific concern about community-based, cost-effective health systems...." tells the program director that some effective research has been done.

Beware of being *too* specific, however. Some proposals are so loaded with buzzwords and key phrases lifted directly from the foundation's publications that the program director begins to wonder if the grantee has any original ideas at all. A proposal that parrots the foundation's published utterances or the jargon of the field sounds like a plagiarized term paper. It is the grant seeker's ability to solve problems in a creative manner that matters to a foundation, not his or her ability to paraphrase.

Another mistake is to send an identical proposal to several foundations simultaneously. While this idea may seduce you with visions of efficiency, it is actually counterproductive in the long term. Such a proposal sounds as warm and caring as a "Dear Resident" letter. By failing to tailor a proposal to the announced priorities of each foundation, you severely limit your chance of success. And if you *are* successful, imagine your embarrassment at having to explain to two foundations how it came to pass that both have fully funded the same major project.

Don't proceed before you have gauged a foundation's interest in a proposal. Pity the foundation staff member who receives an unsolicited proposal of the same cubic volume as *War and Peace,* only to discover after reading dozens of pages that it deals with a project clearly out of the foundation's scope. Much work for the grant seeker—and the program officer—could have been avoided with some prior communication between the two.

Foundation preferences vary, but most prefer that the first contact from the grant seeker be through a letter or phone call, followed up by a short pre-proposal (two to three pages) that summarizes the idea and is suitable for preliminary review purposes. Usually a foundation will request a thorough, detailed proposal only after the pre-proposal steps have been taken.

Meetings between representatives of the grant maker and grant seeker are usually productive. Here, too, be careful to avoid some common mistakes. For example, don't request a "fishing expedition" visit in the hopes that "something may develop." Foundation staff prefer meetings built on promising ideas and definite next steps. They tend to regard agenda-less meetings as counterproductive.

At the meeting itself, be aware of body language, both your own and that of the foundation representative. If your words are confident but your manner is nervous and uncertain, the foundation representative will probably believe what he or she sees rather than what you have actually said. On the other hand, if the program director is listening politely but his or her visage betrays skepticism, take that as a hint that you need to support your position more forcefully.

Finally, if the proposal reaches the stage of a site visit, remember the limits of human endurance. More than one grant seeker has tried to cram so much into a single visit that exhaustion, information overload, and ennui overtake everyone before the session mercifully comes to an end. Remember, you want your climactic presentation at the end of the visit to be heard by an alert and interested program director, not one with aching feet and a splitting headache.

There are several pitfalls to avoid when you are preparing a written proposal. For example, when describing your institution's approach to a problem or the expected outcome, don't use the word "unique" unless you are sure that no one else has *ever* taken such an approach or reached such an outcome. Overuse by the advertising world may have diluted the value of "unique," but to foundation officers it still means "being the only one of its kind." If another institution is already doing your "unique" project, you will appear both uninformed and careless.

Another potential problem is in the purpose of your proposal. Foundations' stated missions vary, but usually they reflect the purpose of improving the quality of human life, not giving aid and comfort to institutions. A grant seeker should be confident that the point of the project being proposed is to improve human well-being, not to add to the greater glory or to ensure the perpetuity of a hospital or university.

A favorite question of program directors is, "What are the grantees bringing to the table?" Staff time, utilities, and meeting space are useful, but these are fixed expenses that would probably be committed anyway. If an idea is truly important, the grant-seeking institution should be committed to it in action as well as in word—and that means that real dollars should be invested in it. You'll find it difficult to convince a foundation to invest money in a project if your institution is not willing to do the same.

A common request is for support to start a "national center" for a special cause or to solve a particular problem. Don't include this sort of ambitious goal in a proposal without first asking the obvious questions: Do *we* have a track record indicative of national leadership in this area? How will other centers across the country react when they hear that we are claiming national leadership? If these questions raise doubts, be cautious about basing requests on such an ambitious claim.

Many proposals fail to provide an adequate answer to the question of "takeover." Foundations are in the venture capital business. The assets of the average foundation could not operate a large university for one year. The forte of foundations is nurturing a good idea, giving it a bit of propulsion, and demonstrating its value until others are willing to take it over and maintain it. A good proposal describes a realistic scenario for the accomplishment of this transfer. A foundation officer is reassured if the possibility of a continuing endowment-draining maintenance expense is removed at the front end of the negotiations.

Every good proposal clearly answers the question, "So what?" You have identified a problem, but so what? Why is it serious? How will society suffer if it is not solved? You have identified a possible solution, but so what? Will this solution really enhance human well-being? How? Answering these questions forthrightly will make your proposal stronger and more attractive.

Finally, there is the unpleasant fact that program directors *can* and *must* say no to many proposals. Even the largest, most affluent foundations receive more requests than they can fund. A regrettable number of good ideas simply must be turned down. Most foundations believe that if your proposal is declined, you deserve an explanation—not necessarily a detailed one but some indication of the reason for the declination.

Whatever the explanation, don't become discouraged and resolve never to try again. Persistence can be a virtue in the world of foundations. But don't just change a few sentences and resubmit the same proposal. Such attempts at shoehorning a declined proposal invariably fail. It wouldn't have been turned down in the first place just because a couple of sentences needed rewriting. And don't resubmit the proposal to a colleague of the program director in the hope that he or she will be more sympathetic. Few foundations are so big that such an end-run will pass unnoticed.

The sins of the grant makers

Enough about mistakes grant seekers make—what about those of grant makers? Here are some that happen all too frequently.

The first is a tendency toward inflexibility. A grant maker would be guilty of inefficient stewardship if he or she plied the grant-making trade without guidelines to organize the foundation's giving. On the other hand, these guidelines should not be graven in stone. A grant maker should be an opportunist when he or she sees that your idea, while technically outside the foundation's priorities, is peculiarly right for its time and place. A grant maker who is too rigid to bend a guideline occasionally when the result would be significant improvement for people is not being a good steward.

Another mistake is to adhere slavishly to the "play-it-safe" mentality. This means the grant maker will fund only the oldest, most prestigious and solid grant seekers. Never mind if such a grant benefits the institution more than it benefits people. Forget that small, unsophisticated, and new organizations are often closest to the people, more attuned to solving their problems, and likely to devise more creative responses. The goal of such a grantor is to avoid risk at all costs: When you take risks, you do not always meet your objectives (*if,* that is, you have dared to set real objectives). Funders rarely fail if they fund only the certainties, but their conservatism may thereby greatly diminish any real contribution to improving the quality of life.

Grant makers are often accused of being inaccessible and intimidating. This charge once had more validity than it does today. In 1956, however, the Foundation Center was created to provide information about foundations to anyone who seeks it. Still, there are obstacles to reaching a grant maker. Part of this may be the result of the grant maker's extensive travel schedule and heavy workload. Whatever the reason, there is little justification for failing to answer a written inquiry or telephone call within a reasonable period of time.

An unhappy by-product of the various tax reform acts passed by Congress since 1969 has been the temptation for the foundation officer to focus on *process* instead of *results*. The benefits promised by a grant proposal may be forgotten while foundation staffers worry about the grantee securing appropriate tax status clearance and complying with the public support test (which was instituted to assure that a nonprofit does not receive too large a proportion of its budget from a foundation or foundations). More than one good idea has gone unfunded because, for instance, a foundation grant would cause an institution to fail its public support test—in short, because a foundation would be considered *too* generous in giving a grant.

And while the program director is focusing on process, he or she does not share this fact with the grant seeker. As a result, most grant seekers regard foundations as black boxes into which proposals are inserted at one end and ejected at the other, with "accepted" or "declined" stamped on them. While it is neither necessary nor desirable that the foundation share every detail of the review process with a potential grantee, you should be told how your proposal will be reviewed, how long it will take, and who will make the decision. Proposal discussions between grant maker and grant seeker should terminate with a candid explanation of the next steps, in which the responsibilities of each party are made clear.

Remember, foundations dispense *venture* capital; therefore, foundations should never fund any project in perpetuity. It is considered desirable to have someone else take over a project as soon as possible, so foundations generally adhere to a three- or four-year-and-out rule. That is, support the program on a declining basis over this period and then hand it over to the owners. This model usually works well if the grantee is a large institution with substantial resources (a university, hospital, or a national youth-serving organization). Problems arise when the grantee is a smaller, less stable organization, with modest financial reserves. Far too often, a good program is brought into existence by foundation funding, nurtured into a useful existence, then allowed to die when the funding disappears after three years. Grant makers could wisely commit for a longer haul, especially if it is likely that a worthwhile program can survive in no other way.

A foundation program director generally ensures that a grant seeker is clearly informed about the implications or intentions of any discussions or interest in a proposal. Failure to do this can create problems. For example, a program director may consider a campus visit to be only a fact-finding tour while the grant seeker takes it as a sign of warm interest and almost certain approval. Therefore, a grant maker should be careful to communicate with clarity and precision.

"No" is not a pleasant word for a grant seeker to hear or a grant maker to say, but it has a fundamental place in the scheme of foundation work. Because of its impact, grant makers must use it wisely and humanely when responding to proposals. Grant seekers complain—and justifiably—that some program directors respond to their ideas with enthusiasm and encourage them to submit a proposal only to decline it later. This is unfair; a grant maker should be cautious about being too encouraging. And sometimes a grant maker's response to a proposal is so indirect and oblique that the grant seeker doesn't know whether it has been declined or not. This is no time for delicacy; you deserve to be told—tactfully but clearly—if your idea cannot be funded by that particular foundation.

Another legitimate complaint is the long lag time between the submission of a grant request and its final disposition. Usually, factors beyond the grant maker's control cause the delay, but occasionally the program director is guilty of procrastination. After months have gone by without a decision, even the most cautious grant seeker may begin to believe that the foundation *must* be interested in the project. If, in fact, the foundation is merely "sitting on" your proposal, it should certainly announce its decision so that you will be free to submit the project elsewhere.

Potential grantees frequently claim that foundation officers enjoy ordering picayune changes. Foundation officers *do* encourage changes in proposals they receive, but the vast majority of these are legitimate: They are necessary to satisfy legal, procedural, or ethical requirements; to meet the foundation's programming guidelines; or to strengthen and stretch the proposal. When the changes proposed by the grant maker are, in fact, minor quibbles over word choices or an attempt to indiscriminately restructure the focus of the proposal, you might do well to look in another direction for support.

As these suggestions show, the key words in any relationship between grant maker and grant seeker are consideration, respect, and the recognition of common interests. When these are present, the results can and will benefit humankind. For grant makers and grant seekers are like love and marriage—as the song tells us, you can't have one without the other.

Section 5

Focused Programs and Foundation Support

Chapter 21

The Foundation Program: In and Out of a Capital Campaign

W. Charles Witzleben
Vice President and Director
Ross, Johnston & Kersting, Inc.

M ost philanthropic dollars come from sources other than private foundations, and yet there is no boost to an institution quite like a significant foundation grant. If, after months or even years of strategizing, the grant you need is awarded, you have acquired not only a sum of money but an interested partner. A foundation investment in your particular program is a vote of confidence not only in that program but in your institution's overall leadership, mission, and future.

Such partners are invaluable, whether or not your institution is in a capital campaign. Even if your college or university is not in line any time soon to receive a $100 million grant such as that given by the Danforth Foundation to Washington University in 1986, seeking foundation partners is well worth the considerable time and effort it takes.

The effort involves studiousness of a sort not applied to any other type of prospective donor, but made necessary by the large quantity of published information on foundations and by the expectation on the part of the foundations that you will acquaint yourself with it. The late Thomas Broce's warning bears repeating:

> In spite of the body of information that has been collected and is regularly and systematically maintained about foundations, most laymen (including most fund raisers) actually know very little about them. Consequently, foundation money continues to go to the few institutions willing to do the work required to gain their support.[1]

Impatience is a quality rarely found in successful foundation grant seekers. And learning about the foundation is only half—the second half—of the battle. First, you must learn about your own institution.

Relating programs to institutional priorities

We all know that foundations exist for the sole purpose of giving away money. This fact leads some development officers to approach a foundation as though it were a pot of gold, waiting to be dipped into. Again, the key word is partnership. Foundations are more inclined to give money to organizations whose priorities are in order and who offer donors an opportunity to make a meaningful contribution toward well-defined goals. In other words, the pot of gold is guarded by guidelines that are enforced by officers and trustees who are unlikely to give in to whimsy.

Therefore, your institution's first order of business, before it seeks foundation support, is to order its priorities. This is the same process that typically precedes a capital campaign: Input from throughout the organization is collected into a body of needs and wants that, when fulfilled through a capital fund-raising effort, will move the institution toward goals consistent with its mission.

Foundations don't care whether this prioritizing has been done as planning for a capital campaign or if you are already in a campaign mode when your request comes to them; their interest is in the program you present. Is the program a significant step forward for the institution and yet in the mainstream of its proven expertise and resources? Is the institution making a significant investment of personnel and internal funds, beyond the foundation grant itself, to ensure the program's success? How will the program evolve, after the foundation's commitment period is over? Does the proposal set forth a method for reporting on the success of the program?

Beyond these specific questions, your institution as a whole is on trial every time you submit a foundation request. Has your institution proven itself to be fiscally responsible? How well does its top leadership speak for the institution? How successful has it been in garnering support from other private foundations? How were these grants managed?

The essence of all these questions is: How well have you set forth your institutional priorities? Only after this has been done—through careful institutional planning endorsed by your leadership—are you ready to seek foundation partners. A foundation cannot (and should not be asked to) set your priorities for you. The relationship of any institution with a foundation must be one of mutual respect. Therefore, don't expect the foundation to define your goals, and don't ask the foundation to violate its particular mission to support your project.

Show your respect for the foundation by submitting a request that is within its guidelines in both content and format. The foundation views itself as having a unique and worthy mission and expects that prospective recipients will approach it with deference and understanding. Waldemar Nielsen states it well in *The Golden*

Donors: "By their special character [foundations] are moral and symbolic entities dealing in matters of the mind and spirit."[2]

If you are dealing with a foundation that awards grants to unusual projects, then respect that foundation's particular ego—its view of itself as a force for good—and offer your project as a means toward fulfilling the foundation's purposes.

Capital campaigns and continuing programs

As you develop a major prospect list for a capital campaign, you will find that private foundations figure prominently. Perhaps the lead gift for your campaign will come from a foundation. (For example, the lead gift for Emory University's last major capital campaign consisted of the entire assets of a private foundation, the Emily and Ernest Woodruff Fund.) But remember that foundations are interested in the merit of your project and not in the current "mode" of your institution—whether you are in the first phase, second phase, or wrap-up of a capital campaign or between campaigns. The foundation must understand your institution and then decide if the project you have brought to it defines the institution and moves it forward.

If you are new to foundation fund raising, you may feel that foundation officers and trustees seem indifferent to your pleas for understanding. Institutions with sophisticated and long-standing public relations officers and those with a long history of successful fund raising have an advantage. But these suggestions may help you take the first steps toward making your institution "known" to the foundation community:

• Don't send every catalog, information brochure, and annual report to the foundation. If you have attended professional conferences and listened to the warnings and entreaties of foundation executives, you have already heard it: "We get so much unsolicited mail that we can't possibly read it all!" If you send published information to the foundation, send only what directly applies to previous discussions with the foundation and send it with a reminder in the form of a cover memo.

• If your institution doesn't happen to be one with instant name recognition and an established reputation (you're not the Metropolitan Museum of Art, Harvard University, or the Brookings Institution), accept the fact that it will take time for a foundation to get to know you. First, let the foundation know that you seek its understanding with the goal of establishing a partnership in the future. Ask the foundation how the relationship can best be pursued.

• And, finally, accept rejection gracefully. A fact of life in seeking foundation support is that there is a lot of rejection waiting for you out there. If statistics help, here's one from David Freeman's *Handbook on Private Foundations*: "It is a fact of foundation life that for every 'yes' answer there will be eight or ten rejected applications, not counting the form appeals."[3]

The theme of all this advice is: *Talk to the foundation.* But as you make personal contact, either on the phone or in person, remember that respect is very important; in your eagerness to get information and to "get your foot in the door," don't forget that the foundation officer's time is valuable.

In the not-too-distant past, development officers could drop in on a foundation executive and expect to be welcomed and heard. It's not so any more. There are so many hungry institutions, so many worthwhile projects, so many development officers knocking on the door, that foundation executives have had to raise the drawbridge in self-defense. In short, the day of the New York junket is over. Ask any development officer who gets no further than the receptionist's desk at a previously friendly foundation, or who has tried in vain to line up a series of foundation visits "just to get acquainted."

Some foundations no longer grant personal interviews for any reason, but most will do so *by appointment* and usually after discussions that set forth the purpose of the meeting. Some foundations will visit with you only if they have invited you to submit a proposal. A still smaller number will make a site visit after your proposal has been submitted, and some may ask for a site visit in connection with an initiative of their own, unrelated to any specific request from you.

Even if a foundation officer grants an interview, it may not really be necessary. Try using the telephone first to explore mutual interests and to discover if the foundation officer or trustees would like to make an appointment. Through a phone call you can also get guidance from the foundation in establishing a timetable; you can learn when you should submit a proposal or if you should submit one at all. Save everyone's time—and your own airfare—by taking care of the groundwork first with a phone call.

Foundation executives have undergone an evolution in their thinking about capital giving. If your institution is in a campaign mode or planning a campaign, you are probably aware that foundations that make grants for capital purposes—"bricks and mortar" and equipment—are becoming more and more elusive. Some foundations have retreated from this area because the tremendous rise in construction costs reduces their impact on the overall project. A $200,000 grant toward construction of a $4 million building meant more, 15 or 20 years ago, than that same grant toward a similar building that now costs $15 million. But some large national foundations—Kresge and Olin are two of the best-known—still give toward capital projects. And local foundations are a good source for smaller capital grants.

In fact, capital grants were the second highest category of eight categories of foundation support, according to the 1986 *Foundation Grants Index* (see Table 1). Foundations gave over $570 million, or 25.7 percent of all dollars awarded by foundations, for capital support.[4] The intense competition for these grants is making them seem rare. Indeed, for an institution seeking a high volume of support but without impressive name recognition and reputation, a significant capital grant can be an impossible dream.

As you prepare to seek capital funds, keep yourself in the competition by making sure that you have the answers to questions relating to your institutional mission: How will this building (or equipment) further your institution's pursuit of excellence in its chosen areas of strength? How have your programs evolved—in both quality and quantity—to lead your institution to this need? The foundation will want to learn how your institutional identity has attracted more and better programs, broader affiliations, increased numbers of students, and so on, as it has moved down its defined path.

Foundations that make large grants for capital purposes are interested in all phases of the building plan and construction. An intelligent, cost-efficient design is your first major hurdle toward finding a foundation partner; with so many demands on their resources, foundations are very wary of waste and very good at spotting a too-elegant or an ill-conceived design.

Although funds for endowment are frequently one of the priorities of a major capital campaign, private foundations are usually not sources for them. Foundations generally want more impact from their investment than can be realized by expenditure of endowment income. And because foundations are themselves endowments, they are usually not excited by the prospect of transferring their assets to another pool of funds. They seek a more active role in making their money work.

Statistics published in the 1986 edition of the *Foundation Grants Index* (Table 1), however, seem to contradict this generalization. According to that report, almost $212 million was given by all types of foundations to endowment in 1986, representing 9.6 percent of all foundation dollars awarded. But a footnote to the statistic states:

> Grants in the endowment category, despite the increase over last year, continue to represent a relatively small proportion of the grants reported; these tend to be comparatively large grants made on a one-time basis to specific institutions.[5]

In contrast to capital campaigns, which seek funds for specific projects, solicitations to private foundations are for general or operating support, defined by the

Table 1: Type of Support Awarded

Type of support	Dollar value of grants	Percent of total
Capital support	$ 570,107,420	25.7
Continuing support	550,145,614	24.8
Endowments	211,885,474	9.6
Fellowships and scholarships	126,222,348	5.7
General/operating funds	280,197,552	12.6
Matching/challenge grants	180,532,635	8.1
Program development	832,659,455	37.6
Research	306,590,704	13.8
Total grants reported	$2,216,647,033	

Adapted from Foundation Grants Index, *1986 ed. Note: Because some grants are included in more than one category (e.g., a challenge grant for construction), total percents equal more than 100, and totals for types of support equal more than total grants reported.*

Foundation Center as grants for ongoing programs, services, or staff positions. According to the *Foundation Grants Index*, community foundations and company-sponsored foundations, both of which have a strong interest in the local community, are much more likely to give for general support than are independent foundations. Community foundations gave 15 percent of the money they awarded, and company-sponsored foundations gave 16.9 percent for general operating funds; in contrast, of the money awarded by independent foundations, only 7.7 percent was allocated to this category.[6]

The reason for this is, again, that providing general operating funds doesn't give much "bang for the buck." Private foundations are generally not interested in keeping your steam plant running, paying faculty salaries, or balancing your budget in times of crisis. Local foundations, whose trustees have close personal ties to your institution, can be exceptions to this rule. But in any case, foundations are not appropriate targets for your annual appeal.

If the foundation and its trustees are all old friends, you could send a special letter of request *in time for the foundation's board meeting,* but don't assume that your long-standing relationship will necessarily bear fruit. Even old, faithful foundation friends have new demands on their resources every year.

What types of programs have special appeal to a foundation? As Table 1 shows, 8.1 percent of all foundation grant dollars were designated as matching or challenge grants in 1986. While this figure does not seem very large, it indicates a trend:

> The percentage of matching and challenging grants increased from 2 percent of the number of grants reported in 1980 to 4.2 percent in the current reporting year. This increase reflects the growing interest among grantmakers and grantseekers in using foundation dollars as leverage for building their financial support base.[7]

Several large foundations—most notably the Kresge Foundation—have used challenge grants, with enormous success, to generate other donations and to inspire recipients to more vigorous fund-raising efforts.

Another trend in foundation giving, and one not reflected in the statistics quoted so far, is to support interdisciplinary and interinstitutional programs. If you look at foundation-initiated programs over the past several years, you will see that foundations are in tune with the new scientific trend of combining the learning of several disciplines in order to understand a problem. The study of some medical problems—and AIDS is the prime example—involves specialists from many different disciplines. We are also seeing a renewed interest in bringing together scholars in various areas of the humanities to shed light on artistic, social, and psychological issues.

Programs that involve more than one institution are popular with foundations as a way to expand the effectiveness of a grant. Even small, local social service agencies can combine efforts and attract larger foundation grants, and for more effective programs, than their individual efforts could have garnered.

Your hard-earned foundation grant can be the beginning of increased attention from other foundations and donors; this is especially true if you have gained support for a well-conducted interdisciplinary or interinstitutional program. But success breeds success in another way too. If you look at the 1986 statistics in Table 1, you see that grants awarded for continuing support amounted to over $550 million, 24.8 percent of all grant dollars awarded and not far behind capital grants as a grant-making category. Continuing support is defined as "renewal grants to the same organization or program."[8] Proving yourself to a foundation is no guarantee of additional grants from that source, but good stewardship should at least ensure you a receptive audience.

Internal goal setting

No matter how small your institution, an important tool for you as a development officer is the annual program plan. Keep on track during the year by outlining your proposed contacts and establishing a timetable for the submission of proposals and for the payout of grants. But don't be too eager to count your foundation money; foundation grants typically have a long gestation period. Initial contact to grant approval can take from several months to several years.

Research, records, and tracking

Although a discussion of research comes at the end of this chapter, research should be your first step, preceding any contact with a foundation. Without this vitally important first step, you will be wasting your own energies as well as the foundation's time with inappropriate requests.

As you research foundations, your goal is to build your own in-house library of materials relating to previous and prospective foundation donors. There are many fine resource books available through the Foundation Center, Taft, and other companies, and these can be invaluable. If your institution seeks support from national foundations, the various newsletters, designed to inform you of changes in leadership or direction and the birth of new foundations, should also be a part of your library. (See the bibliography for a list of resources for research.)

For an in-depth understanding of a foundation's philosophy and programs, however, there is no substitute for its annual report. For small foundations that do not publish an annual report or even a brochure, the IRS return (Form 990) is the only published source. The 990 lists officers and trustees, grants paid out during the past fiscal year, and new grants awarded. IRS returns can be obtained through the Foundation Center or a regional Foundation Center library (see pp. 87-90).

How you manage this flow of information depends on the size of your institution. Some large universities have purchased key-word database systems that allow them to hone in on possible foundation sources for both faculty research projects and institutional programs. Smaller institutions can rely on word-processors to summarize information.

In studying your own needs, remember that information collected indiscriminately, or not properly disseminated once collected, can bury you. The information must get to you in a form that you can comprehend and use; before you phone a foundation, or visit one, you need to have read everything published by that foundation and any information about it in the various directories. The foundation will expect you to have done this as a preliminary to any discussion.

You also need to establish an internal tracking system to monitor activity with all prospects, including foundations. This tracking system accomplishes several purposes:

- it keeps the solicitation process moving forward;
- it tells all fund raisers in your institution who is doing what, so that multiple or conflicting approaches to a foundation can be avoided;
- it informs your "bosses"—the president, the dean, the vice president—of all development activity (thus justifying your budget, or so you hope); and
- it serves as a convenient record of proposals rejected and accepted when the time comes to evaluate the institution's fund-raising programs.

A tracking chart can create good team spirit too. It prompts your fund raisers to sit down and talk out their individual strategies with foundation prospects. This should result in the best possible project being submitted to a foundation with the understanding (if not the agreement) of everyone involved.

In conclusion, the work involved in gaining foundation support can be awesome. But it is work that will lead your institution to see itself in new ways, to strengthen its fund-raising team, to study its information management systems, and to see itself in relation to new competitors and higher standards of excellence. It's well worth the effort.

Notes

[1] Thomas E. Broce, *Fund Raising: The Guide to Raising Money from Private Sources,* 2d ed. rev. (Norman, OK: University of Oklahoma Press, 1986), p. 109.

[2] Waldemar A. Nielsen, *The Golden Donors* (New York: Truman Talley Books, E.P. Dutton, 1985), p. 434.

[3] David F. Freeman, *The Handbook on Private Foundations* (Washington, DC: Council on Foundations, 1981), p. 75.

[4] Clinton, John, ed., *The Foundation Grants Index,* 16th ed. (New York: The Foundation Center, 1987), p. xiii.

[5] Ibid.

[6] Ibid., p. xx.

[7] Ibid., p. xiv.

[8] Ibid., p. xiii.

Chapter 22

Special Issues for Independent Schools Seeking Foundation Support

Virginia D. Howard
Director of Development
The Potomac School

H ow much time should we in independent schools spend researching foundations and writing foundation proposals? While few foundations state in their guidelines support to independent schools as an interest, in this chapter we expore what kinds of foundations under what circumstances might be interested in your school. When time allows, or volunteers are available for research, after annual giving and special event responsibilities are successfully underway, uncovering foundation support for your school's programs can be most exciting.

Exploring the foundation world

National foundations. National foundations offer only limited support to independent schools, especially elementary schools. Only four national foundations consistently support independent secondary schools, and none support elementary schools. The support offered by these foundations is fairly specific and is directed toward certain programs or capital purposes:

• The Edward E. Ford Foundation typically offers challenge or matching grants for capital purposes for endowment and buildings, as well as seed money, equipment, and some scholarship and special projects awards. Grants range from $15,000 to $35,000.

• The Independence Foundation awards grants primarily in the area of student financial aid, especially in the form of student loan funds ranging from $2,000 to $100,000.

• The William R. Kenan, Jr., Charitable Trust gives no grants to day schools and limits secondary school giving to the schools in the eastern seaboard states. For a number of years it has provided a matching fund to the Summer Institute for Newcomers in Advancement, a Council for Advancement and Support of Education (CASE) program. This support reduces participant costs by half.

• The Geraldine R. Dodge Foundation, Inc., concentrates grants to secondary independent schools in the New England and the Middle Atlantic states, and to support projects leading to significant advances in secondary education. Most recently, its grants have supported programs in Chinese studies.

Other national foundations may be responsive if the project for which you seek funding is within their overall guidelines or if your institution has a personal connection through the parent body or the board of trustees, for instance. If you or someone on your board has a business relationship or personal friendship with a member of a foundation's board, this can open the door to consideration of a proposal that would otherwise have been eliminated.

Local foundations. Follow the same strategy with local foundations. Get to know who they are and what projects interest them. Your prospects for support are greater from this group of foundations than from most others. They are concerned about the community served by your school and are often interested in helping your institution broaden its service (e.g., scholarship funding) within that community or in providing seed money for projects that will be. fit the larger community (e.g., summer camps).

Most metropolitan communities publish community directories from which you can obtain names of foundation directors, as well as guidelines for areas of interest and submission of proposals. Again, get to know the executive directors of these community foundations and identify any personal contacts that may exist between your school constituency and the foundation.

Family foundations. Family foundations derive their funds from members of a single family. Generally, family members serve as officers or board members of the foundation and play a key role in grant-making decisions. If a member of the board of directors or the founding donor has a direct family relationship to a student or alumnus at your school, or is otherwise involved in some way, your potential for support is excellent.

Whether such a foundation is national or local, the family tie gives you the opportunity to approach it for support regardless of what the formal guidelines may designate. Don't be discouraged if your initial research reveals that the foundation designates only a particular state for support; the family relationship is often the overriding factor in the decision to make a grant.

Corporate foundations. Corporate foundations give little or no support to independent schools. They are interested in funding research programs at an academic level our students have not attained. They may provide support, particularly gifts of service, or gifts in kind, if the school is located near the corporate head-quarters and a number of employees' children attend. If any member of your school constituency is a CEO of a local company, he or she may be willing to ask neighboring companies to join in providing a small amount of funding, up to $5,000, for example. When peers ask peers to give, no proposal need be written but only a simple letter from one company executive to the other will suffice.

If your school has no such relationship with a corporation's CEO or board of directors, there is little point in approaching that particular company. Many do, however, support independent schools through matching gifts. CASE's Independent Schools Corporate Matching Gifts Initiative program has encouraged many companies to expand their matching gifts to secondary and elementary schools. Corporations move slowly, but your school should be seeing an increase in this type of corporate support in the future.

Foundations with which you have already established a personal, family, or business relationship are going to be the best resource for your school, whether they are local or national.

Enlisting volunteer leadership

The members of the board of trustees constitute the primary volunteer leadership of an independent school. These men and women not only set policies for our institutions, but also provide excellent business and social contacts within our communities and throughout the country. It is important, therefore, that you make them aware of the value of their personal foundation contacts.

Start by giving them a list of community foundation boards and asking them to review possible associations. Often board members have ties with other communities as well, either through their professional lives or through family connections. A member of the board of a school in Virginia, for instance, may hail from Texas where he or she still has family with possible connections to Texas-based foundations.

Parents and alumni of your school may also have important connections. A parent profile for parents of new students should include the question, "Do you serve on a foundation board or can you provide contacts with any foundation?" From time to time, you can send out an alumni questionnaire, perhaps in connection with the creation of an alumni directory, which asks the same question. Ask married women in both groups to put down their maiden names. These may give you leads to foundation contacts.

You may be in for some pleasant surprises. Your school may receive a check for the annual fund written on the account of a family charitable trust representing a foundation you hadn't approached and, in fact, didn't know about. Even if the gift is a modest one, it can alert you to other possibilities, including important contacts this donor may have.

Once you have identified a connection between a member of your school constituency and a foundation, you need to enlist that contact person as a volunteer.

Meet with him or her to review which of your school's areas of need might be of interest to the foundation. You will probably want the contact person to go with you to meet the foundation's executive director to ask the appropriate questions.

When anyone within your constituency identifies himself or herself as having a foundation connection, it probably means that that person is willing to help you approach the foundation for funds. Ask the volunteer to call the foundation and set a time when he or she can take you to meet with the contact. At this meeting, you can ask the contact what the next step should be.

Stay in close touch with your volunteer throughout the process of meeting, proposal writing, review, submission, and follow-up. Whether or not you get the grant, keep the volunteer informed, make him or her feel especially good about helping you in this endeavor, and add a personal thanks to the school's thank-you for the foundation's consideration of the proposal. Remember, keeping your volunteer closely involved in the grant seeking will not only make a good friend for your institution now but a valuable resource for your school in the future.

The importance of nurturing volunteers cannot be overstated. If the grant application succeeds, the volunteer gets the credit; if the grant is denied, the volunteer is made to feel appreciated for his or her effort. The time the volunteer has spent helping you is valuable time—don't waste it. The benefits to your school in funding and in good public relations are incalculable—don't lose them. Independent school development programs are only as good as the volunteer support they generate. Providing communication between your school and a foundation is one of the most effective uses of volunteer time.

Who will do it?

If you run a one-person shop at an independent school, be warned that foundation grants don't just happen. It takes time to develop contacts and to write proposals. A person who focuses on those programs that provide the greatest, most immediate return of income to the school will have little time for anything else. If your board hopes to generate foundation support, you will need additional staff or a volunteer who is able to take that job on as a primary responsibility.

A development office with sufficient staffing may be able to adjust responsibilities within the office so that one staff member can undertake the foundation work part-time. He or she should set aside a certain number of hours each week for foundation research, proposal writing, and the other chores of foundation fund raising. The staff member also needs to have direct access to members of the board and to all development records.

If you don't have enough staff for this arrangement, you may be able to find volunteers to help with research, proposal writing, and follow-up. The board's development committee might include a person willing to take responsibility for the kinds of research and follow-up necessary to generate foundation support. All the better if this person is a foundation director or a member of a foundation board or someone well-connected in the local foundation community. If there is a parent or local alumnus particularly suited for this volunteer role, you might ask him or her to join the development committee expressly for this purpose.

An elementary school should not spend a great deal of staff time and energy in search of foundation grants. Any efforts spent should be devoted to local community foundations that have demonstrated an interest in the school or family foundations with a direct relationship to the school. Corporate foundation support to elementary schools is almost nonexistent and when it comes at all is often in the form of "in-kind" gifts of services.

If your staff or volunteer time is limited, consider buying a COMSEARCH printout, identifying the foundations that have made grants to elementary and secondary schools in the prior year (COMSEARCH printout, *Grants for Elementary and Secondary Education,* is available for $40 from the Foundation Center, 79 Fifth Ave., New York, NY 10003, or call toll-free (800) 424-9836). This useful document can save hours of research time and help focus attention on interests and grant size of those foundations. In addition, I recommend that you buy the annual *Foundation Directory* as an initial resource book for researching connections to individuals serving on foundation boards.

Role of the head

While the primary role of the head of an independent school is to be chief administrator of the institution's academic affairs, he or she must also take a considerable part in meeting today's greatest challenge—finding the voluntary support to provide excellence in academic programs, maintain and add buildings, and create endowments, while holding tuitions to affordable levels.

Many school heads have no training in the "art" of fund raising and have undertaken it reluctantly. Even the most reluctant head, however, enjoys promoting the school or describing a program vital to the school's growth.

But be sure to involve your school head wisely and well. He or she is a busy person and should only be asked to help when you believe such assistance will favorably influence the result. For example, the head could initiate a foundation contact by inviting the executive director to the school for a tour and lunch with the board chair or academic department head of the program for which you are seeking funding. The head may travel with you to the foundation's home office to meet with the executive director.

This type of marketing to foundations is appropriate to the head. It is your job as development officer to brief him or her before the meeting on what type of support the foundation might consider and the range of grant size realistically possible.

You or the staff member or volunteer responsible for foundation support should meet every month with the head to keep abreast of the school's needs and to share information about possible foundation contacts. These meetings will help you determine who will initiate communication with the foundation. The head, representing the school at its highest level, can be most helpful by meeting with the director of the foundation to articulate the school's needs.

The school head should also be alert to possible contacts with the foundation world as he or she meets with constituents; he or she can ask other school heads about foundation support their schools have received and report the information to the development officer.

The headmaster or headmistress of your school often signs the cover letter that goes with the proposal. He or she should also sign the letter thanking the foundation for the grant or (if the grant is not made) for considering the proposal. If the grant is received, the head should sign the follow-up reports that detail how the grant monies were used.

Summary

While private and corporate foundation funding to independent schools is not large, it is significant enough to be worth attention and effort from the development office staff, the board, volunteers, and the school head. Foundation support for our schools will undoubtedly increase if we continue to make ourselves heard. Just remember, if you don't ask, you won't be considered. Know where to ask, what to ask for, how best to ask, and who should ask.

Then you need to thank, to report, and to ask again!

Reference Sources

Broce, Thomas E. *Fund Raising: The Guide to Raising Money from Private Sources,* 2d ed. rev. Norman, OK: University of Oklahoma Press, 1986.

The Foundation Grants Index, 16th ed. Clinton, John, ed. New York: The Foundation Center, 1987.

Freeman, David F. *The Handbook on Private Foundations.* Washington, DC: Council on Foundations, 1981.

Nielsen, Waldemar A. *The Golden Donors.* New York: Truman Talley Books, E.P. Dutton, 1985.

Chapter 23

Fund Raising at Historically Black Colleges: Diversity Endangered

Donald L. Hense
Vice President for Development
National Urban League

(Formerly Vice President for Development and University Relations
Prairie View A&M University)

In the spring of 1987 the Smithsonian Institution mounted "Diversity Endangered," a major poster exhibition to reawaken public interest in the preservation of the world environment. To make the case for the value of plant and animal life, the exhibit contained this caption:

> A full 40 percent of all prescription drugs contain active ingredients originally derived from wild plants and animals...contributing an estimated $40 billion a year to international trade....

The value of the environment should need no such defense. Yet it does—and similarly other seemingly obvious "goods" in our society need a champion when national priorities are being set.

The value of historically black colleges and universities has been so well-documented throughout their history that there would seem to be no need to restate that case. Yet since the advent of "equal opportunity," the debate on black colleges has rarely focused on that value even on the sporadic occasions when these institutions have occupied national attention.

In the United States today, interest in equal educational opportunity is not in vogue. As Stephen Graubard says, "Each crisis seems to have its year...each enjoys attention for the moment, receding into obscurity, not because specific problems have been solved, but because public attention wandered on to something new...."[1] That inattention, that indifference—as with the environment—endangers the diversity of this country's system of higher education and particularly endangers the role of historically black colleges in preserving and expanding that diversity.

The challenge of diversity

In recent years, the National Academy of Sciences and the National Science Foundation have documented critical shortcomings in precollege and undergraduate education (particularly in the sciences, mathematics, and engineering) and how these shortcomings appear to have contributed to the decline of the United States' competitive position in international trade. The post-Sputnik manpower assessment added two additional variables to be considered in the manpower equation: There is a documented decline in the number of white males who pass through our educational system to assume positions in education and industry. Concomitantly, there is an increase in the number of minorities and women who must be trained to fulfill the manpower needs of the country.

Thus, the debate in higher education should never focus on whether or not we need black colleges but on whether we need *any* college or university that does not strive for educational excellence.

The accelerating demographic changes in our society—especially the growth of the Hispanic population in major cities and in the southern states—present unique challenges to all of higher education. To meet these challenges, this nation will continue to need historically black colleges committed to educating our citizens. For as long as there are students, and for as long as those students are provided programs of excellence that enable them to grow intellectually and personally, the need for—and thus the survival of—the historically black college is assured.

The need for a diverse higher education system to serve a diverse population also presents a unique opportunity for this country's philanthropic community, particularly those foundations that have traditionally sought out, and assisted in, the development of innovative programs and curricula. Black colleges must convince foundations that their missions are clearly defined for the populations they choose to serve, and that the programs they have developed, as well as those they will develop in the future, meet the test of competitiveness within the total academic community.

The planning process: A tool to address the challenge of diversity from within

In an environment of change, quality planning becomes crucial. At a recent meeting in Washington, D.C., the Association of Fund Raising Officers invited three people to address the role of planning at their colleges: a president-elect of a black college, a recently elected president, and a seasoned veteran. For most of the workshop, these speakers gave textbook views of the higher education planning process with little discussion of how those views were being implemented. Nebulous activity disguised as planning won't help an institution address the challenges of diversity.

Institutional planning should ultimately shape institutional behavior as well as individual behavior. With strong presidential leadership, the plan should be the joint effort of trustees, faculty, students, and administrators. Alumni, parents, and friends of the college should also be provided some means of legitimate input. The best institutions are not afraid to seek advice from academic specialists, community leaders, and foundation executives in developing a legitimate long-range plan. A foundation is more likely to invest in a specific project if it emanates from well-thought-out institutional priorities, particularly if the foundation has had some input in the development of these priorities.

The model for long-range planning that works best at your institution may be one you developed yourself or it may be adapted from any described in the many publications available on the subject. William Pickett, president of Saint John Fisher College, suggests five essential questions a plan should address:

1. Where are we?
2. How did we get here?
3. Where are we going?
4. Where do we want to go?
5. How do we get there?[2]

If an institution provides for legitimate input from its various constituencies, the planning process accomplishes several things: First, individuals within the institution will take pride in having played an active role in determining its future. Second, the institution will solidify its relationships with many individuals in the community, in corporations, and in foundations who have confidence in the integrity of a planning process that had significant input from the "real world." And finally, a sound document will emerge with many supporters who are prepared to translate the plan into fundable projects to enhance the institution's academic program.

Translating institutional priorities into fundable projects: The need for fund-raising professionals

The literature of advancement addresses the role in the fund-raising process of each of the various constituencies of the institution: Trustees make contact with their peers in industry and in foundations on behalf of the institution; the president—as the chief advancement officer—articulates a vision of the institution; the development officer translates the president's vision into fundable proposals and appropriate programs. Rarely, however, do the articles or books address the reality of implementing small college development programs.

My experience as a consultant to many small colleges suggests that few trustees actively participate in fund raising. Most perceive themselves, particularly if they are alumni, as guardians of institutional traditions or as "containment" officers for the president. Many presidents have had little experience in academic fund raising nor have they had the time to expose themselves to the principles and techniques of the art. And in many cases, the development officer at a small college got "promoted" from the coaching staff because he was well-known to alumni, or he or she is a former dean or department chair being gently "put out to pasture." In such a situation, institutional fund-raising efforts are unlikely to have much success.

For this reason, the institutional development plan should focus on the need to staff the development office with serious full-time professionals. These men and women must have a good knowledge of the fundamentals of institutional advancement as well as the willingness and the resources to seek out and take advantage of continuing professional development opportunities.

Good prospect research is essential

If the trained development officer is the vehicle for the successful marketing of your institution's projects to foundations, good research is the motor. Stories abound in the academic community of the helter-skelter approaches used by some institutions to solicit funds. As resources become more scarce, it becomes less and less likely that these methods will succeed.

Before you approach a foundation, you must have done your homework. Even if your development office is a one-person shop, you should have access to appropriate periodicals, publications, directories, and memberships. Resources such as the publications of the Foundation Center, the Taft Group, and Marquis are *the* basic tools. If you have a more sophisticated program, you'll need access to specialized publications that provide grants resource information according to academic discipline. Access to on-line databases such as IRIS or DIALOG will save you time and money.

You should also get to know colleagues at colleges and universities that are successful in foundation fund raising; don't hesitate to seek their advice about specific targets. Become part of a network and use it. When a foundation is about to develop a new program area, you won't read about it in the standard works. That information becomes "official" or public only after the first round of grants has been made.

Development councils

In the more than 15 years I have spent in academic fund raising, I have discovered that nothing is lonelier or less rewarding than attempting, by myself, to interpret institutional priorities into fundable proposals. This cannot be done in isolation.

Early on I became an advocate of college or university development councils. At Prairie View A&M, the vice president for development chairs a development council composed of the vice presidents of the various divisions and the academic deans. In a small college, the president might chair a council composed of the development officer, deans, key department chairs, and the best faculty. Consultants and other faculty should be brought in as project specialties dictate.

The development council should meet as often as necessary to develop an effective funding strategy to accomplish key elements of the institution's plan. The council should seek to identify clearly the goals, objectives, and target population of each project for which funding is needed so that the development officer, as the key staff person, can provide sound research on funding sources whose priorities match as closely as possible.

The council should then rate potential funding sources according to suitability and develop a systematic plan for the cultivation and solicitation of the top prospects. Critical to this process is control; any contact with a prospect should be reported and recorded at a central source. The development officer can review these records prior to a council meeting to consider funding for a specific project. The records should also include incidental contact with funding source representatives at professional meetings and social gatherings. Records of written or personal contacts should be permanently maintained with the giving history of the individual, corporation, or foundation.

In persuading others to use this system, the development office must convey the value of approaching a donor with a complete history of the donor's involvement with the institution. This prevents making approaches that are likely to be turned down because they don't fit within the donor's priorities. Donors appreciate the continuity and the professionalism.

Developing a cultivation strategy provides you with a great opportunity to consult all the people who participated in developing the planning document— trustees, community people, corporate and foundation executives, and alumni. Whenever possible, even if it requires more work—and it usually does—you should attempt to involve these "volunteers" actively in the cultivation process. Well-prepared volunteers speaking on behalf of the institution and a specific project can be your most effective salespersons. The mere fact of their participation demonstrates that "outsiders" believe in the institution and the project for which funds are being requested.

In the cultivation and solicitation process, the clear articulation of mission, the planning, and the setting of priorities are all brought to bear on the project. And you can learn a lot in this stage. For this reason, if at all possible, write the final proposal after cultivation and solicitation have taken place so that you can incorporate new information in the document.

The proposal

The proposal should reflect the mission, the planning, and the establishment of priorities. Always place the specific project in the larger context so that both project and its context are clearly related to the goals or needs of the institution.

Foundations publish their goals and needs in program guidelines; corporations, in their annual reports; while those of individuals must be deduced from their interests, personal commitments, and professional activities.

Many existing works outline the format a proposal should follow, and I won't attempt to repeat these excellent materials. However, the one element they often overlook is the importance of establishing a broad enough context for the project. Recipients of a proposal must know clearly why the institution has made the project a priority and why they should make it one also.

When you write a proposal, remember that it is hard to give funds away *well*. If your proposal is to succeed, you must be convinced—and your proposal must show it—that you are giving the donor a rare opportunity: a chance to exercise philanthropy in a meaningful way and for a meaningful cause.

Stewardship

The proposal itself is only a small part of the grantsmanship process. By the time you sit down to write the proposal, you, your staff, and your volunteers have already spent a lot of time in the planning and cultivation process. Going through that process and submitting the proposal provide your institution with a golden opportunity for stewardship—whether or not the proposal is funded.

If your proposal is not funded, don't drop the foundation from your list. Consider the rejection as an opportunity to further the relationship and to plan for your next approach. Set the stage by asking for a review of your proposal in writing or by personal appointment. Follow up with telephone conversations about the weaknesses and strengths of the document. Ask the funding source to provide you with technical assistance. But most of all, express your continued appreciation that the foundation considered your institution in its funding process. You may be more successful the next time around.

If your proposal is funded, your goal is not just to use the money wisely, but to use it so well that you will be able to ask the funding agency to invest in the continuation of your project or—better yet—to assist in developing another institutional priority.

An important element in stewardship is to keep the foundation fully informed as to how its funds are being used. One way to do this is to develop a newsletter that reports on the activities funded by the grant. Send the newsletter to the foundation and to others who might be interested in the development of your academic programs. The institution will benefit from the additional publicity, and the funding agency will have its name continuously associated with a project having a positive impact at the institution.

Stewardship also gives you the opportunity to develop a personal relationship with officials of funding agencies. Invite the program officers to your campus to see the direct benefits of their investment. Let them talk to students and faculty who have benefited from programs supported by their funds. Provide them with a forum to talk about their goals and objectives. Invite them to special events, such as convocation or graduation exercises, where they will meet other supporters of your institution. But most important of all, use the funds for the purpose outlined in your proposal, and file complete and timely financial statements.

Conclusion

While we in higher education face many obstacles as we strive to meet the challenges of diversity, we also have many opportunities to integrate people and institutions to meet the requirements of our technological age. The needs of tomorrow's world require that we make significant changes in our educational system to address the challenges presented by a rapidly changing technology and a more diverse population. Only America's position in the global economy in the year 2000 will tell how well we have succeeded.

My special thanks to Gregory Smith Prince, Valerie Lockett, and Edith Chapman for their guidance and assistance in this chapter.

Notes

[1] Stephen R. Graubard, "Thoughts on Higher Educational Purposes and Goals: A Memorandum," *Daedalus,* Fall 1974, p. 2.

[2] William L. Pickett, "The Long-range Planning Process," in *The Successful Capital Campaign: From Planning to Victory Celebration,* ed. H. Gerald Quigg (Washington, DC: Council for Advancement and Support of Education, 1986), p. 10.

Chapter 24

Private Foundation Support for Public Colleges and Universities

Bradford Choate
Director
Corporate/Foundation Relations
The Ohio State University

A s public institutions become more aggressive in their fund-raising efforts, they must put more effort into foundation grant seeking than they have in the past. Traditionally, public institutions have focused their fund-raising efforts on alumni and corporate programs. But today the potential for foundation support to public higher education is very good and getting even better. Although the headlines often announce multimillion dollar foundation programs with captions that read, "Publicly assisted universities and colleges need not apply," trends indicate that the virtual lock private institutions have held on foundation giving may be breaking.

Foundations are becoming more focused in their gift making. And as they focus their giving on narrower issues, giving to publics should increase. Public institutions, especially the large land-grant institutions, are well suited to address the major issues of today's world. If these institutions aggressively pursue foundation giving, they will win the resources they need to attain their missions.

All too often development people at public institutions say, "Foundations will not give to publics so why waste my time?" "It is not worth the effort to go after foundation gifts." "Foundations will not give to the kind of projects we need funded so why bother?" These people are living in the past. The world of foundation giving is changing. It is changing slowly, but it is changing. Those public institutions that understand the change and are aggressive in their fund-raising endeavors will be successful in receiving increased foundation giving.

If you represent a public institution, this chapter will give you a rationale for aggressively pursuing foundation giving to your college or university. If you work for a private institution, I should warn you that I plan to examine—and destroy—some myths that are all too prevalent in the world of foundation grant seeking.

Destroying the myths

When we say an institution is "public" or "private," we are referring to the sources of income that support it. But it might be more accurate if we used these terms to refer to the *control* of the institution rather than its financing. Private colleges and universities have privately appointed boards that control the institution while publics have publicly appointed or, in some cases, elected governing boards.

Most state-assisted institutions do not rely solely on public money to achieve their missions. It is equally true that private institutions do not rely solely on private dollars for survival. Clearly, state-assisted institutions on the whole receive more support from tax dollars than do their private counterparts. Overall, state appropriations to publics far outpace those to privates. This is not to say that private institutions are not receiving significant tax-dollar support.

In fiscal year 1984, for example, federal support comprised over 25 percent of the budget of the private doctoral institutions of this country. At a time when 78 percent of the nation's college students attended public institutions, $3.7 billion in federal grants, contracts, and appropriation support went to private doctoral institutions while $3.3 billion went to public universities.[1]

Much of the federal support to privates was for research. In fiscal year 1985, seven of the top 10 universities receiving federal research and development support were private universities, including the top three (see Table 1 on p. 189).

It can be argued that a typical major private research university receives approximately 45 percent of its income from tax dollars: 15 percent from state sources and 30 percent from federal sources. A typical major public research university also receives approximately 45 percent of its income from tax dollars: 30 percent from state sources and 15 percent from the federal government.

The myth that publics live on tax dollars alone and privates need only private gifts to maintain their programs may have been true in the past. But today all but a small percentage of the private institutions could not survive as they do without tax support, whether in the form of grants and contracts or student financial aid. Conversely, public institutions could not meet the demands being placed upon them by society without private support combined with government support.

The changing foundation scene

What does all of this have to do with the future of foundation giving to higher education? The myth is that publics depend on public funds and privates depend on private funds; the reality is that major universities, both public and private, depend on public funds. The myth is that foundations support only private institutions; the reality is that more and more foundations want to support the best programs, scholars, and departments, regardless of whether they are at public or private institutions. This puts a very real responsibility on development professionals at public colleges and universities to pursue aggressively foundation support for their institutions' goals.

Slowly, but clearly, foundations are following the course set by corporate philanthropists and are increasing giving to public institutions. When the Standard Oils and General Motors of the corporate world first came to the aid of higher education, it was to support private education. For many years, most corporations specifically prohibited giving to "tax-supported" institutions, but by 1985-86, corporate giving was split almost equally between publics and privates. In today's corporate giving world, virtually every corporation in America that contributes to higher education will give to public institutions.

Obviously, corporations did not intend to set as a goal balanced giving to publics and privates. Rather, it was a result of gifts made to accomplish specific results, whether it be scholarship, research, or corporate social responsibility. Corporate donors joined with institutions that were best able to help achieve their goals. In the United States today, corporations have obviously found equally competent universities and colleges on both sides of the public/private fence.

Even though foundation giving to public institutions is increasing, foundations have a long way to go to reach the balance that corporate philanthropists have achieved. While the tradition of foundation giving to higher education is similar to that of corporate philanthropy, foundations have been slower to include public institutions.

Table 2 on p. 190 lists the top 20 universities reporting foundation support in 1986-87. Only five of the top 20 are public institutions. However, contributions to private institutions as a percentage of foundation giving have been declining. The tenth edition of the *Foundation Directory* reported that "Private universities and colleges show the largest decline in the percentage of dollars reported, but allocations for public universities have shown a slight increase."[2]

The desire of foundations to focus their giving programs in order to have a larger impact on society has led them to identify specific areas of interest. As foundations identify the problems they wish to address, they also begin to identify the institutions that can help with those problems. Those institutions that can best work with foundations to solve the identified problems will have the best chance of receiving foundation support.

As foundations become more and more interested in making gifts for specific projects and special-interest areas, the numbers of dollars to the large publics will probably continue to increase. The fact that foundations are moving from contributions for general purposes to contributions for specific projects and special-interest areas may be one reason for the decline in the percentage of foundation dollars to private institutions and the increase to publics. Clearly this is not the only factor leading to change, but it does play a role.

Public colleges and universities are much more involved in fund raising than ever before. As a group, publics were slow to enter the world of private fund raising, and foundations are one of the last constituencies to be seriously solicited. Now many publics are beginning to solicit foundations aggressively, much as they have corporations. This activity is also a major factor for the rise in the percentage of foundation giving to publics versus privates.

This change occurs at a time when foundation giving as a percentage of total giving to higher education is declining. In 1980, foundations provided 23.8 percent of the total voluntary support to education, but this figure dropped every year thereafter, reaching 16.0 percent in 1986. The large, comprehensive public universities will be among the primary recipients of increased foundation support for specific projects and special-interest areas. The rationale for this can be seen in the remarks of Edward H. Jennings, president of The Ohio State University:

> We are well-positioned to respond to the nature of scholarly activity that is changing rapidly and radically. Where else but in a large comprehensive university can society expect progress in biotechnology, which must draw together individuals within the biological sciences, business, chemistry, geology, mathematics, engineering and agriculture?
>
> Where else can society realistically place its hopes for cures for all forms of cancer, when the research involves disciplines as far-ranging as veterinary medicine, genetics, social work, computer science, and all of the health sciences?
>
> Where else can society seek deeper understanding among the diverse peoples of our planet, when such knowledge depends upon the shared research of historians, language professors, geographers, artists, economists, anthropologists, and poets?[3]

As foundations continue to focus their resources on narrow objectives, the large, comprehensive public institutions appear best suited to meet these needs. The few large, comprehensive private institutions will also gain from this trend, but by and large the percentage of foundation dollars to privates will continue to decline while the percentage to publics will continue to increase. The question foundations are asking now and will continue to ask is, "Which institutions can deliver on our stated objectives?" The fact that an institution is publicly or privately controlled will be virtually irrelevant.

Opportunity

In recent years, corporations have become larger donors to higher education than foundations (see Table 3 on p. 191). The future for corporate contributions is unclear, but many philanthropic experts and corporate leaders agree that the growth in corporate contributions will not keep pace with that of recent years. Reports from the Conference Board and the Council for Aid to Education, among others, indicate little or no growth in corporate giving in the near future.[4] If the trend for increased foundation giving to public institutions continues, and increases in corporate giving flatten, additional emphasis on foundation relations will be the rule at the publics.

Another trend of recent years is the decrease in the number of foundations being formed. New tax laws and changes in the economy are often cited as reasons for this fact. According to *America's Wealthy and the Future of Foundations:*

> Foundation formation decreased for about five years following the 1969 Tax Reform Act. Beginning in 1974 there were high levels of foundation formation during four of the next six years, but compared to the 1950s and 1960s there were fewer foundations developed with less than $149,000 and fewer created with assets of $5 million or more. The growth was in foundations with less than $1 million in assets. The first three years of the 1980s showed very few formations, though it will take a few more years to see if that trend persists.[5]

Although it cannot be documented at this point, it would appear that the rate of foundation formation has been increasing since 1984. Six-figure gifts are being made by foundations that only recently came into existence. Whether this is a trend or only coincidence is a matter that will require future study.

Public colleges and universities need to learn how to deal as effectively with foundations and their staffs as they have with corporations and corporate staff. Once public institutions begin to focus attention on foundation solicitations, it is only a matter of time before more foundations that wish to have an impact on areas of special interest realize that when they support public higher education, they can leverage their gifts for even greater impact.

By combining their private dollars with general appropriations, foundations, like other private donors to public institutions, can have a greater impact than they can achieve as the sole source of project support. For example, a $250,000 gift from a foundation can be combined with $250,000 from public sources to fund a $500,000 project. In this "win-win" scenario, the foundation not only gets public recognition for being part of a $500,000 project, it also leverages 250,000 public dollars toward its area of interest.

Although many foundations make general-purpose gifts, most now want to have an impact on a particular problem. Public universities have a tremendous opportunity to solicit foundation support by showing foundations how their funds can be leveraged with general appropriations to have an even larger impact on the issue at hand. This ability to leverage funds, combined with the capacity to bring wide-ranging talents to bear on major societal issues, make foundations and comprehensive public universities logical partners in the philanthropic world.

Notes

[1] "Report on the Future of the Comprehensive State Research Universities and Land-Grant Colleges: Project 2000" (Washington, DC: National Association of State Universities and Land-Grant Colleges, 1986), p. 5.

[2] *The Foundation Directory,* 10th ed. (New York: The Foundation Center, 1985), p. xxvii.

[3] Dr. Edward H. Jennings, address to the Harvard Club of Central Ohio, February 26, 1987, Columbus, Ohio.

[4] See Paul Desruisseaux, "Corporations' Gifts Are Unlikely to Grow This Year and May Even Fall, Board Warns," *Chronicle of Higher Education,* November 12, 1986, pp. 37, 39.

[5] Teresa J. Odendahl, ed., *America's Wealthy and the Future of Foundations* (New York: The Foundation Center, 1985), p. 82.

Table 1: Federal Obligations for Research and Development:
Top 20 Institutions Ranked by Amount Received (Fiscal Year 1985)

Rank	Institution	Dollars in thousands
1.	Johns Hopkins University	$429,180
2.	Massachusetts Institute of Technology	187,649
3.	Stanford University	174,961
4.	University of Washington	146,179
5.	University of California at Los Angeles	128,211
6.	Columbia University, Main Division	127,331
7.	University of Wisconsin at Madison	124,604
8.	Cornell University	119,966
9.	Harvard University	109,414
10.	Yale University	109,227
11.	University of Michigan	108,035
12.	University of California at Berkeley	106,710
13.	University of California at San Diego	103,603
14.	University of Minnesota	103,272
15.	University of Pennsylvania	103,119
16.	University of California at San Francisco	98,536
17.	University of Southern California	89,646
18.	University of Illinois at Urbana	83,122
19.	Pennsylvania State University	76,723
20.	New York University	74,577
	Total	$2,604,065

Source: National Science Foundation.

*Table 2: Top 20 Doctoral Institutions
Reporting the Most Foundation Support, 1986-87*

Institution	Amount
Washington University	$69,100,064
* University of Texas-System Summary	54,149,981
* University of California-System Summary	42,830,673
California Institute of Technology	42,650,836
Harvard University	41,743,000
* University of Minnesota	36,762,952
Stanford University	32,952,333
Yale University	26,943,821
New York University	22,778,750
Columbia University	22,177,906
Duke University	21,299,194
Cornell University	19,587,752
* University of Wisconsin-Madison	18,487,337
University of Miami	17,586,505
Massachusetts Institute of Technology	16,266,711
University of Pennsylvania	16,197,073
Johns Hopkins University	15,823,634
Princeton University	15,032,404
University of Southern California	14,304,762
* University of Washington	14,171,053

* Public doctoral institutions

Compiled from Council for Aid to Education, Voluntary Support of Education, 1986-87.

*Table 3: Estimated Total Voluntary Support of Higher Education
by Corporations and Foundations, 1969-70 to 1986-87
(Millions of dollars)*

Year	Foundations	Businesses, Corporations
1969-70	$ 434	$ 269
1970-71	418	259
1971-72	523	275
1972-73	524	320
1973-74	535	354
1974-75	497	357
1975-76	549	379
1976-77	558	446
1977-78	623	508
1978-79	701	556
1979-80	903	696
1980-81	922	778
1981-82	1,003	976
1982-83	1,018	1,112
1983-84	1,081	1,271
1984-85	1,175	1,574
1985-86	1,363	1,702
1986-87	1,513	1,819

Source: Council for Aid to Education, Voluntary Support of Education, 1986-87.

Career Development for the Foundation Relations Professional

Rita Bornstein
Vice President for Development
University of Miami

T here is no job in development more directly connected to the primary goals of the academy—teaching, research, and public service—than that of director of foundation relations. This position is one of the most interesting and challenging in academic fund raising.

The foundation office serves as a key nexus between the academic and development spheres within an institution and between the institution and the foundation world. It takes an individual of uncommon intelligence, skill, and character to manage effectively both internal relations with the community of scholars and external relations with foundation representatives.

Characteristics of a successful foundation relations officer

What do we look for in a foundation relations officer? Fundamental to success in this position is competence in the research techniques necessary to match institutional needs with appropriate funding sources. Also critical is the ability to understand and interpret programmatic and research ideas from many disciplines. The effective presentation of these ideas depends on persuasive communication skills in writing and in ordinary discourse.

Much more is required, however, than a good brain and a silver tongue. The foundation relations officer must possess highly developed interpersonal skills.

193

He or she must possess a sincere interest in other people; particularly important is the ability to listen carefully and to elicit confidence. Success in the job also involves an unusual mixture of aggressiveness and deference—he or she must be willing to initiate contact when necessary (the so-called "cold call") or to take a back seat during interactions between foundation and institutional representatives.

This exceptional individual is called upon to be a good manager: to plan, organize, execute, and follow up on the numerous internal and external activities necessary for success. Such skills are especially important in the foundation relations office where the pattern of work is not clearly delineated and must be defined and constructed by the incumbent.

Finally, the foundation relations officer must consider it a privilege to ask for support for the important purposes of his or her institution. To be effective, he or she must embody the values and perspectives of that institution. More than any other person, the foundation relations officer speaks on behalf of the whole array of programs and research as well as the history, mission, and goals of the institution.

The foundation relations officer and the faculty

It is upon the work of the foundation relations officer that the trust and involvement of the faculty are built. Although the professoriate increasingly recognizes the importance of financial support from private sources, a traditional suspicion and disdain toward fund raising linger. In many institutions, development is still perceived as commercial in orientation and, as such, is considered to be necessary but extrinsic to the intellectual work of the academy.

If the foundation officer fails to be responsive to faculty concerns, relations will be strained. But if the officer provides leadership in proposal development, prospect cultivation, and stewardship, faculty support for development will follow.

The foundation officer serves as honest broker among institutional units that are competing to submit proposals or make cultivation calls to foundations. This role requires the acumen to identify proposals poorly conceived or written, ideas without funding potential, and projects low on the institution's priority list. The officer must also possess the sensitivity, strength, and confidence to provide appropriate feedback to the parties involved.

The foundation officer can have a direct and important influence on institutional planning. As academic goals and priorities are developed, he or she is in a unique position to provide information and advice based on a specialized knowledge of national funding patterns and trends.

The faculty may fear that the development tail will wag the academic dog.[1] However, institutional priorities for research, programs, and facilities have always been influenced by available funding, both government and private. The savvy foundation relations director, recognizing faculty sensitivity, works collaboratively with the academic leadership to ensure inclusion of fund-raising realities in institutional planning.

194

Relationships with foundation representatives

The director of foundation relations is the primary link between the institution and the foundation world. He or she develops and manages the institution's relations with appropriate foundation representatives. In order to build these relationships, the director must spend considerable time away from the home office visiting with program officers, alone or with other institutional representatives, to assess areas in which foundation interests and institutional programs may intersect.

The network of important giving officers developed by the foundation relations officer can result in highly productive, long-term relationships for the institution. This is a major responsibility because the academic reputation of a college or university among foundation executives carries great weight. Since the foundation relations director is most often the person who interprets the institution to the foundation, fluff and hype or a lack of seriousness and forthrightness can damage a college or university's image in New York.

Pathways to foundation fund raising

WANTED: A person with the knowledge and enthusiasm to encourage the development of fundable proposal ideas, the intelligence to separate the chaff from the wheat in the dozens of proposals that flow through the office, the confidence and skill to serve as both cheerleader and traffic cop while maintaining excellent relations with the faculty and ably representing the institution to the foundation world.

What are the career paths that bring such a person to a college or university foundation office? People most often come to foundation relations work via one of three avenues: another position in higher education development, a development position elsewhere in the nonprofit sector, or a non-development job within or outside the academy. Promotion from within a development office is good for employee morale, so when there is a vacancy in foundation relations, the annual fund director and other directors of development will usually be considered. Internal candidates have the advantage of familiarity with the division and the institution.

The most common route from elsewhere in an institution is the sponsored research office, an area where the candidate has learned grant writing and proposal processing and become familiar with the academic interests of the professors. People in other departments on campus are far less aware of the type and scope of development activities. Applicants from other nonprofits bring expertise in fund raising, and those from local organizations also have a knowledge of the community. These candidates, however, often lack an understanding of higher education.

The foundation relations office is an excellent entry point into development for those with a doctoral degree. In the early 1980s a number of Ph.D.'s made the transition to development. Reasons for this move included a contraction of the job market in several academic disciplines, the inability or unwillingness of some individuals to relocate, the increasingly attractive salaries in development (often eclipsing those available to young professors), and the desire for a more active, varied, and administrative worklife than that afforded by research and teaching. By 1986, according to one survey, 12.8 percent of advancement professionals had doctoral degrees, and 38.2 percent had master's degrees.[2]

Although success in foundation relations does not depend on advanced degrees, the ideal candidate is a Ph.D. with good human relations skills. The foundation officer with an advanced degree is most likely to have legitimacy with the faculty. Master's and professional degrees are also highly desirable, but the Ph.D. best provides the research orientation that enables the officeholder to understand and communicate with faculty and to interpret their ideas to the outside world.

No discussion of career paths to foundation relations is complete without mention of the significant increase in the proportion of women entering the field of development. Some of these women are coming directly from business or law school. Many women who, in an earlier period, might have become nurses or teachers, come to development work from other professions in search of a sense of mission and social purpose. Women who have spent much of their lives in community service now hope to put their commitment and dedication into a profession that promises prestige and financial rewards.

Development as a profession

Foundation relations officers who bring expertise, a special commitment to the academy, and a sense of service can have a profound effect on the status of development work. In the past, fund raising has been called a trade, a business, or, at best, a minor or semiprofession. Slowly this image is changing, but the field still lacks the power of better established professions.

James L. Fisher, then president of the Council for Advancement and Support of Education, in remarks to the CASE Colloquium on Professionalism in 1985, urged that "We ... define ourselves more surely as professionals." As Fisher said, although today "We are accepted at the academic conference table, [it is] largely out of a pressing need for us rather than out of appreciation for what we are and what we do as professionals."[3]

Two characteristics of the major professions are the service orientation of its practitioners and their expertise. Robert L. Payton, scholar in residence at the University of Virginia, in his seminal paper "Major Challenges to Philanthropy," directs our attention to the difference between fund raisers who view philanthropy as simply a job and those who are drawn to it as a "calling."[4]

Foundation relations officers most likely to feel "called" to support the mission of higher education through philanthropic endeavor may well be those prepared for the intellectual life of the academy and rooted in its processes of research and distribution of knowledge. Also, as noted above, the women now attracted to foundation relations demonstrate an especially powerful drive to improve society through higher education. From whatever background, the individual who goes beyond the specific job requirements and commits himself or herself to the mission of the institution advances the occupational status of development.

Robert Bellah and his co-authors in *Habits of the Heart* define "work" in its highest sense as commitment combined with expertise. They write:

> In the strongest sense of a "calling," work constitutes a practical ideal of activity and character that makes a person's work morally insepara- ble from his or her life. It subsumes the self into a community of dis- ciplined practice and sound judgment whose activity has meaning and value in itself not just in the output or profit that results from it.

Service on behalf of the social aims of higher learning is a worthy goal for de- velopment and, coupled with a growing knowledge base and expertise, serves to elevate the status and prestige of development both within and outside the acade- my. The foundation relations officer who reflects the values and standards of aca- deme enhances the legitimacy of development with internal and external consti- tuencies, especially in the foundation world and certainly with the faculty.

Professional growth

The key to career advancement and personal satisfaction for the foundation officer is professional growth. Most people come into development with little understand- ing of either higher education or philanthropy. To be credible as a spokesperson for an institution, the officer's knowledge of particular projects and programs must be framed in a broader context. That context includes the evolution and structure of the institution as well as the history and organization of higher education.

The able foundation officer can provide specific information of interest to the external world, including data on student enrollment and SAT scores, faculty num- bers and qualifications, size of alumni body and level of financial support, gift in- come and its relationship to the institution's budget, and so on. In addition, however, he or she should be able to describe the important eras, events, legends, and leaders in the institution's history.

The foundation relations officer may also be drawn into discussions about gener- al higher education issues, such as the tenure process, conflicts between public and private universities, and admissions practices. The individual without an un- derstanding of such concerns may be taken less seriously than one able to partic- ipate knowledgeably in the dialogue.

Of equal importance is a knowledge of the history of philanthropy with a spe- cial focus on foundations and their impact on higher education and society. To fully understand the evolution and decision-making processes of foundations, the foundation relations officer needs to be familiar with relevant legislation and tax codes.

To serve an institution well, while at the same time advancing his or her own career, the foundation officer must master the technical knowledge available, de- velop the judgment that comes with experience in the field, adhere to the highest ethical standards in the profession, and earn the respect of clients.

His or her superiors will use several criteria to judge the foundation officer's success and ability to take on greater responsibility. These include:
- achieving a significant number of successful proposals and appropriate contacts;
- making creative contributions to institutional planning;
- experiencing growth in the profession;
- achieving a high level of involvement as a member of the development team; and
- contributing to the profession by conducting research and writing articles on fund-raising concerns and providing seminars and workshops at professional meetings.

Career paths for the foundation relations officer

A variety of career possibilities are open to the successful foundation relations officer. There is always the option of staying on the job. In this field, longevity increases effectiveness—there is no substitute for relationships developed over the years with both internal and external constituents and for the broad knowledge of an institution's research and programmatic needs that comes with long experience. Institutional officials are well advised to provide rewards sufficient to retain an outstanding foundation relations officer for as long as that individual is challenged by the position.

The foundation officer may consider a move to sponsored research if he or she has reason to view it as preparation for advancement in the provost's office. The many research projects and programs that exist throughout an institution may offer possibilities for greater administrative responsibility.

Sometimes the foundation relations officer moves on to another development position such as that of director of development for a particular program or school within the institution. This is a good career decision if the new position requires a broader range of development skills (e.g., direct mail, telephone solicitation, major gift fund raising, publications, and alumni relations).

The foundation relations office may also be a direct stepping stone to top administrative positions in development. The opportunity to work closely with the president and the chief development officer puts the foundation relations director with administrative potential in a good position for advancement in the development hierarchy.

The director of foundation relations who leaves academe can shift from grant seeker to grant maker in the foundation or corporate world. The business and public sectors also offer opportunities in research, market analysis, community relations, and general administration.

In many colleges and universities, the foundation relations officer has responsibility for both foundation and corporate fund raising; this provides exposure to two very different constituencies. Corporate fund raising involves regular contact with corporate executives who serve as volunteers and prospects. These contacts will help professionals who wish to situate themselves in the business world.

Whatever the career plans of the foundations relations officer, wholehearted participation in the life of the institution and its community is a must. Relationships developed with faculty, administrators, and community leaders at campus and community events extend the reach of the foundation relations officer, provide stimulation and ideas for the operation of the office, and create the network necessary for the next job move.

The professional network should extend beyond the local community to the national community of development officers. Professional colleagues at other institutions can provide information about available positions and offer career guidance, references, encouragement, and support. Such a local and national web of relationships offers incalculable opportunities for personal friendship, professional growth, and advancement.

Notes

[1] Leon E. Trachtman, "Where Advancement Fails," CURRENTS, September 1987, p. 13.

[2] Judy VanSlyke Turk, "The Changing Faces of CASE," CURRENTS, June 1986, p. 12.

[3] James L. Fisher, "Keeping Our Place at the Academic Table," CURRENTS, June 1985, p. 12.

[4] Robert L. Payton, "Major Challenges to Philanthropy," A Discussion Paper for Independent Sector, 1984, p. 65.

[5] Robert N. Bellah and others, *Habits of the Heart: Individualism and Commitment in American Life* (New York: Harper and Row), 1986, p. 66.

Bibliography

Adapted from Prospect Research: A How-to Guide, *ed. Bobbie J. Strand and Susan Hunt (Washington, DC: Council for Advancement and Support of Education, 1986). Revised and updated by Susan Hunt.*

PRICES CURRENT AS OF JANUARY 1989.

Free publications

Watch for announcement of free publications and free reprints in periodicals and advertisements. The *Foundation Directory* and other similar sources list foundations that publish and will send annual reports. Many of the larger foundations will continue to send reports, newsletters, and other materials free of charge.

Prospect information

America's Hidden Philanthropic Wealth, 2d ed. The Taft Group, 5130 MacArthur Blvd., NW, Washington, DC 20016-3316. 1988, $147. Tomorrow's potential foundation giants. Identifies hundreds of small private foundations—each backed by a wealthy sponsor capable of propelling it to the center of the philanthropic scene. Six indexes—headquarters state, state of major grant recipients, name and title, major grant recipients by category, typical recipients, alma mater.

America's Newest Foundations: The Sourcebook on Recently Created Philanthropies, 2d ed. Taft Group. 1988, 365 pp., $89.95. Highlights more than 545 up-and-coming foundations created since 1980. Includes profiles of new major grant-making organizations—with giving priorities, contact information, major grant types, geographic giving preferences, and total giving. Indexed by state; grant type; areas of interest; donors, officers, and trustees; and grant recipients by location.

America's Wealthiest People: Their Philanthropic and Nonprofit Affiliations. Taft Group. 1986, 78 pp., $57.50 plus $5 shipping. Biographical directory with profiles of over 500 of America's wealthiest individuals and families.

America's Wealthy and the Future of Foundations. Published by the Foundation Center and co-sponsored by the Council on Foundations and the Yale University Program on Non-Profit Organizations. Teresa J. Odendahl, ed. 1987, $24.95

(paper) or $34.95 (hardcover). Examines the complexity of attitudes, motivations, economic forces, and policy regulations that lead wealthy people to commit private resources to public endeavors. Order from the Foundation Center, Dept. FC, 79 Fifth Ave., New York, NY 10003, or call (800) 424-9836.

Annual Register of Grant Support. Marquis Who's Who, Inc., 200 East Ohio St., Chicago, IL 60611. Includes details of the grant support programs of government agencies, public and private foundations, corporations, community trusts, unions, educational and professional associations, and special-interest organizations. Covers a broad spectrum of interests including academic and scientific research, travel and exchange programs, publication support, equipment and construction grants, in-service training, and competitive awards and prizes in a variety of fields.

ARIS Funding Reports. Academic Research Information System, Inc., The Redstone Bldg., 2940 16th St., Suite 314, San Francisco, CA 94103, (415) 558-8133. *Biomedical Sciences Report* and *Social and Natural Sciences Report*, annual subscription (eight issues a year with supplements), $180 each; *Creative Arts and Humanities Report,* annual subscription (eight issues a year), $105. Information about grants, contracts, fellowships, and scholarships in the arts, humanities, and sciences.

Associates Program. The Foundation Center. Annual fee of $350 entitles an Associate to toll-free telephone reference service, access to custom searches of the Foundation Center's computerized databases, and billing privileges. Call (800) 424-9836 for information.

The Big Foundations. Waldemar A. Nielsen. Columbia University Press. 1972, 475 pp., $17 (paperback) or $37.50 (hardcover). Research on and analysis of the 33 largest foundations.

Chronicle of Higher Education. 1255 23rd St. NW, Washington, DC 20037. Annual subscription, $55. Weekly publication with news and classified job listings.

Chronicle of Philanthropy. New from the publishers of the *Chronicle of Higher Education.* Covers the news of corporate and individual giving, foundations, fund raising, taxation regulation, management, and more. Biweekly newspaper; annual subscription, $57.50.

Compilation of State and Federal Privacy Laws. Privacy Journal, P.O. Box 15300, Washington, DC 20003, (202) 547-2865. 1988, $26. Includes all states with categories within each state.

COMSEARCH Printouts. Foundation Center. Subjects are grants listings categorized into 31 highly targeted subject fields: education, health, cultural activities, welfare, and other. $20 per subject (paper); $8 per subject (microfiche); $125 for complete set of 31 subjects (microfiche). Also available: broad topics covering 26 key areas of grant making ($40 each); special topics (most frequently requested listings) for $20 each; and geographic categories (two cities, 11 states, and seven broad regions) for $35 each. For more information, contact the Foundation Center.

Congressional Staff Directory. P.O. Box 62, Mt. Vernon, VA 22121, (703) 765-3400. *Congressional Staff Directory,* $45; *Federal Staff Directory,* $50; *C.S.D. Advance Locator,* $15; *Judicial Staff Directory,* $50. Annual directories containing everything you always wanted to know about Washington.

Cumulative List of Organizations Described in Section 170(c) of the Internal Revenue Service Code of 1954. IRS Publication 78. Superintendent of Documents, U.S. Government Printing Office, Washington, DC 20402, (202) 783-3238. Annual subscription (looseleaf manual plus updates), $38. The official list of organizations to which contributions are tax deductible. All organizations listed have 501(c)(3) status; organizations not listed, however, may also have 501(c)(3) status under a different or previous name or under a group ruling. (Churches and some organizations, such as those with annual budgets of less than $25,000, are not technically required to apply for 501(c)(3) status.)

DIALOG Information Services, Inc. 3460 Hillview Ave., Palo Alto, CA 94304, (800) 3DIALOG. On-line information service with over 250 databases available. Material such as references to published and unpublished literature, the full text of articles, newswires, financial data, directory listings, and statistics, etc., may be accessed. Write for full list of databases.

Forbes. 60 Fifth Ave., New York, NY 10011. Biweekly, $48 per year.

Fortune. Time and Life Building, Rockefeller Center, New York, NY 10020-1393. Biweekly, $47.97 per year.

Forum. Donors Forum of Chicago, 53 W. Jackson, Suite 401, Chicago, IL 60604, (312) 431-0260. Bimonthly newspaper for the philanthropic community. Library open to the public for research on grant-making prospects (cooperating collection of the Foundation Center network).

The Foundation Directory, 11th ed. The Foundation Center. 1987, $85. Information on foundations with assets in excess of $1 million or grants over $100,000. More than 5,000 foundations included. Entry includes name, address, giving interests, limitations, type of support awarded, financial data, officers and directors, and grant application information. Indexes by state and city locations, personnel, fields of interest. *Foundation Directory Supplement* (11th ed., $50), published in alternate years, offers updates on more than 1,200 *Directory* foundations. *Foundation Directory* and *Supplement* as a set, $120.

Foundation Fundamentals, 3rd ed. The Foundation Center. $9.95. General background information: What are foundations? How do you identify foundations interested in your organization; how do you present your ideas to a foundation?

The Foundation Grants Index, 17th ed. The Foundation Center. 1988, $55 plus $2 postage and handling, prepaid. Published each summer. Lists more than 43,000 grants of $5,000 or more. Listed alphabetically by foundation by state.

Foundation News—The Magazine of Philanthropy. Council on Foundations. Bimonthly, $29.50 per year. Provides in-depth coverage of current philanthropic activities and issues and includes regular features on community foundations, corporate giving, legislation and regulation, international programs, books, and the views of foundation leaders.

"Fund-Raising Ideas and Techniques." Fund-Raising Institute, Box 365, Ambler, PA 19002-9983. Catalog of available "How-to" guides.

Giving USA. American Association of Fund-Raising Council Trust for Philanthropy, 25 W. 43rd St., New York, NY 10036, (212) 354-5799. $35. One-year subscription ($65) includes *Giving USA, Giving USA Updates,* and "Compilation of State Laws Regulating Charitable Solicitations."

The Golden Donors. Waldemar A. Nielsen. Truman Talley Books, E.P. Dutton. 1981, 468 pp. Begun as an updating of an earlier study (*The Big Foundations*), this book reveals profound and complex changes in the nonprofit sector as a whole and the environment in which it functions.

Grant Proposals that Succeeded. Public Management Institute, 358 Brannan St., San Francisco, CA 94107, (415) 896-1900. 240 pp., $25. A useful evaluation tool for grant proposals; includes examples of successful applications for research grants, training grants, arts and humanities grants, grants ranging from $5,500 to $450,000, and foundation grants. Critiques from grants experts show why these applications succeeded.

Handbook of Institutional Advancement, 2d ed. A. Westley Rowland, gen. ed. Jossey-Bass, Inc., 433 California St., San Francisco, CA 94104. 1986, $47.95. A practical guide to institutional advancement; see, especially, "Raising Funds from Foundations" by Mary Kay Murphy (pp. 278-291) and "Building a Donor Information Base" by Bobbie J. Strand (pp. 337-349).

The Handbook on Private Foundations. David F. Freeman. Council on Foundations. 1981, $15. Written for current and prospective grant makers, handbook covers all aspects of foundation philanthropy and includes appendices outlining applicable laws, regulations, and details.

How to Write Successful Foundation Presentations. Joseph Dermer. Taft Group. $14. Examples of actual grant-winning presentations that have secured grants from $5,000 to $200,000.

The Information Report. Washington Researchers Publishing, 2612 P St. NW, Washington, DC 20007, (202) 333-3533. Annual subscription, $120. Monthly publication providing specific sources of information crucial to business researchers.

International Foundation Directory, 4th ed. Gale Research Co., Book Tower, Dept. 77748, Detroit, MI 48277-0748, (800) 223-GALE. 1986, $95. Emphasizes foundations, trusts, and other similar nonprofit institutions that operate on an international basis.

Michigan Foundation Directory. League for Human Services, 300 N. Washington Sq., Suite 401, P.O. Box 10195, Lansing, MI 48901-0195. Contact your regional Foundation Center library for information about a foundation directory for your state (see pp. 87-90).

National Data Book, 12th ed. The Foundation Center. 1988, 2 volumes, $65. Very basic information on more than 25,000 foundations. Alphabetical and geographic volumes. Includes name, address, principal officer, financial data, annual report information.

The New Grants Planner: A Systems Approach to Grantsmanship. Public Management Institute. 397 pp., $49. Manual helps simplify the grantsmanship process and maintain a Grants Readiness System, allowing you to respond quickly to grant opportunities. Includes forms, worksheets, and "Grants Blueprint and Grants Forecaster"—a budgeting and flow chart system that cuts proposal writing time by 10 to 25 percent.

The New How to Raise Funds from Foundations. Joseph Dermer, ed. Taft Group. $13.95. New strategies and techniques in cultivation. A basic manual.

People in Philanthropy: A Guide to Funding Connections, 8th ed. Taft Group. 1988, 512 pp., $127. Concise biographical profiles of more than 8,500 of the most influential philanthropic decision makers in America. Indexed by place of birth, state of office, state of philanthropy, industry affiliation, nonprofit affiliation, philanthropic affiliation, and alma mater.

Philanthropic Digest. Brakeley, John Price Jones, Inc., 1600 Summer St., Stamford, CT 06905, (203) 348-8100. $59.50 for 12 monthly issues with special supplements each year. Now also available on disk. Recaps $1 million-plus grants and corporate grants of more than $100,000. Special analyses of health and arts added in 1987. Grants are keyed into five major gift categories: arts, education, health, social services, and religion. Information received directly from hundreds of grant makers and recipients.

The Profiles System. Profiles Donor Research, Inc., 380 Lexington Ave., Suite 19011, New York, NY 10168, (212) 490-6688. A donor research service developed for use by nonprofit institutions.

The Proposal Writer's Swipe File: 15 Winning Fund-Raising Proposals. Jean Brodsky, ed. Taft Group. $18.95. Six professional proposal writers invite you to steal ideas from their grant-getting works. Outstanding examples presented just as they were submitted. Suggestions for title pages, budget, layout, etc.

Prospect Research: A How-to Guide. Bobbie J. Strand and Susan Hunt, eds. Council for Advancement and Support of Education (CASE). 1986, 150 pp., $18.50, members; $23.25, nonmembers. Improve your investigation skills with this guide to researching major donors. Contains chapters by experts in the research field, including Bobbie Strand; Mary Kay Murphy; Emily Pfizenmaier Henderson; Alfred Blum, Jr.; Marc W. Jaffe; Betty Taylor Bright and Bruce Flessner. Order #26701 from CASE Publications Order Dept., 80 S. Early St., Alexandria, VA 22304 (postage and handling charge, $2).

Prospecting: Searching Out the Philanthropic Dollar. James Hickey and Elizabeth Koochoo. Taft Group. 69 pp. plus Forms Kit (donor record forms, prospect record forms, individual and corporate donor fact sheets, and more), $23.95. Includes information on collecting research materials, organizing a record-keeping system, assessing donor potential, etc.

"Public Management Institute Catalog." Public Management Institute. Catalog of books for nonprofit fund raisers.

The Raising of Money: Thirty-Five Essentials Every Trustee Should Know, plus "A Guide for the Professional." James Gregory Lord. Third Sector Press, 2000 Euclid Ave., P.O. Box 18044, Cleveland, OH 44118, (216) 932-6066. 1984, $34.50.

Source Book Profiles. The Foundation Center. Annual subscription fee for set of 500 (125 per quarter), $295. Previous sets may be ordered. Analyses of the largest foundations. Subscribers receive 125 profiles per quarter, along with revised indexes by name, subject interest, geographic limitations.

Taft Directory of Nonprofit Organizations: Profiles of America's Major Charitable Institutions. Taft Group. 1988, 535 pp., $97. Gives you the facts on America's 1,129 largest nonprofit organizations, who runs them, how they allocate their resources, who funds them, etc. Cross-referenced by areas of activities, headquarters state, executive officers, board officers, and donors.

Taft Foundation Information System. Taft Group. $397 plus $15 handling. Includes *Taft Foundation Reporter* (containing financial data on major foundations, officers, and directors; areas of interest; etc.); *Foundation Updates* (monthly periodical of foundation changes and major developments); *Foundation Giving Watch* (monthly periodical of foundation news, trends).

The Taft Nonprofit Executive. Taft Group. Monthly newsletter, $97 per year.

VU/TEXT Information Services, Inc. 325 Chestnut St., Suite 1300, Philadelphia, PA 19106, (800) 258-8080. Costs per connect hour. No charge for subscription, initial charge for user manual includes training. Database of 30 full-text newspapers around the country, including 29 exclusive to VU/TEXT (*Boston Globe, Detroit Free Press, Miami Herald,* etc.).

The Wall Street Journal. 200 Burnett Rd., Chicopee, MA 01020. Annual subscription, $119.

The Wall Street Journal Index. Index of articles by company, industry, topic, etc.

The Wall Street Transcript. Covers brokerage firm research reports, publishes text from newsletters, has regular interviews with security analysts and money managers, indexes all mentions of stocks from previous issues.

Writing Winning Proposals. Judith Mirick Gooch. CASE. 1987, 87 pp., $18.50, members; $23.25, nonmembers. A step-by-step guide for people in education who are writing proposals to foundations and corporations. Covers researching your prospect, organizing your material, preparing a budget, writing the proposal, and follow-up. Also includes a bibliography for proposal writers. Order #28101 from CASE Publications Order Dept., 80 S. Early St., Alexandria, VA 22304 (postage and handling charge, $2).

About the Editor

Mary Kay Murphy

Mary Kay Murphy learned the craft of foundation fund raising at the Georgia Institute of Technology, both before and during the Institute's $202-million capital campaign. She knows the ins and outs of successful cultivation of foundation support. She is credited with raising over $13 million from national, community, and local foundations during the campaign. She is currently director for development at Georgia Tech.

In addition to editing this book, she has lectured throughout the country on the topic for CASE, the American Association for State Colleges and Universities, and the National Society of Fund Raising Executives.

She is an active member of CASE, serving as chair-elect of the CASE District III board and as chair for CASE's Matching Gift Forum, Corporate and Foundation Support, and Major Donor Research Conferences. She is a frequent contributor to CURRENTS.

Murphy serves on the NSFRE Executive Committee and has been chair of the Society's public relations and audit committees, as well as president of the Georgia chapter. For two years, she was Georgia coordinator for the American Council on Education's program for women in higher education administration.

A native of Colorado, she has lived in Atlanta since 1960. She earned her Ph.D. in higher education administration at Georgia State University and her master's degree at Emory University. She is listed in *Who's Who of the South and Southwest* and *Who's Who of American Women*.

Other CASE Publications for the Development Professional

Special Events: Planning for Success, by April L. Harris, 75 pages, #25301.

The Successful Capital Campaign: From Planning to Victory Celebration, edited by H. Gerald Quigg, 188 pages, #29701.

Prospect Research: A How-to Guide, edited by Bobbie J. Strand and Susan Hunt, 150 pages, #26701.

Writing Winning Proposals, by Judith Mirick Gooch, 87 pages, #28101.

Institutional Image: How to Define, Improve, Market It, by Robert Topor, 68 pages, #23801.

Your Personal Guide to Marketing a Nonprofit Organization, by Robert Topor, 153 pages, #24201.

The New Guide to Effective Media Relations, edited by Nancy Raley and Laura Carter, 101 pages, #24402.

For a catalog listing all CASE publications and current prices, write:

> CASE Publications Order Department
> 80 S. Early Street
> Alexandria, VA 22304

Orders may also be placed by calling (800) 336-4776.